# ROTISSERIE LEAGUE BASEBALL

# ROTISSERIE LEAGUE BASEBALL

## 1987 Edition

### Edited by
### Glen Waggoner and Robert Sklar
### Introduction by Steve Wulf

**The Rotisserie League**

Lee Eisenberg • Rob Fleder • Peter Gethers
Bruce McCall • Daniel Okrent • Michael Pollet
Cary Schneider • Robert Sklar • Cork Smith
Harry Stein • Glen Waggoner • Steve Wulf

BANTAM BOOKS
TORONTO • NEW YORK • LONDON • SYDNEY • AUCKLAND

ROTISSERIE LEAGUE BASEBALL

*A Bantam Book / March 1984*
*Bantam Second Edition / April 1987*

**Library of Congress Cataloging-in-Publication Data**

Rotisserie League baseball.

1. Rotisserie League Baseball (Game)   I. Waggoner,
Glen.   II. Sklar, Robert.   III. Eisenberg, Lee, 1946–
IV. Rotisserie League.
GV867.3.R67   1987      794      86-47880
ISBN 0-553-34393-9 (pbk.)

*Published simultaneously in the United States and Canada*

---

---

PRINTED IN THE UNITED STATES OF AMERICA

CW      0  9  8  7  6  5  4  3  2  1

# Contents

# Me and Dale

## An Introduction to Rotisserie League Baseball By Steve Wulf of the Wulfgang

"So, how's your Rotisserie League team doing?"

That's a question that we, the members of the original, accept-no-substitutes Rotisserie League have often been asked over the years. The query usually comes from Rotisserian disciples who own teams in offshoot leagues, and, with all humility, there are a lot of brethren out there. Much in the manner of the golf goof who tells you what club he used on the 186-yard 14th, these gentle souls want to tell you how they acquired Eric Davis for Mookie Wilson, or somesuch. While we find these encounters touching, we also find them . . . I'm looking for the right word here . . . boring is too strong . . . sleep-inducing is too mean . . . entrancing, yes that's it, we find them entrancing.

The Rotisserie League has spread from coast to coast and to at least one foreign country (Canada counts) since our first book, the one in the green cover, came out in 1984. Green, by the way, is bad news in the book business, so there's no telling what we could have done in another color, like blue. The Rotisserie League also touches the fringes of celebrity. Film genius Ron Howard, formerly Opie (please whistle the theme from *The Andy Griffith Show*), plays in a facsimile league, as does Fred Grandy, Gopher on *The Love Boat*, and now a congressman from Iowa.

(Time out for a trivia question: Who actually owns The Love Boat? Answer below.)

We have Pulitzer Prize winners, media moguls, jailbirds, Bryant Gumbel, Jim Kaat, and several members of the San Francisco Giants front office hooked on the Rotisserie way. Why, Peter Golenbock, the author of many sports books filled with many misspellings, has been a member of the American Dreams League for a whole year, which qualifies him to write a book about the Rotisserie League for Random House even though we own the copyright. But that's okay, because we are as one in the Rotisserie world, and, besides, we are going to sue his ass.

(.rennerbnietS egroeG)

Nothing, though, quite prepared us for what we consider the greatest day in Rotisserie League history. It was May 7, 1985, to be exact, and I was standing behind the batting cage at Shea Stadium. Although I am sometimes mistaken for Frank Cashen, I am in truth a writer and editor for *Sports Illustrated*. Baseball is my beat, but I do know Paulina Porizkova personally. On this particular late afternoon, I was trying to look like I belonged while the Atlanta Braves jumped in and out of the batting cage— "More top hand," I said to Horner—when all of a sudden I heard the words:

"So, how's your Rotisserie League team doing?"

I turned around, fully expecting to come face-to-face with a fellow Rotissrian. But instead, my eyes encountered the *rave* in *Braves*. I hoisted my gaze upward, and squinting into the sun (I forgot my eyeblack) I recognized, could it be, yes, Dale Murphy, center fielder for the Braves, two-time National League MVP, hero to millions. Half-blinded by either the sun or a dream, I rubbed my eyes. Fortunately, I still had the gift of gab.

"Huh?" I said to Dale.

"I asked how your Rotisserie League team is doing," said Dale.

"Fine, but how do you know I have a Rotisserie League team?"

"I read the book. It was pretty funny. Someday, if I had the time, I'd like to get into a league with my father."

"Dale, pardon me for being flabbergasted. Not so much because *you* read the book. I frankly didn't think anybody read it."

Before I continue with this epic confrontation, I would like to correct one common misconception about Dale Murphy. His goodness and consideration are well documented and, if anything, underestimated. We know that he is a devout Mormon and a family man as well as a marvelous ballplayer. He is the closest thing we have to Gary Cooper, and I know one beat writer who stayed with the Braves simply because he liked watching Murphy every day.

Yet I often hear people say that Murphy is nice but bland, friendly but essentially boring. Nothing could be farther from the truth. He has a probing mind and a delightful sense of humor. I got to know him a little when I did a story on him several years ago. Two of the things I learned about Dale were that he loved Frank Capra movies and that he liked to play Whack-A-Mole in arcades. Now, if that doesn't tell you something about the man, I don't know what does.

And now back to the cage.

"One of my favorite things in the book," said Dale, "was Dale Day." (For the benefit of the millions of you who didn't read the first book, and to refresh the memories of the tens of you who did, Dale Day was a promotional idea of Rob Fleder, owner of the Fledermice. Everyone named Dale got in free and was photographed with the Dale of his or her choice: Murphy, Berra, or elderly cowgirl Evans.)

"You know, Dale, the guys aren't going to believe this."

"Who owns me?"

"As a matter of fact, I do."

"You do? How much did you pay for me?"

"Fifty dollars."

"FIFTY DOLLARS!!!"

"I don't mean to put any pressure on you, but that is the highest any player has ever gone for in the league."

"Gee, I'll try to do better." (We both laughed at that because, at the time, Murphy was tearing up the National League.) Who else is on our team?"

I then proceeded to go over my roster with him, and Dale nodded when he liked one of his ersatz teammates and didn't nod when he didn't. Murphy may be a great ballplayer, but his judgment turned out to be no better than mine—he told me to hang on to José DeLeon, who went on to lose 19 games. Just before he slipped into the cage to take his swings, Dale said, "You know, I wish I had the time to do something like that. It sounds like fun."

That was the end of the conversation but the beginning of a sensation. I called Beloved Founder and Former Commissioner-for-Life Dan Okrent of the Fenokees that evening to relate the meeting, and by the end of the night, I had repeated the tale to almost everyone in the league. Other real ballplayers had expressed a mild interest in the Rotisserie League before, most notably infielder Mike Ramsey and pitcher Dave LaPoint, the first two speakers at our annual spring training banquet. But Dale Murphy was, if you'll pardon the expression, a whole new ball game.

For a while, I basked in the glow of my close encounter. But then I began to see the signpost up ahead. We had entered the Twilight Zone. The Rotisserie League had gone through the looking-glass, or rather, through the box score. For years, we had been poring over the names in the boxes, drafting them, trading them, waiving them, claiming them, calling them up. What we did was great fun, but it was also impersonal, and I thought if the players knew, they might find it a little demeaning. I mean, what right did I have to "own" Dale Murphy or even Sammy Khalifa—although to tell you the truth, I didn't feel so bad about Sammy. And now Dale Murphy knew that I and thousands of other Rotisserians were watching him, not as fans do, but as owners.

Worse yet, I began to think, what if the players become Rotisserians themselves? What if they carry on their own leagues in the sanctity of their clubhouses? What if they find themselves pitching against one of their own hitters, or hitting against one of their own pitchers? I envisioned the scenario of Dave LaPoint, nursing a comfortable lead in a real game, serving up a fat one to Dale Murphy so that he could improve the home run totals for his own LaPoint LaBlanks. I saw a proliferation of such scandals, I saw the Commissioner stepping in to halt these insidious leagues, I saw mandatory Rotissitesting for all major league teams. ("I'm sorry, LaPoint, but the amount of USA Today newsprint on your fingers exceeds the acceptable limit. Book 'im, Bart.")

My fears subsided with time, of course. But they lay dormant inside the Rotisserie compartment of my brain, sandwiched between my memory of trading Willie McGee for Tony Scott and my impatience with Brad Komminsk. Then one day last September, I found myself on assignment in Atlanta-Fulton County Stadium. It was late afternoon, and the sun was giving me a serious case of the squints. The Braves were taking BP—"You're opening up too soon," I told Oberkfell—and who should appear beside me but Dale Murphy. We exchanged pleasantries, and then I said, "Dale, there's something I want to ask you."

"Sure," he said. "Go ahead."

"Do you remember our talk about the Rotisserie League last year?"

"Well, sort of."

"Does it bother you that other people—besides the Braves, I mean—own you?"

"Nah, I'm just sorry I'm not having a better year for them."

Pause. Then I said, "Did you ever get into a Rotisserie League?"

"Just didn't have the time," he said as he headed off into the outfield.

A few minutes later he returned.

"Besides, if I did get into one," said Dale, "I could be accused of insider trading."

Phew.

# Ground Rules

## How to Play the Game

All you need to play Rotisserie League Baseball is a handful of fellow fanatics, a good head for baseball, the willingness to devote most of your waking hours to cooking up deals and scouting players—and this book.

If you're one of the 50,000 or so intelligent, imaginative, right-thinking souls who also bought (and loved) the first Rotisserie League Baseball book, you'll probably check out the new rules set forth in the "Official Constitution of Rotisserie League Baseball (Revised)" on pages 10–30, and then get on back to developing your draft plan and trading strategy. That's fine. Just remember to take a look at all the other new stuff later, when you have some free time. (For Rotisserians, a little window opens up when the regular season ends. The playoffs and the World Series are, for our purposes, utterly anticlimactic, since their box scores are pitifully devoid of meaning. This is the time of year for relearning our children's first names.)

If you're among the 262,300,000 who did *not* buy the first book, shame on you. Here are some pointers for making best use of this one. Take a pass on the "Official Constitution" for now. First skim "The Rules, Simplified," then flip to "1987 Player Ratings" and learn what we think ballplayers ought to be paid.

Then come back to the "Constitution," master it, and you're on your own (which, as it's now your book as well as ours, is fair enough).

How you use it, of course, is entirely up to you, although we do modestly recommend that you consider its every word as Revealed Truth.

# The Rules, Simplified

The rules of Rotisserie League Baseball are exquisitely complicated, especially when you come to grips with long-term contracts, disabled lists, farm systems, waivers, September roster expansion, and the like. Nobody ever said owning your own baseball team was easy. Neither is life, and Rotisserie League Baseball is surely bigger than *that*. But the basics are simple enough.

1. Teams are assembled at a free-agent draft auction that takes place on the first weekend following opening day in the major leagues.

2. Each team is composed of 23 players taken from the active rosters of National or American League teams. You should have 10 teams in a Rotisserie League stocked with National Leaguers, 12 if you use the American League.

   • Teams drawn from the National League have five outfielders, two catchers, one second baseman, one shortstop, one middle infielder (either 2b or ss), one first baseman, one third baseman, one first or third baseman, one utility player who may qualify at any nonpitching position, and nine pitchers.
   • For American League versions, substitute a designated-hitter for the utility player.

3. Players are acquired at an open auction. Spending is limited to $260 per team. Teams may spend less. The order of auctioning players doesn't matter. The first bidder opens with a minimum bid of $1 for any player he chooses. The bidding then proceeds around the room (at

minimum increments of $1) until only one bidder is left. The process is repeated, with successive owners introducing players to be bid on, until every team has a full complement of 23 players.

4. A player is eligible to be drafted at any position at which he appeared in 20 or more games the preceding year. If he did not appear in 20 games at any one position, he is eligible for the position at which he appeared the most times. Once the season commences, a player qualifies for a position by playing it at least once.

5. Cumulative team performance is tabulated in four offensive and four pitching categories:
   • Composite batting average
   • Total number of home runs
   • Total RBIs
   • Total stolen bases
   • Composite ERA
   • Total wins
   • Composite pitching Ratio of walks and hits to innings pitched (Bases on Balls + Hits ÷ Innings Pitched = Ratio)
   • Total saves

6. In each of the eight categories, teams are ranked from first to last. For example, in a ten-team league, the first-place team will receive ten points, the second-place team nine, on down to one point for last place. The team with the most total points wins the pennant. The most accessible source for statistics is *USA Today* (American League stats on Tuesdays, National League on Wednesdays if they follow their 1986 schedule).

7. Prize money is distributed as follows:
   • 50% for first place
   • 25% for second
   • 15% for third
   • 10% for fourth

8. Trading is permissible from draft day through June 15. After every trade both teams must be whole—that is,

they must have the requisite number of players at each position. The transaction fee for trades is $10 per trade, regardless of the number of players involved.

9. If a player is put on the disabled list, sent to the minors, or released, he may be replaced by a player from the free-agent pool of unowned talent. The price for calling up such a player is $20 until the All-Star break, $40 thereafter. Replacement must be made by position: you cannot replace a disabled catcher with an outfielder, even if the free agent pickings at backstop are slim. The original player may be put on a team's reserve list for an additional $10 fee. When he is healthy, the reserved player may be activated upon payment of another $10 fee, at which time the free agent called up to replace him must either be moved to another slot where a natural opening exists or released. As with trades, all reserve-list moves must result in a team having the requisite number of players at each position.

Okay, you've got a lot of questions, and two of them get answered right now:

*"Do I have to play for money?"* No. We do, but you can play for nothing, or more, or something less than our stakes, which work out to be about $350–$450 per team once all fees are paid. Just be sure that you keep the ratio of "acquisition units" to players for each team at 260:23. Similarly, the number of units for fees and salaries should be proportional to those used in our system.

*"What do I do if it's May 15 and I've just gotten around to reading this book? Wait till next year?"* No, that's the old pre-Cashen Met mentality. Start putting together a league immediately, deduct all stats that accrue prior to your draft auction, and restrict yourself to one month of trading. Next year, start from scratch.

The rest of your questions are dealt with in the pages that follow. If not, write us c/o The Rotisserie League Baseball Association, 211 West 92nd Street, Box 9, New York, NY 10025, and complain—or ask us for answers. We'll do our best.

Batter up.

# Official Constitution of Rotisserie League BASEBALL

### PREAMBLE

We the People of the Rotisserie League, in Order to spin a more perfect Game, drive Justice home, kiss domestic Tranquility good-bye, promote the general Welfare from Tidewater, where it's bccn tearing up the International League, and secure the Blessings of Puberty to ourselves and those we've left on Base, do ordain and establish this Constitution for Rotisserie League Baseball, and also finish this run-on sentence.

### I. OBJECT

To assemble a lineup of 23 National League or American League baseball players whose cumulative statistics, compiled and measured by the methods described in these rules, exceed those of all other teams in the League.

### II. TEAMS

There are 10 teams in a duly constituted Rotisserie League composed of National League players, 12 if composed of American League players.

**NOTE:** Do *not* mix the two leagues. Bryant Gumbel does, and he's got a job that requires him to get up at 4:30 in the morning, for Ueberroth's sake! It's unrealistic and silly, and it deprives you of the pleasure of owning Luis Aguayo. For other reasons not to merge the two leagues, see page 31.

## III. ROSTER

A team's active roster consists of the following players:

### 1. NATIONAL LEAGUE VERSIONS
5 outfielders, 2 catchers, 1 second baseman, 1 shortstop, 1 middle infielder (either second baseman or shortstop), 1 first baseman, 1 third baseman, 1 first *or* third baseman, 1 utility player (who may play any non-pitching position), and 9 pitchers.

### 2. AMERICAN LEAGUE VERSIONS
The same, except that the utility player is replaced by a designated hitter.

## IV. DRAFT DAY

A major league player draft in the form of an open auction is conducted on the first weekend after Opening Day of the baseball season. Each team must acquire 23 players at a total cost not to exceed $260. A team need not spend the maximum. The League by general agreement determines the order in which teams may nominate players for acquisition. The team bidding first opens with a minimum salary bid of $1 for any eligible player, and the bidding proceeds around the room at minimum increments of $1 until only one bidder is left. That team acquires the player for that amount and announces the roster position the player will fill. The process is repeated, with successive team owners introducing players to be bid on, until every team has a squad of 23 players, by requisite position.

> **NOTE:** Don't get hung up on the bidding order; it's irrelevant. Do allow plenty of time; your first draft will take all day.
>
> If possible, recruit someone who is not an owner to conduct the auction for you. Keeping track of the players you want is tough enough. Keeping track of who everyone has,

and how much everyone has spent, taxes the capacity even of Beloved Founder and Former Commissioner-for-Life Okrent, who will *not* be available for your draft.

Unlike the big league version, Rotisserie League baseball can be played for very little money, or none at all. Our stakes require a $350–$450 investment per team, depending on the number of trades and call-ups over the course of a season, but you can play for pennies, Cracker Jacks, or nothing at all and still have fun. Or you can play for more and add new meaning to the word "anxiety."

- Players eligible at more than one position may be shifted during the course of the draft.
- No team may make a bid for a player it cannot afford. For example, a team with $3 left, and two openings on its roster, is limited to a maximum bid of $2 for one player.
- No team may bid for a player who qualifies only at a position that the team has already filled. For example, a team that has acquired two catchers, and whose utility or designated hitter slot is occupied, may not enter the bidding for any player who qualifies *only* at catcher.
- Players who commence the season on a major league team's disabled list *are* eligible to be drafted. If selected, they may be replaced (see below, **Article XII,** for details).

**NOTE:** Final 25-man (24 if big league owners continue to play hard ball) rosters for all 12 National League or all 14 American League teams will be needed on Draft Day. Getting them is a pain, as newspapers are generally careless about reporting last-minute player moves before Opening Day. Appoint a committee, or obtain them with your membership in the Rotisserie League Baseball Association (see pages 190–191 for details).

Immediately following the major league draft, a minor league player draft shall be conducted, in which each Rotisserie League team may acquire players who

(a) are not on any National/American League team's active roster and

(b) still have official rookie status, as defined by major league baseball.

**NOTE:** The major-league rule reads: "A player shall be considered a rookie unless, during a previous season or seasons, he has (a) exceeded 130 at-bats or 50 innings pitched in the major leagues; or (b) accumulated more than 45 days on the active roster of a major league club or clubs during the period of a 25-player limit (excluding time in the military service)." And he has an agent.

- Selection takes place in two rounds of a simple draft, not an auction.

  In the first season the selection order shall be determined by drawing paired numbers from a hat (that is, positions 1 and 20, 2 and 19, and so on in a ten-team league).

  In subsequent years teams select in reverse order of the final standings of the preceding season's pennant race.
- The price and subsequent salary upon activation of each Farm System player drafted is $10.
- See **Article XIII** for operational rules governing Farm Systems.

## V. POSITION ELIGIBILITY

A player may be assigned to any position at which he appeared in 20 or more games in the preceding season. If a player did not appear in 20 games at a single position, he may be drafted only at the position at which he appeared most frequently. The 20 games/most games measure is only used to determine the position(s) at which a player may be drafted. Once the season is under way (but after Draft Day), a player becomes eligible for assignment to any position at which he appears at least once.

**NOTE:** The best sources for determining player eligibility are the National League's *Green Book* and the American League's *Red Book*. Both list appearances by position under fielding averages. The *Red Book* lists all players who appeared as designated hitters the preceding season. Circulating an eligibility list by position before Draft Day saves a lot of time. Prepare one yourself in March, when the *Green Book* and *Red Book* are published. Or obtain it with membership in the

Rotisserie League Baseball Association—our list is available at least 3 months earlier, so you'll be able to spend the winter doing something worthwhile (see pages 190–191 for details).

## VI. FEES

The Rotisserie League has a schedule of fees covering all player personnel moves. No money passes directly from team to team. No bets are made on the outcome of any game. All fees are payable into the prize pool and are subsequently distributed to the top four teams in the final standings (see below, **Articles VIII** and **IX**).

1.  **BASIC:** The cumulative total of salaries paid for acquisition of a 23-man roster on Draft Day may not exceed $260.

2.  **TRANSACTIONS:** $10 per trade (no matter how many players are involved) or player activation (from Reserve List or Farm System). In a trade, which team pays the fee is subject to negotiation.

3.  **CALL-UP FROM FREE-AGENT POOL:** $20 until the All-Star Game, $40 thereafter until season's end.

4.  **RESERVE:** $10 for each player placed on a team's Reserve List (see **Article XII**).

5.  **FARM SYSTEM:** $10 for each player in a team's Farm System (see **Article XIII**).

6.  **ACTIVATION:** $10 for each player activated from the Reserve List or Farm System.

7.  **WAIVERS:** $10 for each player claimed on waivers (see **Article XIV**).

8.  **SEPTEMBER ROSTER EXPANSION:** $50 (see **Article XV**).

## VII. PLAYER SALARIES

The salary of a player is determined by the time and means of his acquisition and does not change unless the player becomes a free agent or is signed to a guaranteed long-term contract (see below, **Article XVI**).

- The salary of a player acquired in the major league draft is his auction price.
- The salary of a player called up from the Free Agent Pool during the season is $10.
- The salary of a player activated from a team's Farm System during the season is $10.
- The salary of a player claimed on waivers is $10.
- The salary of a player called up during September Roster Expansion as an extra (i.e., 24th player) is $25 if he is drawn from the Free Agent Pool (see below, **Article XIV**).

**NOTE:** Because you can commit only $260 for salaries on Draft Day, and because you will keep some of your players from one season to the next, salaries are *very* important, particularly after the first season ends and winter trading begins. Would you trade Rickey Henderson for Oddibe Mc-Dowell? George Steinbrenner and Lou Piniella wouldn't trade Henderson for the 1927 Yankees, but a smart Rotisserie League owner just might deal him for Oddibe Young Again. Rickey's salary in the Junior League, an officially authorized Rotisserie League using American League players, is a whopping $56, the highest in organized baseball (Rotisserie League Baseball, that is). McDowell only makes $10, and the $46 difference is enough to buy a Jack Morris *and* a Carney Lansford.

Maintaining accurate, centralized player personnel records (i.e., salary and contract status) is *the most important* task of the League Secretary, who deserves hosannas of praise from the other owners for all the work he does.

## VIII. PRIZE MONEY

All fees shall be promptly collected and wisely invested by the League Treasurer, who is empowered to subject owners to public humiliation and to assess fines as needed to insure that payments are made to the League in a timely fashion. The interest income from this investment can be used to defray the cost of a gala postseason awards ceremony and banquet. The principal shall be divided among the first four teams in the final standings as follows:

- First Place—50%
- Second Place—25%
- Third Place—15%
- Fourth Place—10%

**NOTE:** The Junior League throws a bone of $260 to the fifth best team. Call it balm for the best of the also-rans.

## IX. STANDINGS

The following criteria are used to determine team performance:

- Composite Batting Average
- Total Home Runs
- Total RBIs
- Total Stolen Bases
- Composite ERA
- Total Wins
- Composite Pitching Ratio of walks and hits to innings pitched (Bases on Balls + Hits ÷ Innings Pitched = Ratio)
- Total Saves

Teams are ranked from first to last in each of the eight categories, and given points for each place. For example, in a ten-team league, the first-place team in a category receives ten points, the second-place team 9, and so on down to 1 point for last place. The team with the most total points wins the pennant.

**NOTE:** Pitchers' offensive stats are *not* counted, mainly because they don't appear weekly in *USA Today* or *The Sporting News*. Nor are the pitching stats of the occasional player called in to pitch when the score is 16–1 and the relief corps is hiding under the stands (Astro infielder Craig Reynolds had a 27.00 ERA in 1986, not great but good enough to top Padres' pinch hitter Dane Iorg, who carded a 36.00 as a pinch pitcher).

- In cases of ties in an individual category, the tied teams are assigned points by totaling points for the rankings at issue and dividing the total by the number of teams tied.
- In cases of ties in total points, final place in the standings is determined by comparing placement of teams in individual

categories. Respective performances are calculated and a point given to each team for bettering the other. Should one team acquire more points than the other, the team is declared the winner of the tie. Should the points be equal, the tie stands.

**NOTE:** In the early days of Rotissehistory (i.e., 1980), the Sklar Gazers and the Eisenberg Furriers finished in a flat-footed tie for second with 52 points each. Only seven categories were employed at that time (Wins were added in 1981). The Gazers were ahead in four categories, the Furriers in three, so the Gazers got second place and the bigger check, while the Furriers got heartburn.

## X. STATS

The weekly player performance summaries published in *USA Today* beginning in early May constitute the official data base for the computation of standings in Rotisserie baseball.

**NOTE:** Box scores in daily newspapers are riddled with errors, and official scorers occasionally change rulings. *USA Today* is the final word. When we first started out, we used *The Sporting News.* That was when *TSN* cared more about baseball than about all the Stanley Cup skate-offs, NBA playoffs, and NFL summer camping rolled into one (which, by the way, is how the Rotisserie League's Founding Fathers view them). Not for nothing was the Holy Bible known to baseball people as *The Sporting News* of religion. But that was then, and this is now. *The Sporting News* has passed from the last Spink to new owners who seem intent on taking the "Sporting" part seriously—that is, to cover other sports at the expense of baseball. Also, when we first started out, *USA Today* had not yet been born. With stats that are a lot fresher (one-day lag vs. seven for *TSN*), *USA Today* is Rotisserie League Baseball's official newspaper of record.

• The effective date of any transaction for purposes of statistical calculation is the Monday (AL) or Tuesday (NL) **immediately after** the deadline for reporting transactions to the League Secretary.

**NOTE:** This is because cumulative weekly stats appear in *USA Today* on Tuesday for AL games through the preceding Sunday and on Wednesday for NL games through the preceding Monday. Reporting deadlines should be established as close to these breaks as possible but not later than the start of any game at the beginning of a new week. We use noon on Monday (Junior League/AL players) and 2:00 P.M. on Tuesday (Rotisserie League/NL players). Why the difference? Might as well ask why the strike zones in the two leagues are different.

- Transactions recorded **on** Draft Day, including trades and call-ups to replace disabled players, are effective retroactive to Opening Day. Transactions occurring **after** Draft Day but **before** the closing date of the first cumulative summaries to appear in *USA Today* in May are effective the Monday (AL) or Tuesday (NL) immediately after the first closing date.

**NOTE:** It's a lot simpler than it sounds. Really.

- Performance stats of a player shall be assigned to a Rotisserie League team **only** when he is on the active 23-man roster of that team.

**NOTE:** It is common for a player to appear on the roster of more than one Rotisserie League team during the season because of trades and waiver list moves. Even a player who is not traded may spend time on a team's Reserve List, during which period any numbers he might compile for his major league team do not count for his Rotisserie League team.

- Standings shall be tabulated and issued in a regular and timely fashion, as determined by the League owners.

**NOTE:** Keeping score (see pages 176–188) is the only part of Rotisserie League Baseball that isn't any fun. It's eight or nine hours of number-crunching for each standings report if you're not computerized, a couple of hours of data entry if you are. It's especially important to have weekly standings during the April–May–June trading period, however, and teams still in the race will want weekly standings as the season draws to an end. So divvy up the workload (if some poor innocent won't volunteer), hire someone to do it for you, or become a member of the Rotisserie League Baseball Association and subscribe to its statistical service (see page 191).

## XI. TRADES

From the completion of the draft auction until noon Thursday of the All-Star game break, Rotisserie League teams are free to make trades of any kind without limit, *so long as the active rosters of both teams involved in a trade reflect the required position distribution upon completion of the transaction*. From the All-Star break through August 31, trades may take place *only* between teams contiguous in the preceding week's standings. Trades made from the day after the season ends until rosters are frozen on April 2 prior to Draft Day are **not** bound by the position distribution requirement.

**NOTE:** This means that if Team A wants to swap Darryl Strawberry to Team B for Fernando Valenzuela anytime between Draft Day and the trade deadline, Team A will have to throw in a bum pitcher and Team B a duff outfielder to make the deal. During the off-season, the Strawman could be dealt for Fernando even-up.

- Trades do not affect the salaries or contract status of players.
- Each trade is subject to the $10 transaction fee. The fee is not affected by the number of players involved in the trade.

**NOTE:** Unless you want knife-fights to break out among owners, prohibit all trades involving cash, "players to be named later," or "future considerations." Trust us.

## XII. THE RESERVE LIST

A team may replace any player on its 23-man roster who is

- placed on a **disabled list,**
- **released,**
- **traded** to the other league, or
- **sent down** to the minors by his major league team.

To replace such a player, a Rotisserie League team must release him outright, waive him (see below, **Article XIV**), or place him on its Reserve List. A team reserves a player by notifying the League Secretary and paying the $10 transaction fee. A reserved player is removed from a team's active roster at the end of the stat week (i.e., on Monday or Tuesday) during which formal notification is given, and placed on the team's Reserve List. There is no limit to the number of players a team may have on its Reserve List. Reserving a player protects a team's rights to that player. *A suspended player may not be reserved, released, or replaced.*

**NOTE:** When we first wrote that, we were thinking about the old-fashioned things players would do to get themselves suspended—Bill Madlock hitting an umpire (1980), say, or Gaylord Perry throwing a spitter (1962 to 1983), although he was suspended only once for doing it (in 1982). Then came the drug suspensions of 1984. We chose to consider those players as if they were on the disabled list, and we allowed teams to reserve and replace them.

- Once a specific action has been taken to remove a player from its 23-man roster (via release, waiver, or placing him on the Reserve List), a team is then free to select any eligible player from the Free Agent Pool of players not already owned by another Rotisserie League team. The salary assigned to a player so selected from the Free Agent Pool is $10; the call-up fee is determined by the time of the season in which the call-up is made (see above, **Article VI**).
- The call-up takes effect as soon as it is recorded by the League Secretary, although the player's stats do not begin to accrue to his new team until Monday (AL) or Tuesday (NL) of the week the League Secretary records the call-up.

**NOTE:** On a black *Monday* in May your third baseman, Mike Schmidt, goes into the hospital for arthroscopic surgery on his knee. On *Tuesday* the Phillies get around to announcing officially that Schmidt has been placed on the 21-day disabled list. On *Wednesday* you tab Padre utility man Jerry Royster to fill in for your beloved Schmidty. The valuable Royster qualifies everywhere, and on *Thursday* he drives in two runs and steals a base. His stats don't start counting for you until next Tuesday, but you're thinking he'll help you in steals while Schmidt is mending. On *Friday* Royster goes 4 for 4. Oh, boy! On *Saturday* he pulls a hamstring trying to beat out an infield hit (he's out). On *Sunday* the Padres say he'll be out about 10 days but will not be put on the disabled list at this time. Knowing hamstrings, you figure he'll come back too soon, pull it again, and then be put on the DL. In the meantime, what you have is zip—no stats, no hot streak, no way to replace him, and the likelihood that he won't steal any bases even if he does come back and doesn't hurt himself again. Good morning, black *Monday*.

- When a player on a Reserve List returns to active major league duty, he must be **reinstated** to the active 23-man roster of his Rotisserie League team **two weeks** after his activation, or be **waived**. Failure to notify the League Secretary shall be considered a waiver of the player on the Reserve List.

**NOTE:** Intended to prevent stockpiling of players, this rule is tricky to monitor. Daily newspaper transaction columns, and the telephone sports-information lines, are unreliable about reporting major league roster moves. The clock starts ticking when the League Secretary *is made aware of* a player being reactivated. By the way, "two weeks" means two full reporting periods and may actually be as much as two weeks plus six days (as in the case of a player being reactivated the day after a reporting deadline).

- When a player is reinstated to the active 23-man Rotisserie League roster from a team's Reserve List, the player originally called up to replace him must be waived, unless he can be shifted to another natural opening on the roster for which he qualifies. If the replacement player has been traded, reserved, released, *or* waived within the Rotisserie League, the player acquired in his place must be waived or put into a natural roster opening if one exists. A reinstated player may not displace any player on the active 23-man roster **other than** his original replacement **or** the player for whom the replacement has been traded. The rule holds through successive replacements that may occur for the duration of the season.

**NOTE:** The intent of all this is to minimize the benefit a team might derive from an injury. Say Kirk Gibson is injured and you call up Dan Pasqua to replace him. Gibson comes back. What you'd like to do is activate Gibson, keep Pasqua, and waive your fifth outfielder, Mickey Hatcher, who hasn't had an at-bat in six weeks. Our rules say you can't, on the premise that *a team should not be helped by an injury to a key player*. We know the big leagues don't handle it this way, but art does not always imitate life. Without restrictions of this sort, a team might draft a bum and hope that it would be "lucky" enough for a good player at that position to go on the 15-day DL (with a minor injury, of course), thus giving it a chance to acquire a quality player that got passed over in the draft or a hot rookie who's just been promoted.

- Placing a player *on* the Reserve List and activating a player *from* the Reserve List are *each* subject to a $10 transaction fee.

## XIII. FARM SYSTEM

If a Farm System player is promoted to the active roster of a major league team at any time during the regular season *prior to* September 1 (when major league rosters may expand to 40), his Rotisserie League team has **two weeks** after his promotion to **activate** him (at any position for which he qualifies) *or* **waive** him.

- The fee for activating a player from a team's Farm System is $10.
- If a Farm System player is activated, the player displaced from the 23-man roster to make room for him must be placed on waivers, **unless** the Farm System player can be activated into a natural opening, in which case no waiver is required. Example: One of your pitchers is placed on a major league disabled list; you reserve him and activate a pitcher from your Farm System who has been called up by his major league team.

- Once brought up from its Farm System by a Rotisserie League team, a player may not be returned to it, although he may be placed on a team's Reserve List in the event he is returned to the minor leagues by his major league club.
- A Farm System player not brought up to a team's 23-man roster during the season of his initial selection may be kept within the Farm System in subsequent seasons upon payment of an additional $10 per year, so long as he retains official rookie status and the League Secretary is duly notified on April 2 each year when rosters are frozen (see also **Article XVII**).
- At no time may a team have more than **four** players in its Farm System.
- A Farm System player may be traded during authorized trading periods, subject to prevailing rules governing transactions, as may a team's selection rights in the minor league draft.

**NOTE:** This means that a team could acquire and exercise as many as four Farm System draft picks, providing that it does not exceed the maximum of four players in its Farm System at a given time.

## XIV. OUTRIGHT RELEASE AND WAIVERS

Under certain conditions, a Rotisserie League player may be released outright or placed on waivers.

- When a team activates a player from its Reserve List, the player called up earlier to replace him *must* be placed on waivers (see **Article XII**).
- When a team activates a player from its Farm System, except into a natural opening (see **Article XIII**), the player dropped from the 23-man roster to make room for him **must** be placed on waivers.
- A player no longer on the active roster of his major league team and whose Rotisserie League position is taken by a player activated from the Reserve List or Farm System may not be placed on waivers but **must** be released outright.

**NOTE:** This is to prevent a team from picking up a player on waivers merely for the purpose of releasing him and replacing him with a player of higher quality.

- The *waiver period* begins at noon on Monday (AL) or Tuesday (NL) after the League Secretary has been notified that a player has been waived and lasts one week, at the end of which the player shall become the property of the lowest-ranked team to have claimed him. To make room on its roster, the team acquiring a player on waivers must assign the player to a natural opening or waive a player at the same position played by the newly acquired player.
- *Waiver claims* take precedence over the replacement of an injured, released, or demoted player. That is, a player on waivers in a given week may be signed by a team with a roster opening at his position only if no other team lower in the standings claims the player on waivers.
- A team may acquire on waivers *no more* than one player in a given week.
- A player who *clears waivers*—i.e., is not claimed by any team—returns to the Free Agent Pool.
- The fee for acquiring a player on waivers is $10. The salary of a player acquired on waivers shall be $10 or his previous salary, whichever is greater, and his contract status shall remain unchanged.
  - A player may be given his *outright release only* if he is
    - (a) unconditionally released,
    - (b) placed on the "designated for assignment" list,
    - (c) sent to the minors,
    - (d) placed on the "disqualified" list, or
    - (e) traded to the "other" major league.

**NOTE:** A suspended player may not be released or replaced. A Rotisserie League owner is held strictly accountable for his players' deportment, and must bear the consequences of their transgressions.

## XV. SEPTEMBER ROSTER EXPANSION

If it chooses, a team may expand its roster for the pennant drive by calling up **one** additional player after September 1 from the Free Agent Pool, its own Reserve List, or its own Farm System.

- The order of selection for September Roster Expansion is determined by the most recent standings, with the last-place team having first selection, and so on. This selection order pertains until midnight, September 2 *only,* after which time a team forfeits its order in the selection process, though *not* its right to make a selection. Selection after midnight, September 2 is on a first-come, first-served basis.
- The performance stats of a player called up during September Roster Expansion start to accrue on the Monday (AL) or Tuesday (NL) after the League Secretary has been notified of the player's selection.
- The fee for expanding the roster in September is $50.
- The salary assigned to a September call-up from the Free Agent Pool is $25. The salary of a September call-up from a team's Reserve List or Farm System is the salary established at the time he was previously acquired (i.e., on Draft Day, or subsequently from the Free Agent Pool, or via waivers).

**NOTE:** A device for heightening the excitement for contending teams and for sweetening the kitty at their expense, September Roster Expansion will generally not appeal to second-division clubs (who should, however, continue to watch the waiver wire in the hope of acquiring "keepers" for next season at a $10 salary). Of course, there are always exceptions. A ninth-place Junior League club snapped up Don Sutton as its September player when he came over to the AL in 1982 on the grounds that he'd be worth keeping at $25 the next season. He wasn't, but it seemed like a good idea at the time.

## XVI. THE OPTION YEAR AND GUARANTEED LONG-TERM CONTRACTS

A player who has been under contract at the same salary during two consecutive seasons and whose service has been uninterrupted (that is, he has not been waived or released, although he may have been traded) must, prior to the freezing of rosters in his third or option season, be

- released,
- signed at the same salary for his option year, or
- signed to a guaranteed long-term contract.

If **released,** the player returns to the Free Agent Pool and becomes available to the highest bidder at the next draft auction. If signed at the same salary for an **option year,** the player must be released back into the Free Agent Pool at the end of that season. If signed to a **guaranteed long-term contract,** the player's salary in each year covered by the new contract (which commences with the option year) shall be the sum of his current salary plus $5 for each additional year beyond the option year. In addition, a signing bonus, equal to one half the total value of the long-term contract, but no less than $5, shall also be paid.

> **NOTE:** This rule is intended to prevent blue-chippers, low-priced rookies who blossom into superstars, and undervalued players from being tied up for the duration of their careers by the teams who originally drafted them. It guarantees periodic transfusions of topflight talent for Draft Day and provides rebuilding teams something to rebuild with. And it makes for some interesting decisions at roster-freeze time two years down the pike.
>
> Here's how it works. Let's say you drafted Andres Thomas of the Atlanta Braves for $3 in 1986, a fair price then for an unproven talent. It's now the spring of 1988 and Thomas, who has become the best all-around shortstop in the league, is entering his option year. Only a Charlie Finley would let him play out his option; only a Calvin Griffith would trade him. You compare Thomas' stats with those of other players at various salary levels, assess your needs, project what's likely to be available in the upcoming draft, cross your fingers against injury—and sign him to a four-year guaranteed contract. Thomas' salary zooms to $18 ($3 plus $5 plus $5 plus $5), but he's yours through the 1991 season. His signing bonus, which does not count against your $260 Draft Day limit, is $36 (one half of 4 × $18). If he continues to blossom, you've got a bargain.

- In determining a player's status, "season" is understood to be a full season or any fraction thereof.

NOTE: Thus, a player called up from the Free Agent Pool in the middle of the 1986 season and subsequently retained at the same salary without being released in 1987 (even though he may have been traded) enters his option year in 1988 and must be released, signed at the same salary for an option year, or signed to a long-term contract.

- Option-year and long-term contracts are entirely transferable, both in rights and obligations; the trade of a player in no way affects his contract status.
- If, during the course of a long-term contract, a player is traded from the National League to the American League (or vice versa), the contract is rendered null and void. The team that loses the player's services shall be under no further financial obligations.
- In all other cases—specifically *including* permanent disability or sudden loss of effectiveness—a team must honor the terms of a long-term contract, as follows:

     A player with such a contract *may* be released (that is, not protected on a team's roster prior to Draft Day), but a team that chooses to do so must pay into the prize pool, above the $260 Draft Day limit, a sum equal to **twice** the remaining value of the player's contract. The player then reenters the Free Agent Pool.

NOTE: This is an escape hatch for the owner who buys a dog but can't stand fleas. It's costly, but it's fair. After all, the Mets had to buy out the remainder of George Foster's contract in order to make room for Mookie Wilson and Lenny Dykstra in the same outfield.


## XVII. ROSTER PROTECTION

For the first three seasons of the League's existence, each team must retain, from one season to the next, *no fewer than* **7** but *no more than* **15** of the players on its 23-man roster. After three seasons, this minimum requirement is eliminated, the maximum retained.

**NOTE:** After three seasons, a team might find it impossible to retain a specific minimum because too many players had played out their option.

- The names of players being retained must be recorded with the League Secretary by midnight, April 1. Specific notice must also be made at that time of any guaranteed long-term contract signings and Farm System renewals.

**NOTE:** The April 1 Roster Protection deadline was originally set to correspond with the end of the major leagues' spring interleague trading period, a rite of spring that no longer exists. We've stuck to April 1 anyway, because it gives us a couple of weeks to fine-tune draft strategies. Until you know whom the other teams are going to keep, you won't know for sure who's going to be available. And until you know how much they will have to spend on Draft Day, you won't be able to complete your own pre-Draft budget. So April 1 it is; don't fool with it.

- The cumulative salaries of players protected prior to Draft Day are deducted from a team's $260 expenditure limit, and the balance is available for acquisition of the remaining players needed to complete the team's 23-man roster.
- The League Secretary should promptly notify all teams in the league of each team's protected roster, including player salaries, contract status, and amount available to spend on Draft Day.
- Failure to give notice of a guaranteed long-term contract for a player in his option year will result in his being continued for one season at his prior year's salary and then released into the Free Agent Pool. Failure to renew a Farm System player's minor league contract will result in his becoming available to all other teams in the subsequent minor league draft.
- A Farm System player whose minor league contract is renewed on April 1 and who subsequently makes his major league team's active roster may, at his Rotisserie League owner's option, be added to the protected list of players on Draft Day (and another player dropped, if necessary, to

meet the 15-player limit), or he may be dropped and made available in the draft auction. He may not be retained in his Rotisserie League team's Farm System.

## XVIII. SUBSTANCE ABUSE

After one year from the ratification of this article the manufacture, sale, or transportation of intoxicating liquors within, the importation thereof into, or the exportation thereof from the United States and all territories subject to the jurisdiction thereof, for beverage purposes is hereby prohibited.

**NOTE:** The Rotisserie League is convinced that you have to take a stand somewhere.

## XIX. GOVERNANCE

The Rotisserie League is governed by a Committee of the Whole consisting of all team owners. The Committee of the Whole may designate as many League officials as from time to time it deems appropriate, although only two—the League Secretary and the League Treasurer—ever do any work. The Committee of the Whole also designates annually an Executive Committee composed of three team owners in good standing. The Executive Committee has the authority to interpret playing rules and to handle all necessary and routine League business. All decisions, rulings, and interpretations by the Executive Committee are subject to veto by the Committee of the Whole. Rule changes, pronouncements, and acts of whimsy are determined by majority vote of the Committee of the Whole. The Rotisserie League has three official meetings each year: Draft Day (the first weekend after Opening Day), the Trade Deadline Meeting (at the All-Star break), and the Gala Postseason Banquet and Awards Ceremony. Failure to attend at least two official meetings is punishable by trade to the Minnesota Twins.

## XX. YOO-HOO

To consecrate the bond of friendship that unites all Rotisserie League owners in their pursuit of the pennant, to symbolize the eternal verities and values of the greatest game for baseball fans since baseball, and to soak the head of the League champion with a sticky brown substance before colleagues and friends duly assembled, the **Yoo-Hoo Ceremony** is hereby ordained as the culminating event of the baseball season. Each year, at the awards ceremony and banquet, the owner of the championship team shall have a bottle of Yoo-Hoo poured over his or her head by the preceding year's pennant-winner (or by the most recent victor, in the event of successive championships). The **Yoo-Hoo Ceremony** shall be performed with the dignity and solemnity appropriate to the occasion.

> **NOTE:** If Yoo-Hoo, the chocolate-flavored beverage once endorsed by soft drink connoisseur Yogi Berra, is not available in your part of the country, move.

# Five Things You Should
# *Never Do*

**1. Don't screw around with defensive statistics.** Fairly regularly, we hear that the thing wrong with Rotisseball is that defense doesn't count. All right, we say, how do you make it count? Not fielding averages, for Dick Stuart's sake. Ken Singleton, who runs just fast enough to get to one ball a week, led American League outfielders in fielding percentage a few years ago. Errors? In 1981 Ozzie Smith made more errors than Bill Russell. Even more important, neither *USA Today* nor *The Sporting News* publishes weekly fielding stats, and without weekly stats you've got no way to compute weekly standings, and without weekly standings you've got nothing to live for.

**2. Never, ever join a league which uses both American League and National League players.** In such mutant organizations, a GM inevitably puts together a team made exclusively of first-rank players. In a league of ten 23-man teams drawn from all 624 major leaguers (assuming the owners don't fudge on the 24-man rosters), you need only draft from the top 33% of available players. That's too easy. In an AL league of twelve teams, you use 276 of 336 available players, or 82%. In a ten-team NL league, you use 230 of 288, or 80%. The result, if you stick to one league, is that you have to find a decent second-string catcher, decide which utility infielder has the most speed, figure which fourth and fifth outfielders will get more playing time, and pick a middle-inning reliever who won't slaughter your ERA and Ratio. In other words, you gotta have depth. You know how Joe Garagiola always says pennants are won by the team with the best bench? For once, Joe's right. It's easy to put together a team of stars and near-stars; try doing it with Jim Pankovits and Mike Fischlin, and you'll get a real sense of GM agony. And yes, the 24-man rosters do make it tougher. But it still beats working.

**3. Don't let your computer tell you how to play.** Just because you can manipulate numbers virtually without limit doesn't mean you should. One league we know of decided to make it truly scientific. In computing the standings in their ten-team league, the secretary gives ten points to the league leader in, say, home runs, one point to the team with fewest home runs, and points in between based on the *proportion* of home runs to the gap between first and last. Thus, if Team A leads with 150 taters, and Team B is last with 50, then a team with 140 four-baggers gets nine points even if three other teams have 145 (they'd each get 9.5).

The league's participants claim that this system is fairer. They're decent enough people who know something about baseball, but where **we** come from, "fairness" isn't the point. Do the Phillies get a special bonus when they win 13–0, or are the Royals penalized when they win 2–1? It's not how much you win by that counts, unless you're playing "Major League" Indoor Soccer.

**4. Don't tinker with the size of rosters.** We've already done that. Initially, the Rotisserie League had 22-man rosters. We added a ninth pitcher in 1983 to make us dig deeper and appreciate the value of middle-inning relievers. Why not 25-man rosters? Well, part of it is that when you get down to the last spots on your team, and you've got to decide between Chris Speier and Tim Flannery (if you don't know much about them now, you soon will), you've got problems enough. Moreover, after the draft you've got to have enough unowned talent around so that you can make call-ups from the Free Agent Pool to replace players who are injured, released, or sent to the minors. Otherwise, after the trading deadline, you'll be beset by sorrow, anomie, and a desperate longing for action. Of course, if you are compelled to go with only eight teams in an NL league or ten in an AL version, you can—and should—use 25-man rosters. But trust us: 23 is all the traffic can bear in a 10-team NL Rotisserie League or the 12-team AL variant.

**5. Don't fiddle with the All-Star break trading deadline.** As in the variety of baseball that Reggie and Pete and the others play, the trading deadline protects the Integrity of the Game. Without the deadline early enough in the season so that the standings aren't remotely set in stone, you'll run the risk of Finleyesque player-dumping by the dog-end teams. Suppose it's September 1 and your team is composed of Dale Murphy, Fernando Valenzuela, and 21 guys named José Uribe. You're hopelessly in last, so why not trade the too-expensive contracts of Dale and Fernando to a first-division team for a brace of low-salaried young players who can help you next year? Without the trading deadline you could, but if you did, the contenders you didn't trade with would bury you under second base. We've eased the withdrawal from wheeling and dealing with the Contiguous Trading rule, but don't go beyond that and allow open-ended trading right on through the season. Unless, of course, you enjoy chaos, anarchy, and civil war.

# Iron Hand in a Catcher's Mitt

## The Lonely Job of a Rotisserie League Commissioner

*We are proud—nay, honored—that the normally silent (the way we normally like him) Commissioner for Life of the Rotisserie League, Corlies M. "Cork" Smith, has deigned to descend Mount Olympus to offer his observations and insights on the inner workings of his exalted role in our game. We would have preferred that he explain once and for all what kind of damnfool name "Corlies" is, but we decided to humor him. Gas on, Your Corkship:*

As I perch in my legendary aerie high atop the Savoy Plaza in towered midtown Gotham, I have little to look forward to but my customary three-hour lunch among the grifters at fabled Toots Shor's. Perhaps I should be thinking instead of Runyon's or the Sporting Club. Frankly, I may be out of touch. For I am Commissioner for Life of the one-and-only, the original Rotisserie League, which is probably also unique in that it has had *two* Commissioners for Life, both of whom are more or less still alive.

Although I am often compared (usually favorably) to the late, great General William ("Spike") Eckert in my impotence, I was not snatched from the obscurity of military retirement to be the pious front for a bunch of greed-obsessed owners of major league baseball teams. I swear this on the grave of Walter O'Malley.

No, I earned my spurs, or wristbands, or whatever it is that commissioners wear. I was one of the original owners in the Rotisserie League. The gonfalon of the Smith-Coronas fluttered proudly, if limply, from the center-field flagpole of Smith's Folly, the spacious, natural-turf ball yard where the Coronas went through their stumbling paces and where designated hitters were denied admittance. In that maiden year of 1980 the Coronas finished an honorable seventh. We were models of consistency for the next three seasons: We finished last, last, and last. I was gradually overtaken by the unthinkable: that I wasn't very good at this squirrely game. My fellow owners had been quick to grasp my proclivity for *ejaculatio praecox*. Let one of my thumpers go 0-for-8, or an ace twirler have a couple of bad outings, and he was banished from the Corona clubhouse. How else explain my swapping Darryl Strawberry, *even-up*, to the Fenokees for Eric Show, or Bob Welch to the Brenners for speed merchant Frank (You Can't Steal First Base) Taveras?

When I apprised my fellow Rotisserians of my irrevocable decision to flog my franchise to the lowest bidder, they were of course appalled. After all, where else were they ever going to find so rich a farm club? It must be said that the then reigning Commissioner (also an owner) had evoked occasional murmurs about self-interest as he handed down his otherwise arbitrary fiats from his palatial manse in the Berkshires. The fact that his team languished consistently in the depths of the second division kept his peers from being mutinous, just sullen. So, by sudden acclamation, the switch was made: One Commissioner-for-Life took up the fungo of authority from another.

The job, as has been rumored, is not all beer and bratwurst. For example, as Czar I feel obligated to attend spring training rituals in Clearwater. I actually *go* to Grapefruit League games and cast a critical eye over the hot young prospects. My vassals (as I now see the owners) *talk* about going to the ball park. But in reality they spend most of their daylight hours in pursuit of the dimpled pellet, surely heresy to anyone who understands that there is only one game. So while I study the pheenoms from the vantage point of the Commissioner's box at Jack Russell Stadium, they curry sunstroke on the links or fondle the latest illegal putter in the pro shop. While in Florida we do have a rules-change and policy meeting at which I preside. It's just like real life. The Owners decide what they're going to do and inform the Commissioners of their decision; he gets to announce it. In theory I get to vote in the event of a tie, but it hasn't come up yet and I doubt that it will since they are a fair and reasonable, if slightly hysterical, lot. I am also empowered to exercise a veto over any act that I, in my infinite Commissionerhood, deem to be detrimental to the good of the league. This hasn't come up either, but such action would be subject to review by the membership. See?

(Interesting sidelight: Did anyone ever even *hear* of *Mrs.* Bowie Kuhn or *Mrs.* Peter Ueberroth? Well, my wife, the divine Sheila C., is agreeably visible at Rotisserie League outings. In the days of the Coronas the current Czarina performed yeowoman work as the official money laundress. Today, she handles the onerous chores of First Lady with grace and aplomb. Any owner who thinks he can get at me through her is probably right.)

Another of my heavy duties is to run the annual player draft each April (it's always held the first Sunday *after* Opening Day, since the major league rosters have to be final). My most compelling qualification for this job is that my dining room table is bigger than theirs—and yours, too, come to think of it. (I know, I know—a lot of guys *think* they have a big one, until they see mine. Why, even Dave Winfield . . . but that's another story.)

Basically, I act as auctioneer. An owner will name a player and enter a bid (usually a dollar); the bidding then proceeds around the table until the high bidder "signs" that player; then the next owner names another player; and so forth until every roster is filled. It's my task to see that it all goes in orderly fashion and to keep close tabs on how much each owner has left to spend. All of this high-powered stuff takes place at the now-alas-dark headquarters of Smith's Folly, a.k.a. the Coronas front office. There have been rumors that the old apple orchard is to be leveled to make way for a midget-auto racing velodrome. Not as long as I draw breath.

My penultimate act each year is to pass out the winnings, a gratifyingly phony bit of largesse since it's not my dough. There I am faced with ten freshly scrubbed owners, all dressed to the twos. One of them is going to be very happy; one pretty darn happy; one happy enough; and one will get his bait back (the 10% for fourth place usually roughly matches what the owner has put in over the course of the season). But there are in attendance six others, all of them just as mind-bogglingly self-serving as the winners. They take it all in good grace, and I can say to their credit that not one of them has ever said, "Wait till next year."

From my point of view the highlight of the season comes with the solemn presentation of the Golden Spike (the William Eckert Award). This eccentrically obscene piece of brass is given annually to "that owner who has best emulated the high standards set by the revered Commissioner of the Rotisserie League." In a nutshell, the prize goes to the team that finished last. It is three years since the Commissioner, out of his own heart and pocket, generously donated the Golden Spike to posterity. It is some measure of the regard in which the Eckert Award is held that not a single winner/loser has ever taken it home after the cheering stopped.

# Scouting Report

## 1987 Player Ratings

After Rotisserie League Baseball arrived on the planet Earth in a spherical, white, hand-stitched spaceship from Mars around 1980, thousands of red-blooded American men and women would never approach the grand old game of baseball the same way. It used to be that we were happy to read the same old stories about the Twins' pennant chances or the odds on Pete Rose getting 10,000 hits. But when we became Rotisserie League owners our thirst for baseball knowledge took quantum leaps—explicable only because of the extraterrestrial intelligence that originated the game.

Hang Pete's hits, Rotisserie owners want to know who among his half dozen rookie outfielders is going to get playing time. Who will be the Twins' stopper—if anyone? Will the Dodgers' catcher at San Antonio leap over the Dodgers' catcher at Albuquerque before both of them fail to make the grade in Chavez Ravine? Why has Joe Blow sat out three days in a row? Will Harry Hangnail's injury put him on the DL? Maybe in the old days you were really a fan and you knew the starting lineups of just about every major league team. Now, Mr., Mrs. and Ms. Rotisserie Owner, you try to know by heart the benches, the bullpens, probably the Triple A and Double A prospects, and possibly the first fifty or so names in the high school draft—heck, some of you have been out there scouting them.

Still, you wake up in the morning groggy from the questions that have swirled through your overheated mind and disturbed your unquiet sleep. Some of you are brazen enough to ring up a team's publicity department and say, "Hi, this is Redford Roberts from the *American Literary Historical Review*, uh, how's Jack's ankle?" Others pore over the stats pages of the local rag as if you would win World Series tickets if you could find your license plate number hidden among the agate type.

You won't find any tickets or any news on Jack's ankle tucked away in this Scouting Report, but its aim is to answer just about every other question you might have about hundreds of major league ballplayers prior to your Rotisserie League's annual April draft, and, of course, the most important question of all—how much is the guy worth?—when you're belly up to the table with a bunch of other boys and girls and the Commissioner is cruelly crowing, "All right, your key to the title, here he is, Roy Hobbs, $32, do I hear more, going once, going twice . . ." The following descriptions and price judgments have been produced by various expert owners in the Rotisserie League, checked for four-letter words by the editors, and run past Johnny Carson's writers for added laughs. Each player's 1986 stats in the four Rotissecategories of offense or pitching are listed after his name.

Publishers can't get books out overnight, of course, so you might find Rick Rhoden still among National League pitchers instead of with the Yankees, assuming, that is, that Syd Thrift finally gave in and accepted Don Mattingly for him. So you need to supplement this wisdom with slightly more up-to-date reports. The best daily source—you might argue if you live in a world-class sportspage city like Boston, Los Angeles, or Philadelphia, but the rest of us have no options—is *USA Today*, with its spring training reports from every major league camp and authoritative transactions column. Among the weeklies, Peter Gammons' "Inside Baseball" in *Sports Illustrated* is a must. *Baseball America* is a biweekly that is indispensable for following the stats of your and everybody else's Farm System players.

It surely can be no coincidence that the years since Rotisserie League Baseball came down from—oh, you've heard that one—have seen a proliferation of baseball annuals addressed to the more than casual fan. The only ones that go back to pre-Rotisserie years are TSN's *Baseball Register* and *Official Baseball Guide* and *The National League Green Book* and *The American League Red Book*, the latter two of which have only been widely disseminated in post-Rotisserie times. There's *Baseball America's Statistics Report, The Bill James Baseball Abstract, The Elias Baseball Analyst, The Scouting Report, Bill Mazeroski's Baseball, The Sporting News Baseball Yearbook,* and who knows what else. Buying all those books is an incentive to do well in Rotisseball—you'll probably have to finish first or second to be able to afford them. To get a head start on finishing high, you've got the right book in your hand.

---

### BASEBALL AMERICA

*Baseball America* is still a well-kept secret from many Rotisserie League owners and GMs, but it ought not to be. Formerly known as "the Baseball Junkie's Newspaper" until being a junkie, of any sort, suddenly went out of fashion, it now carries the moniker "Baseball News You Can't Get Anywhere Else . . . ," and for once a claim is true. *Baseball America* covers the farm systems, the minor leagues, college baseball, winter ball, and all points in between. It is the *absolute* source for printed public information about players *not* in the major leagues. Recently, trying to broaden its appeal, it has increased coverage of major league doings with a columnist for each of the four divisions, as well as running Dick Old—er, Young. Let's hope *Baseball America* doesn't decide that the way to big bucks is to recycle baseball star quotes clipped from out-of-town newspapers, the way all too many daily sports columnists and other papers fill up their allotted white space. Put Dick out to pasture, do what you do best, *Baseball America*. All us junkies will love ya, even if you can't call us that anymore (18 issues a year for $24.95 from *Baseball America*, P.O. Box 2089, Durham, NC 27702). And tell 'em you read about it in *Rotisserie League Baseball*.

---

# NATIONAL LEAGUE

## *Warmup*

National League baseball is getting harder and harder these days to tell apart from World Cup soccer. Score a run early in the game and then play defense . . . play for a scoreless tie in nine and hope to win in overtime—oops, extra innings. Watch for Dottore Giamatti to put in a new rule soon: All ties after 12 innings will be decided by a home run contest—bring in the batting practice pitchers and see if anyone can bloop it out of the park. If you think a walk, a stolen base, a groundout advancing the runner, and a squeeze bunt are more fun to watch than Babe Ruth pointing to the descamisados in the Wrigley Field bleachers and then blasting one out, then National League Rotisserie play is for you.

They steal more bases in the Senior Circuit, that's for sure, and—whether the cause is mighty pitchers or puny hitters—score less runs, hit fewer home runs, and have lower pitching earned run averages and hits/walks ratio. It doesn't necessarily hold that the royal road to Rotisserie League championships using National League players is to build around speed and pitching—after all, you get 10 points for leading the league in home runs even if the numbers are modest—but it is a fact that recent winners in the original Rotisserie League have constructed their teams around, yes, speed and pitching.

You don't have to be greedy like the Stein Brenners and have Vince Coleman's 107 stolen bases *and* Eric Davis's 80 *and* Mitch Webster's 36 on your team to be a contenda, but you do need to keep your eye on stolen base totals, see if any of the speedsters can help with batting average, home runs, and runs batted in, and try to acquire three or four players who will steal 25 or more bases for you. For pitching, there are two schools of thought: Emphasize starters, stress relievers. If you have a Mike Scott on your team— better yet, if you can cheaply acquire a mediocre pitcher who will turn into a Mike Scott the way Mike Scott did—you will get many innings of low run, low ratio baseball. But the risk of stocking up on starters is that a poor season—for example, Rick Mahler's 4.88 ERA and 1.59 ratio in 1986—will give you headaches for every one of the 200-plus innings he worked. Going for the relievers gives you a head start in saves while it usually leads to lower earned run averages and ratios, since relievers who are ineffective are not used. However, you will probably sacrifice some points in the win column.

No Angels, but quite a few Giants and Pirates have danced on the heads of pins as the sagest Rotisserie minds have pondered these matters. Write us a letter when you've solved them.

## On the Mound

The Rotisserie owner who spends the off-season toting up prospective home runs and stolen bases has a fool for a general manager. Year after year, pennants are won with strong arms. It's the pitching that conquers: rotation starters with stingy earned run averages and ratios, on teams with .500 records or better, plus the blue-chip stoppers you can nearly count on the hand of Mordecai Brown. Keep in mind, too, the tenth man on your staff: the ball park. Bandboxes such as those in Atlanta, Chicago, and Philadelphia should make you think twice about any hurler, while the cavernous parks in Montreal, St. Louis, and Houston more than justify your spending a few more bucks on pitchers there. You should also value the talented *setup* relievers on decent ball clubs: Tim Burke, Ron Robinson, Charles Kerfeld, among others. They not only have the generally good numbers associated with relief pitchers, they also contribute their fair share of saves and can reasonably be expected to pitch in with ten or so wins.

**RICK AGUILERA.**    10 Wins, 0 Saves, 3.88 ERA, 1.280 Ratio
    The Mets are so pitching deep—at all levels of their organization— that Aguilera could be the pitcher to be traded should any offensive need arise. A very good pitcher who'll get better. $10.

**DOYLE ALEXANDER.**    6 Wins, 0 Saves, 3.84 ERA, 1.296 Ratio
    A hard call. He loves playing for Bobby Cox and he gets the ball over. Nothing spectacular, though. He might be a more tempting pick if he pitched in another ball park. $5.

**MIKE BIELECKI.**    6 Wins, 0 Saves, 4.66 ERA, 1.560 Ratio
    Anyone for a good class-action suit against *Baseball America*? Amid all the hype, and in their cover story, they forgot to mention a little detail called the strike zone. $3–$5.

**VIDA BLUE.**   10 Wins, 0 Saves, 3.27 ERA, 1.366 Ratio
Oakland was yesterday. $4.

**TOM BROWNING.**   14 Wins, 0 Saves, 3.81 ERA, 1.212 Ratio
He's good but he's not *that* good. Just take a look at his supposedly phenomenal rookie season. Still, except for his earned run average, he came back strong after a terrible start in '86. He's gritty and could actually grow into what some people mistakenly thought he was. $10–$14.

**DON CARMAN.**   10 Wins, 1 Save, 3.22 ERA, 1.229 Ratio
Pitched very well after being converted to a starter and may be worth much more in the rotation than in the pen. Still something of an enigma—shades of Mark Davis. $10–$12.

**TIM CONROY.**   5 Wins, 0 Saves, 5.23 ERA, 1.544 Ratio
May be the best arm on the Cardinals, *when healthy*. Rotisserians who remember when he broke in at Oakland were impressed enough to persuade some who refuse to recognize the existence of the American League—but those 1986 numbers are pretty powerful unpersuaders. Could he be the Mike Scott of '87? $1.

**DANNY COX.**   12 Wins, 0 Saves, 2.90 ERA, 1.132 Ratio
Rounded into form after his scrape with a Florida seawall and should be as good as new in '87. If you look for the Cardinals to bounce back, Cox should figure to win in the high teens. $10–$14.

**RON DARLING.**   15 Wins, 0 Saves, 2.81 ERA, 1.198 Ratio
So what *was* a nice boy from Yale doing at Cooter's Executive Burgers? For this we sent him four years to college? The scuffle didn't hurt his work, however, and Darling has shown signs of cutting down on the walks, which makes him prime, grade-A, Rotisserie beef. $17–$22.

**DANNY DARWIN.**   5 Wins, 0 Saves, 2.32 ERA, 1.087 Ratio
He absolutely has the worst luck of any pitcher now pitching. Good ratio, good ERA, and little to show for them. Teammate Rick Manning took to paying Brewers $50 for every run they drove in while Darwin was pitching. You can probably pick him up for a buck or two, but he's worth more now that he's pitching indoors. $6.

**STORM DAVIS.**   9 Wins, 0 Saves, 3.62 ERA, 1.396 Ratio

With Tudor and Ojeda coming over from the American League and burning up the National, some may imagine Davis can do the same. But he's neither left-handed nor an ex-Red Sox pitcher. $9.

**JOHN DENNY.**   11 Wins, 0 Saves, 4.20 ERA, 1.372 Ratio

Not the world's most friendly human being: throws bats at TV cameras and beats up on sportswriters. On second thought, what's so bad about that? $7–$10.

**JIM DESHAIES.**   12 Wins, 0 Saves, 3.25 ERA, 1.271 Ratio

Crafty Rotisserians will take a long look. He's a left-hander with better than average ball movement and pitches under the Dome. On the debit side, he tends to be wild high and prone to gopher attacks. $9.

**DAVE DRAVECKY.**   9 Wins, 0 Saves, 3.07 ERA, 1.259 Ratio

Year after year, one of the more underrated southpaws for Rotissepurposes. His major league ratio through 1985 was a glittering 1.177, his ERA 3.05. Last season he was hampered by a gimpy elbow, so exercise caution. If he's healthy, jump on him. $10–$14.

**DENNIS ECKERSLEY.**   6 Wins, 0 Saves, 4.57 ERA, 1.340 Ratio
See Rick Sutcliffe.

**SID FERNANDEZ.**   16 Wins, 1 Save, 3.52 ERA, 1.233 Ratio

It's truly awesome how few hits he allows per nine innings. His walk ratio also is maturing with time. In the end, he may prove as good as Gooden, though be careful: He became erratic late in the '86 season, and the Mets may have soured on him—unless his seventh-game World Series heroics redeemed him. $20–$25.

**BOB FORSCH.**   14 Wins, 0 Saves, 3.25 ERA, 1.213 Ratio

Back from the grave with a surprisingly potent performance. Great ratio and ERA most of the season, with considerable slippage in the last month or so. He's earned a nod in this year's planning, with caution: Rick Reuschel pulled the same Lazarus trick in '85, but crept back into the cave a season later. $5–$7.

**DWIGHT GOODEN.**   17 Wins, 0 Saves, 2.84 ERA, 1.108 Ratio

No, he ain't God, man. But he may be God's son. $28–$30.

**KEVIN GROSS.**  12 Wins, 0 Saves, 4.02 ERA, 1.382 Ratio
There were those who thought he'd go to the head of the class in '86, but they were wrong. But there may be hope for him yet. $7–$10.

**BILL GULLICKSON.**  15 Wins, 0 Saves, 3.38 ERA, 1.246 Ratio
Stick with him. A notorious slow starter, he gets serious in the heat and humidity of late July. He looked for a while like he might turn into a 20-game winner, but it doesn't seem likely anymore. But you can count on 15 and a decent ratio. $12–$15.

**ANDY HAWKINS.**  10 Wins, 0 Saves, 4.30 ERA, 1.400 Ratio
Go know. He had a crummy season in '84, won 18 games in '85, then fell off again last year. Riskier than this they don't come. $4.

**OREL HERSHISER.**  14 Wins, 0 Saves, 3.85 ERA, 1.293 Ratio
Wha' happened? After two extraordinary years, he nearly lost it in '86. Don't ask for an explanation, but it says here that Hershiser will someday soon become one of the great relievers in the league. $20–$24.

**JOE HESKETH.**  6 Wins, 0 Saves, 5.01 ERA, 1.487 Ratio
The reason Blue Cross won't return Edgar Bronfman's phone calls. Hesketh is a truly sad case: a fine, young lefty who's chronically accident-prone. There's hope he makes it again, but this is hard ball. Be wary. $3–$7.

**RICK HONEYCUTT.**  11 Wins, 0 Saves, 3.32 ERA, 1.222 Ratio
After arm problems in '85, he bounced back to enjoy the kind of superb season he used to have in the Junior Circuit. No reason it shouldn't continue. $12–$15.

**LAMARR HOYT.**  8 Wins, 0 Saves, 5.15 ERA, 1.497 Ratio
Like Lonnie Smith and Darrell Porter, he seemed better off as a party animal. After drying out last spring, he *really* lost control, which was one thing he always had going for him. $6–$8.

**CHARLES HUDSON.**  7 Wins, 0 Saves, 4.94 ERA, 1.549 Ratio
They say he's got problems contentratin'. You can be sympathetic but grow tired of waitin'. $2.

**BOB KIPPER.**   6 Wins, 0 Saves, 4.03 ERA, 1.377 Ratio
Rushed unmercifully fast to the big leagues, he'll come into his own this year or next. In Rotisserie League Baseball, as in good comedy, timing is everything. $3.

**BOB KNEPPER.**   17 Wins, 0 Saves, 3.14 ERA, 1.140 Ratio
With Jesus as his Pitching Coach, who's to worry? It used to be Knepper would give you good seasons every other year. Now he's a blue-chipper—at least until the Astros start playing outdoors in Houston again, or in Washington, D.C., whichever comes first. $20–$25.

**MIKE KRUKOW.**   20 Wins, 0 Saves, 3.05 ERA, 1.057 Ratio
Always a gamer, even when he toiled for worse teams than the Giants. Last season was no fluke. $13–$19.

**MIKE LACOSS.**   10 Wins, 0 Saves, 3.57 ERA, 1.219 Ratio
He owes Roger Craig his firstborn *and* a player to be named. Further proof that you don't need much else if you master the you-know-what fastball. Another candidate to be the next Mike Scott. $6–$8.

**ED LYNCH.**   7 Wins, 0 Saves, 3.73 ERA, 1.283 Ratio
Doesn't walk anybody, which in Wrigley Field is hardly a compliment. $2–$3.

**RICK MAHLER.**   14 Wins, 0 Saves, 4.88 ERA, 1.590 Ratio
Gives fresh vision to the tired cliché "winning ugly." Horrendous ratios, mediocre ERAs haven't stopped him from winning a goodly number of games the past two seasons. But it may be his luck is running out. $1–$5.

**ROGER MASON.**   3 Wins, 0 Saves, 4.80 ERA, 1.433 Ratio
Here's a guy to keep your eye on. He brings pretty impressive minor league numbers to the party and under Craig's tutorship could make it big. May be a bargain in your draft. $2–$5.

**GREG MATTHEWS.**   11 Wins, 0 Saves, 3.65 ERA, 1.259 Ratio
May emerge as a stalwart. His rookie season lived up to reasonable expectations after less than a full season at Triple A. Definitely recommended. $9–$12.

**BOB OJEDA.**   18 Wins, 0 Saves, 2.57 ERA, 1.091 Ratio
   They said post-Fenway Tudor wouldn't last and they'll say it about this guy, too. But he's for real—as long as he keeps the ball down as consistently as last year. $13–$16.

**DAVID PALMER.**   11 Wins, 0 Saves, 3.65 ERA, 1.350 Ratio
   By the time you read this he may be pitching in Japan. Before his chronic injuries he showed enormous potential. What poisoned it was the time last year that he threw at Strawberry and Strawberry charged the mound. Palmer then responded by hysterically tossing his mitt in Strawberry's face. *Sayonara.* $1.

**ALEJANDRO PENA.**   1 Win, 1 Save, 4.89 ERA, 1.486 Ratio
   Last year the smart owner bought him for a buck and hoped for the best. He may never regain his former heat, but if he's sound enough to pitch, he'll pitch relatively well. Certainly a dollar's worth. $1–$4.

**SHANE RAWLEY.**   11 Wins, 0 Saves, 3.54 ERA, 1.370 Ratio
   Obtained from the Yankees in exchange for Marty Bystrom, he proved again (before suffering an injury in August) that Steinbrenner doesn't know his pinstripes from his prison stripes. $12–$15.

**RICK REUSCHEL.**   9 Wins, 0 Saves, 3.96 ERA, 1.340 Ratio
   The man who fell to earth. On the bright side, he's eligible once again for Comeback Player of the Year. Odds are he won't win it. $3–$6.

**RICK RHODEN.**   15 Wins, 0 Saves, 2.84 ERA, 1.131 Ratio
   At the time of this writing he's still under house arrest. They don't call Syd Thrifty for nothing. You'd think Rhoden would have gotten some early parole for good behavior. $12–$15.

**BRUCE RUFFIN.**   9 Wins, 0 Saves, 2.46 ERA, 1.244 Ratio
   Within two years, barring injury, he'll be the class of the Phillies' staff. Take that for what it's worth. Right now it's easy to be high on him. As they say in Paris, he's got pwoz. $10–$14.

**NOLAN RYAN.**   12 Wins, 0 Saves, 3.34 ERA, 1.129 Ratio
   Not only can he still win, he's also not as wild as he used to be. Washed up he ain't. $14–$20.

**SCOTT SANDERSON.**   9 Wins, 1 Save, 4.19 ERA, 1.190 Ratio
See Rick Sutcliffe. $6–$9.

**MIKE SCOTT.**   18 Wins, 0 Saves, 2.22 ERA, 0.923 Ratio
Doesn't matter if it's the split finger or the sandpaper, Scott
has emerged as one of the premier Rotisserie pitchers. A guy or
two like this on your staff and your numbers are safe even from the
likes of Rick Mahler. $20–$25.

**ERIC SHOW.**   9 Wins, 0 Saves, 2.97 ERA, 1.306 Ratio
Remember, politics don't count. Like Dravecky, a solid and
consistent pitcher (lifetime ratio before '86, 1.26, ERA 3.35). He
kept his earned run average under 3.00 last season despite tendini-
tis in his right flipper. $14–$17.

**BRYN SMITH.**   10 Wins, 0 Saves, 3.94 ERA, 1.308 Ratio
The Rotisserie owner who had him last year was begging for
mercy. To say he slipped from his 18 wins in '85 is an understate-
ment. $8–$12.

**ZANE SMITH.**   8 Wins, 0 Saves, 4.05 ERA, 1.534 Ratio
Possibly the ugliest pitcher since Don Mossi. (Hmm, maybe
he should have asked for Sid Bream's old chin.) When he's on,
Smith throws a nasty slider, mean and down, which could make
him a dominant pitcher, even in the Launching Pad. $4.

**MARIO SOTO.**   5 Wins, 0 Saves, 4.71 ERA, 1.514 Ratio
He's had two disappointing seasons in a row, so look for him
to go cheaper than usual. But even at that he's scary. Odds are that
his shoulder is a lot worse than he's letting on, which could explain
all the home runs he's giving up. He could go the way of Joaquin
Andujar—to the American League. $10.

**RICK SUTCLIFFE.**   5 Wins, 0 Saves, 4.64 ERA, 1.483 Ratio
Some days he has great stuff, other days he doesn't, and others
still he's on the DL. It's your guess. People who can predict the
future would not be writing books about fantasy baseball. $10–$14.

**JAY TIBBS.**   7 Wins, 0 Saves, 3.97 ERA, 1.319 Ratio
This is his pivotal year. He walks too many and hitters wait on
the fat ones. But signs show he's got the stuff to be an effective

low-ball pitcher, which in Olympic Stadium could mean *bien plus*. There's a chance that he's for real. $5.

**STEVE TROUT.**   5 Wins, 0 Saves, 4.75 ERA, 1.627 Ratio
See Rick Sutcliffe. $3–$5.

**JOHN TUDOR.**   13 Wins, 0 Saves, 2.92 ERA, 1.142 Ratio
Whatever hit the fan (not baseball fan, the air-circulating kind) at the deciding game of the '85 World Series showed no ill effects in '86. Tudor had another great year, carving a place at the top of those whose numbers are invaluable to a serious Rotisserie contender. $20–$27.

**FERNANDO VALENZUELA.**   21 Wins, 0 Saves, 3.14 ERA, 1.155 Ratio
The best starting pitcher in the league. The only worry is his arm, which has yet to show any strain from all those innings and all those screwballs. $24–$30.

**BOB WALK.**   7 Wins, 2 Saves, 3.75 ERA, 1.362 Ratio
There are worse fifth starters, which more and more people will recognize this year. $2–$5.

**BOB WELCH.**   7 Wins, 0 Saves, 3.28 ERA, 1.196 Ratio
Something of an off year in '86, following his fantastic second half in '85. If he stays with the Dodgers he's capable of winning 15 games or so, with good numbers. You could—and will—do a lot worse. $13–$18.

**ED WHITSON.**   1 Win, 0 Saves, 5.59 ERA, 1.612 Ratio
Now that the nails in his New Jersey driveway are history, Whitson may again find happiness among the tract homes of San Diego. Looking on the plus side, you could say he's got something to prove. Looking on the minus, you probably said that a year ago, too. $1.

**FLOYD YOUMANS.**   13 Wins, 0 Saves, 3.53 ERA, 1.201 Ratio
In case you missed it, he was Dwight Gooden's teammate in high school, blah, blah, blah. Golly, what a staff that musta been, blah, blah, blah. Well, sports fans, someday Floyd Youmans

will stand on his own two feet, and throw his own hummer, and then maybe we won't have to hear the deep background anymore. A budding superstar, to coin a phrase. $14–$20.

## Out of the Bullpen

If relief pitching is a dangerous job, how about being a Rotisserie owner of a relief pitcher? It's an experience every Rotisserian has had, with the worst and with the best—runners on second and third, slugger coming up, the manager walks slowly to the mound, waves an arm, wants the righty—oh, no, your guy! Slow minutes of agony while he comes in from the pen, warms up, throws high outside, low inside, a belt-high fast ball, pow! Fifty thousand screaming fans and you've got your head buried in your hands, silently praying, beam me up, Scotty, get me out of this. Well, being a Rotisserian can't be all fun, can it? Championships can be won with little or no relief—the Stein Brenners did it in '86—but you miss the agony and ecstasy of the game. And aren't they more important than a check and a trophy?

**PAUL ASSENMACHER.**  7 Wins, 7 Saves, 2.50 ERA, 1.274 Ratio
The man throws dangerous curves, and he's got what it takes to be an occasional stopper and a very good setup man. With a dismal Atlanta rotation, look for him to win in double figures. $8–$12.

**STEVE BEDROSIAN.**  8 Wins, 29 Saves, 3.39 ERA, 1.251 Ratio
Bedrock provides many classic moments like the nightmare described above. Two out, bottom of the ninth, ahead by a run, he'll walk the bases loaded and . . . $20–$24.

**TIM BURKE.**  9 Wins, 4 Saves, 2.93 ERA, 1.471 Ratio
A valuable eighth or ninth man because he tends to win quite a bit for a reliever. 1986 showed that his talent's for real—of course, he may end up a starter in '87. $10–$12.

**JOHN FRANCO.**  6 Wins, 29 Saves, 2.94 ERA, 1.327 Ratio
A little guy with a lot of moxie and a slider with fangs. The best left-handed reliever in the National League. $27–$33.

**GENE GARBER.**  5 Wins, 24 Saves, 2.54 ERA, 1.231 Ratio
Depends on Sutter's health and whether Al Hrabosky makes a comeback. $15–$18.

**SCOTT GARRELTS.**  13 Wins, 10 Saves, 3.11 ERA, 1.255 Ratio
Returned to the pen three months later than the Rotisserie League owner who kept him at $10 predicted, but better late than never. Gold as a reliever, pewter as a starter. Surely Roger Craig understands that now. $25 as a closer, $8 as a starter.

**GOOSE GOSSAGE.**  5 Wins, 21 Saves, 4.45 ERA, 1.376 Ratio
Still blazing after all these years, but with Lance McCullers coming of age, the Padres might well unload him, his scowl, and his salary. High ERA and ratio take the edge off his saves. $25–$30 on past performance, but might be on the high side.

**KEN HOWELL.**  6 Wins, 12 Saves, 3.87 ERA, 1.525 Ratio
By September this year Tom Lasorda will have a short man with more than twenty saves. It won't be Howell, or his pen pal Tom Niedenfuer, either. $10.

**BARRY JONES.**  3 Wins, 3 Saves, 2.89 ERA, 1.340 Ratio
See Don Robinson.

**CHARLES KERFELD.**  11 Wins, 7 Saves, 2.59 ERA, 1.206 Ratio
You gotta love the guy, blubber and all. Will get some saves and his share of wins. Eventually he will take over the stopper's chores, which makes him a good investment. $11–$17.

**LANCE McCULLERS.**  10 Wins, 5 Saves, 2.78 ERA, 1.184 Ratio
See The Goose. $18–$23.

**ROGER McDOWELL.**  14 Wins, 22 Saves, 3.02 ERA, 1.155 Ratio
Will he be the main man or the setup man in '87? Orosco's gutsy playoffs and World Series may have rewritten the script. If you think McDowell's the one, with a 30-plus save year in the offing, the price will run $33–$38.

**TOM NIEDENFUER.** 6 Wins, 11 Saves, 3.71 ERA, 1.438 Ratio
See Ken Howell. $10.

**JESSE OROSCO.** 8 Wins, 21 Saves, 2.33 ERA, 1.222 Ratio
Smart money was saying that Randy Myers would take Orosco's place as the bullpen lefty sometime before or during the '87 season. Were two World Series saves a gallant farewell, or a return to Number One? $15–$18.

**TED POWER.** 10 Wins, 1 Save, 3.70 ERA, 1.295 Ratio
Who? Maybe he'll be a starter. $5–$8.

**JEFF REARDON.** 7 Wins, 35 Saves, 3.94 ERA, 1.225 Ratio
They say he came up with a third pitch last year that right-handed hitters found demoralizing. Since Buck Rodgers isn't one to mess around with committees, there's no reason to think Reardon won't be worth a dollar a save again this year. Still, that ain't cheap. $38–$40.

**DON ROBINSON.** 3 Wins, 14 Saves, 3.38 ERA, 1.270 Ratio
There's an outside chance he'll be the stopper. The same goes for Barry Jones, who's six years younger. Flip a coin, then spend $12 and keep your fingers crossed.

**RON ROBINSON.** 10 Wins, 14 Saves, 3.24 ERA, 1.311 Ratio
He says he wants his role better defined. Fair enough. Ron, you're too sound to be wasted in long relief and you lack the stuff of a true closer. Why don't you ask Pete if you can start? $7–$10.

**DAVE SMITH.** 4 Wins, 33 Saves, 2.73 ERA, 1.089 Ratio
Virtually unhittable for much of last season, he fell victim to a nagging back, and not for the first time. If he's healthy he'll rack up 20–30 saves. $25–$30.

**LEE SMITH.** 9 Wins, 31 Saves, 3.09 ERA, 1.229 Ratio
It must be truly one of the most hair-raising jobs in life: standing in against Lee Arthur Smith with two strikes and his fast ball working in the Wrigley Field twilight. He's the best argument to go to law school. $35.

**BRUCE SUTTER.**  2 Wins, 3 Saves, 4.34 ERA, 1.390 Ratio
Seek the advice of a qualified physician.

**TODD WORRELL.**  9 Wins, 36 Saves, 2.08 ERA, 1.225 Ratio
So imposing, it's hard to accept he was only a rookie last year. Herzog says he wouldn't trade him for any other stopper in baseball. Whitey don't lie. Will save 30 or more. $38–$41.

## Behind the Plate

When the time came for the New York Mets to make their first selection in the expansion draft prior to the 1962 season (a lineal precursor of the first Rotisserie League Draft, which followed only 18 years later), whom did they select?

The old Dodger Gil Hodges, a sure-fire bet to please the team's soon-to-be fans? A .300 hitter like Richie Ashburn, who could lead off and give the team a shot of instant class? A righty slugger like Frank Thomas, whose stroke was tailor-made for the left-field seats in the Polo Grounds, where Bobby Thomson had consummated the Little Miracle of Coogan's Bluff in 1951?

No, the Mets might be new kids on the block, but they knew how to build a ball club. They picked journeyman backstop Hobie Landrith, late of the San Francisco Giants (.239 BA, 2 home runs, 10 RBI in 1961). Casey Stengel put it all into perspective: "You gotta have a catcher. If you don't have a catcher, you'll have a lot of passed balls." You could look it up.

In a twisted way, that's what Rotisserie League rules tell you. You gotta have a catcher. Two catchers, in fact. Only a few can help you, and a lot can hurt you. Truth is, the offensive talent to be found at this position is as thin as a rookie's scrapbook. Once you get past Gary Carter there's a big drop into Jody Davis-Tony Pena territory. After that, for every Bo Diaz there are two Sal Buteras.

Here's a look at the top 12 National League receivers. Savor their names, but realize that by the end of the draft you'll be bidding up a Bruce Bochy or a Dann Bilardello, and maybe having to settle for a Junior Ortiz or a Steve Lake.

At least they'll cut down on your passed balls.

**ALAN ASHBY.**   .257 BA, 7 Home Runs, 38 RBI, 1 Stolen Base
No power, but the 35-year-old Ashby will hit for a decent average (.262 in 191 at-bats in 1984, .280 in 189 in 1985) if he

doesn't have to catch too much. Problem is, Mark Bailey flopped in 1986, and Ashby was behind the plate almost every day. A lot of low-average at-bats that aren't offset by a sackful of homers and ribbies can hurt you. $2.

**BOB BRENLY.** .246 BA, 16 Home Runs, 62 RBI, 10 Stolen Bases

Manages to hit 15–20 home runs a year, although a lot of them must come with the bases empty (only 56 RBI in 440 at-bats in 1985, 62 in 472 in 1986). But the guy has a batting average that only Ozzie Virgil or Mike Heath could envy (below .225 in two of the past four seasons). And while his defensive limitations used to earn him a little time at first or third, the arrival of Will Clark, the emergence of Chris Brown, and the superior defensive skills of Bob Melvin could mean that Brenly is a short-timer in San Francisco—or, infinitely worse for a Rotisserie team owner, a part-timer. $13.

**GARY CARTER.** .255 BA, 24 Home Runs, 105 RBI, 1 Stolen Base

Forget that he can't throw anyone out. Forget that he's the most unpopular player in the National League among his peers. (In Montreal, "The Kid" was called "Lights"—as in "Lights . . . Camera . . . Action!"—because of his craving for media attention.) But remember that Carter is one of the few hitters, and the only catcher, who consistently delivers 25–30 home runs and 100 RBI. Most seasons he will surpass the second-best receiver in the league by half a dozen dingers and 30 ribbies. His batting average, though, is a good 25 points lower than other blue-ribbon thumpers like Schmidt, Parker, Horner, and Murphy. And what about the knees? If the Mets run away with the NL East again, and if they're smart, Carter could sit a lot in the last third of the season to rest his gams. Good for him, good for the Mets, but bad for your pennant drive. Beware of long-term contracts, and consider trading him if he has a hot first half. Always a good idea to check in with Gary's orthopedist just before Draft Day. $33.

**DARREN DAULTON.** .225 BA, 8 Home Runs, 21 RBI, 2 Stolen Bases

Comes as an entry with John Russell. Their platoon looked like it would deliver 30–35 home runs and around 100 ribbies before Daulton tore up his knee. Both have good power, and both fare better when they don't have to face pitchers from the "wrong" side. If Daulton recovers, go for both halves of the platoon. The pair for $12.

**JODY DAVIS.**   .250 BA, 21 Home Runs, 74 RBI, 0 Stolen Bases
Jody's the easiest Davis in the National League to keep straight. He hits for a lower average and steals fewer bases than Chili, Eric, and Glenn. But Wrigley Field always gives Jody a good shot at 25 home runs. A bleeding ulcer or some other Kishkah problem hurt his production in 1985, but he recovered fast enough to be Carter's backup in the 1986 All-Star game. Always a good idea to check in with Jody's gastroenterologist just before Draft Day. $22.

**BO DIAZ.**   .272 BA, 10 Home Runs, 56 RBI, 1 Stolen Base
When he left the platoon in Philadelphia for the Reds it seemed like Bo was ready to put up some startling numbers at Riverfront Stadium. No such luck. Maybe he misses Ozzie Virgil. Diaz can crunch the ball, but he'll be 34 on Opening Day 1987. And Carlton Fisk still is the exception who proves the rule. $8.

**MIKE FITZGERALD.**   .282 BA, 6 Home Runs, 37 RBI, 3 Stolen Bases
Figure Gary Carter's successor out. His bat was so weak in the spring of 1986 that the Expos made Sal Butera their starting catcher shortly after the season began and shipped Fitzgerald to Indianapolis. Then he comes back, goes on a tear—before an injury ended his season early—and finishes second only to Scioscia in the all-receivers batting race. Maybe he didn't like Indianapolis. $9.

**MIKE LAVALLIERE.**   .234 BA, 3 Home Runs, 30 RBI, 0 Stolen Bases
After Mike Heath fell into a funk upon seeing all those spacious National League outfields, eventually to be traded back to the snugger confines of Tiger Stadium, LaValliere was rushed in from the bullpen to handle the Cardinals' catching chores. Youth is on his side, but there's little evidence in his minor league numbers to expect much better than what he accomplished at the plate in '86. $4 tops.

**TONY PENA.** .288 BA, 10 Home Runs, 52 RBI, 9 Stolen Bases

When Terry Kennedy went to the Orioles, the question became, what *other* team would get Pena, and in what league? However, Pena made a comeback in average in '86, so Sid Thrift may just keep him. $17.

**JOHN RUSSELL.** .241 BA, 13 Home Runs, 60 RBI, 0 Stolen Bases

See Darren Daulton.

**MIKE SCIOSCIA.** .251 BA, 5 Home Runs, 26 RBI, 3 Stolen Bases

Has his name misspelled more often than any backstop since Jim Pagliaroni, and hits for the best average of any National League catcher other than Tony Pena—though 1986 was pretty much lost to injuries and the Dodgers' swoon. Scully, Garagiola, and colleagues have made the entire nation aware that Scioscia is a superior and aggressive blocker of home plate, so count on him to spend even more time on the mend in the future. $15.

**OZZIE VIRGIL.** .223 BA, 15 Home Runs, 48 RBI, 1 Stolen Base

Everyone figured Ozzie for 30 flares or more once he got to the Launching Pad. Ozzie fell short of that mark. In fact, he almost fell short of hitting .200. It's the old Kingman Perplex—how much power do you have to get to give away all those outs? Look for him to bounce back to somewhere between 1984 (.261) and 1985 (.246). And fire at least 20 flares. $16.

## At the Corners

Let us talk first basemen—broad shoulders of the diamond, hog butchers to the baseball world. Along with his major league colleagues, any Rotisserie League GM who is even passingly bright will—*must*—look to the position as a power source. That's why Terry Francona, even with his lifetime .290 batting average, can't land a steady job.

A competent RL first sacker need not possess so much as a modicum of grace. The mere thought of stealing a base may require him to sit for a moment in the shade to catch his breath. His batting average can hover forever on the dark side of .260. But to earn the big bucks, he must be there with his 22–30 taters and 80–plus ribbies.

Which means, the history books tell us, that Dick ("Dr. Strangeglove") Stuart would have been a Rotisserie League Hall of Famer while Vic Power, with his customary dozen home runs and sixty-some RBI to accompany his annual Golden Glove, would barely have been mediocre.

But there is some justice, and its name is Marv Throneberry: He stunk both ways.

**SID BREAM.**   .268 BA, 16 Home Runs, 77 RBI, 13 Stolen Bases

Of the large, powerful first basemen to emerge recently from their once-vaunted minor league system, Bream was clearly least valued by the Dodgers, despite his 69 home runs in 2½ years at Albuquerque and his .370 batting average there in '85. Pittsburgh was desperate enough to give Gumby a chance, however, and he came through with decent enough numbers—including a bit of speed—to give him, at 26, the possibility of being a fixture at Three Rivers for a decade or so. $25.

**GREG BROCK.**   .234 BA, 16 Home Runs, 52 RBI, 2 Stolen Bases

He was going to make us forget Garvey. He was going to outslug Mike Marshall. He was all set for Cooperstown. Now, after four years, and with Pedro Guerrero likely to take over and make us forget him, Greg Brock, 29, may be flat out of chances, at least in Los Angeles. $6.

**JACK CLARK.**   .237 BA, 9 home Runs, 23 RBI, 1 Stolen Base

Went from a bad park for a right-handed power hitter to a worse one. A free agent after the 1986 season (most of which he spent on the disabled list), he could end up anywhere in 1987. Dream about Wrigley (Awesome!), fantasize about the Launching Pad (Dynamite!), but don't count out Tiger Stadium (Omigod!). Even with Busch as home base, he produced 31 dingers in 674 at-bats. But it took him two years to get that many, as he's played only 57, 126, and 65 games in the past three seasons. $27.

**WILL CLARK.**   .287 BA, 11 Home Runs, 41 RBI, 4 Stolen Bases

Will he or won't he? Young and obviously talented, but 1986 was disappointing—a tough injury, world-class hype, and major league pitching were a lot for a guy with only 65 Double A games on his professional résumé to handle. More likely a Keith Hernandez hitter than a Bob Horner. $18.

**GLENN DAVIS.** .265 BA, 31 Home Runs, 101 RBI, 3 Stolen Bases

After just a year and a half in the bigs, Davis has, in Rotisserie League terms and "real" ones alike, proven himself the most valuable first baseman in the National League. He hits for big power. He drives in bushels of runs. He even hits for decent average. He's only 26 and just reaching his peak. And if you're looking for human interest on your ball club, he even comes with a terrific story for your media guide: the one about how, as a teenage runaway from Florida, he was taken in by another family named Davis in Texas—which is how he became the "brother" of the San Diego Padres'. But pathos you can find on afternoon TV. This kid can flat out play ball. $36.

**NICK ESASKY.** .230 BA, 12 Home Runs, 41 RBI, 0 Stolen Bases

Pete seems to like him, which is a major plus, but like him or not, some are giving odds that he'll be in another uniform in '87. He has great power, as he has shown in spurts, but even in the minors he never put together a mind-boggling season. Still, at 27, he's just entering the power hitter's prime—and his main rival for the position, if he remains in Cincinnati, is 46. $13.

**ANDRES GALARRAGA.** .271 BA, 10 Home Runs, 42 RBI, 6 Stolen Bases

Large and Baby Bull strong, Galarraga demonstrated great power and equally great inconsistency in his rookie year. The Expos brought him along slowly after a horrible spring, and he was performing decently when he went under the 'scope to fix a gimp knee. This is the kind of guy who can burn you bad if you go big for him at the draft, because even the best rookies have a lot to learn, and who knows yet whether Galarraga spent enough time in school last season? A contending team will pass him by, a team building for 1988 will pay too much now in hope of a big dividend later. $16.

**STEVE GARVEY.** .255 BA, 21 Home Runs, 81 RBI, 1 Stolen Base

In his best years (we're talking the Dodger Blue period, 1977–80), the man with the Popeye forearms and the Jack Armstrong persona was the model of what a Rotisserie League first baseman ought to be—33/115/.297, 21/113/.316, 28/110/.315, 26/106/.304. That's why Garvey cost $35 the year the Rotisserie League came into being. But in his first three years as a Padre he averaged only 13 home runs and 75 RBI a season. In 1986 he rallied in the power categories, but John Kruk could see a lot of work at first in 1987 as Garvey copes with the reality that 38 may be young for a senator but old for a ballplayer. $17.

**PEDRO GUERRERO.** .246 BA, 5 Home Runs, 10 RBI, 0 Stolen Bases

If he can do what he did before the injury (albeit minus the stolen bases), he's worth as much as any offensive player in the league. But he'll have to do it, all out, for more than a few weeks to prove that the leg is sound enough to warrant your making him *número uno* on your payroll. And he'll almost certainly be doing it at first base. $25–$30.

**KEITH HERNANDEZ.** .310 BA, 13 Home Runs, 83 RBI, 2 Stolen Bases

The knock on Keith, for our purposes, is that most years he struggles to reach double figures in dingers. A problem, a *big* problem, for a Rotisserie League GM. And his perennially golden glove is of no use to him in our brand of baseball. Still, Hernandez is something of an exception to the first-base rule, especially if you've already got one boomer—a Schmidt, a Davis—on board at the other corner spot. With that steady stroke and all those at-bats, and batting third in that lineup, he will not only pump up your batting average but also help keep your RBI total respectable. His box score will rarely knock your eyes out over morning coffee, but his numbers will always look pretty doggone good on your side of the ledger come October. $24.

**BOB HORNER.** .273 BA, 27 Home Run, 87 RBI, 1 Stolen Base

The goods. The gen-u-ine article. A Jack Clark and then some—and then *plenty*—including, alas, the fragility. At his best, he's as good as they come. But invest 10%-plus of your budget in a bona fide buster who, until 1986, never played a full season? Could be the stuff of dreams—or a season-long nightmare. Whichever, you won't sleep easily from April to October. $35.

**PETE ROSE.** .219 BA, 0 Home Runs, 25 RBI, 3 Stolen Bases

The odd truth is that, even in his glory days, Charlie Hustle wouldn't have fetched a high price in a Rotisserie League draft—except when he played second base. First base is big buster territory. Singles don't do it. And Peter never even had all that much speed; it just seemed like he did. $1.

Like big league clubs, Rotisserie League teams have come to accept something less offensively of third basemen than of the thumpers on first. Though it is axiomatic that the position has never been more respected, a large part of that new respect—thank you, Brooksie and Graig—has to do with the business (irrelevant showboating for our purposes) of diving stops and beeline throws from knees. Who cares if a third baseman gets his uniform dirty? We're looking for 20 home runs and 80 RBI, .280 BA and a few stolen bases, and hang the number of E-5's. Obviously, however, getting down to cases, there is one towering National League exception to the prevailing hot-corner rule. . . .

**BUDDY BELL** .278 BA, 20 Home Runs, 75 RBI, 2 Stolen Bases

Funny, in his best years with Texas, he was always mentioned in colossal three- and four-for-one deals that the Rangers supposedly spurned with monotonous regularity. But in his entire career, until this year, he had never hit more than 18 home runs in a season—or four less than Tim Wallach has *averaged* in his five full seasons with Montreal. Bell was playing in a terrible place for right-handed hitters, you say? Sure, but what about Olympic Stadium in Montreal, which Pete Rose says is the worst hitter's park, bar none, that he's ever played in? Except for 1979, when he had 101, Bell's highest RBI total in his 16-year career was 83 (1980 and 1984), and his next best was last year's 75. Wallach has *averaged* 80 RBI since 1982. We're not trying to put Bell down; he's a fine player. But how come Wallach has never figured in four-for-one trade talks? Could it have something to do with the lack of appropriate recognition that comes with playing in Canada? Ask Tim Raines. $18.

**CHRIS BROWN.** .317 BA, 7 Home Runs, 49 RBI, 13 Stolen Bases

Once known by his teammates as "The Tin Man" (he allegedly lacked heart), Brown made a lot of converts in 1986 with a new, improved attitude and a higher batting average. But what happened to the power potential he showed in his rookie season? Better a Tin Man with 20–25 dingers than a team player who hits singles. The skills are obviously there, but so is the head. A tough call, but it says here that 1987 is when Chris Brown puts it all together—power, average, and heart. But will it be in San Francisco? $22.

**RON CEY.** .273 BA, 13 Home Runs, 36 RBI, 0 Stolen Bases

The Cubs have been looking for a way to ditch the Penguin, his salary, and his attitude for a couple of years, and they may just end up eating the big contract that has one more year to run. If he's still around in '87, he'll still pop the pelota over the ivy once and a while, despite decreasing run production. $6.

**PHIL GARNER.** .265 BA, 9 Home Runs, 41 RBI, 12 Stolen Bases

Still hard to think of Phil Garner as a third baseman, isn't it? In fact, he's only half a third baseman (see Denny Walling, below), but he's all gamer. With only a few bucks left at the end of the draft, you could do a lot worse. $5 ($6 if he grows back his moustache).

**HOWARD JOHNSON.** .245 BA, 10 Home Runs, 39 RBI, 8 Stolen Bases

The one Met who, having endured a so-so 1986, might be a bargain in 1987. A good bet. The man can crush the ball and just needs playing time. Problem is, where is Davey Johnson going to play Hojo? We say third until Dave Magadan proves he's ready. $13.

**RAY KNIGHT.** .298 BA, 11 Home Runs, 76 RBI, 2 Stolen Bases

Along with most of his teammates, Knight got too much ink in 1986 for your—and his—own good. Closely examined, his heralded comeback year was nothing to rave about. After a brilliant April and May, it was merely so-so. Mets management recognized this, even if fans and press didn't. Will he catch on in '87, and where? $10 if he's a regular.

**BILL MADLOCK.** .280 BA, 10 Home Runs, 60 RBI, 3 Stolen Bases

Maybe it's been that incredible, unending string of injuries, but Mad Dog hasn't had a classic Madlock year since 1983. Moreover, even healthy and younger he never hit more than 19 home runs in a big league season. Still, classic Madlock is pretty swell, and it's hard to bet against his attitude. $8.

**JIM MORRISON.** .274 BA, 23 Home Runs, 88 RBI, 9 Stolen Bases

Where did all those 1986 home runs come from? From getting enough at-bats to hit them, that's where. Morrison once hit 15 in Chicago, when he got 604 at-bats. His next-highest at-bat total—537—came in (you guessed it) 1986. (Before last season the most at-bats he got in Pittsburgh was 304, in 1984.) Teams seem to find it difficult thinking of Morrison as a regular, probably because he's been so useful coming off the bench. $11.

**GRAIG NETTLES.** .218 BA, 16 Home Runs, 55 RBI, 0 Stolen Bases

He's got to run out of gas one of these years. Doesn't he? The lowest batting average of his career in 1986 suggests that 1987 may be the year. If it's not, you could have a huge bargain. $5.

**KEN OBERKFELL.** .270 BA, 5 Home Runs, 48 RBI, 7 Stolen Bases

His Atlanta Brave nickname is 5-0-2-0, for the box score line that means 5 at-bats, 0 runs, 2 hits, 0 runs batted in. It's one of baseball's abiding puzzles—how a lifetime .286 hitter can log 400 or so at-bats each year with so few RBI. By all means draft him—but as a second baseman (if he qualifies). $5.

**TERRY PENDLETON.** .239 BA, 1 Home Run, 59 RBI, 24 Stolen Bases

Looked like a lefty Madlock when he first came up. Still does, except when he comes to bat. He'll steal a couple of dozen bases, but he's got to hit better than .240 to earn better than an average Rotissesalary. $12.

**MIKE SCHMIDT.** .290 BA, 37 Home Runs, 119 RBI, 1 Stolen Base

There are Rotisserie League thinkers—admittedly not the deepest in the Free World—who began insisting two or three seasons ago that Schmidt was slipping. Since then, bad back and arthroscopic surgery and no one batting behind him and all, he's averaged better than 35 home runs and 100 RBI a year. Entering the 1987 season, he still looks to be one of the top four or five offensive forces in the game. Money in the bank. Blue-chipper. So what if he doesn't steal the 10–12 bases a season he used to swipe before he started going downhill? $38.

**TIM WALLACH.** .233 BA, 18 Home Runs, 71 RBI, 8 Stolen Bases

Forget last year's injuries, this guy's the real thing. A bona fide 20–25 home run, 80–85 RBI kind of guy. He won't carry a club, Montreal's or yours, but he delivers value. $24.

**DENNY WALLING.** .312 BA, 13 Home Runs, 58 RBI, 1 Stolen Base

The Astros had to trade Danny Heep a couple of years ago because no one in the front office could tell him and Denny Walling apart. The one who stayed in Houston is the other half of the Astros' third base platoon, the one who's not Phil Garner. Danny—no, *Denny*—is five years younger and worth a couple of dollars more. $7.

## Up the Middle

Much as it will hurt some of you baseball purists out there, it must be said: A winning Rotisserie League team does *not* have to be strong "up the middle." If the truth be told, very fine Rotisserie clubs, even *championship* teams, have been constructed with no middle to speak of at all. Which is not to say that it wouldn't be nice to have a keystone combination of Ryne Sandberg and Ozzie Smith on your ball club, or Hubie Brooks and Juan Samuel, for that matter. It's just to acknowledge that it's possible to buy your speed in the outfield and your power in the corner positions, and leave other owners to fight over the relatively shallow pool of talent up the middle.

What should you look for, ideally, in a middle infielder? Well, ideally you want production in each of the four offensive categories. But this is not Eden, and you can count the available four-category middle infielders on one hand. Realistically, you can hope to get a decent batting average and some speed and modest RBI production (40 or more) from second and short. There are a few guys at these positions with serious power, a few with dazzling speed, even fewer with both—and they will cost you dearly. There are many more who will go to the plate 500 times and hit .220.

You can choose to go after the Rolls-Royce middle infielders and make them as central to your team as they are to a big league club. Just be aware that in the great free market of the Rotisserie draft, the demand for these guys is high and the supply low; they are priced accordingly. A prudent middle course would be to go after your basic, generic guys—workaday players who will give you a few steals and maybe hit for average, with the odd home run every month or so. Finally, you might opt for the radical approach and make your selection of middle infielders an exercise in damage control. Buy your offense in the outfield and at the corners, where it's more plentiful (and, you hope, cheaper), and use whatever you have left shrewdly to select middle infielders who, above all else, will not hurt you.

**WALLY BACKMAN.**  .320 BA, 1 Home Run, 27 RBI, 13 Stolen Bases

If he could hit lefties, he would have had enough at-bats in '86 to contend for the batting crown. As the left-handed-hitting half of the Mets' platoon, he's still a very valuable demiplayer. $8.

**RAFAEL BELLIARD.**  .233 BA, 0 Home Runs, 31 RBI, 12 Stolen Bases

He is strictly a glove man, a major league shortstop who makes up for his lack of size (5'6", 150 pounds) with heart and hustle. You've got to like him, but you don't have to own him. $1.

**HUBIE BROOKS.**  .340 BA, 14 Home Runs, 58 RBI, 4 Stolen Bases

As a shortstop, Brooks makes one heck of a third baseman. But who cares about his range? Here's a highly productive hitter with power. A season-ending injury kept his numbers down in '86 and cost him a shot at the batting crown, but there's no indication that he won't be back at full strength in '87. Get out your checkbook. $26.

**BILL DORAN.**  .276 BA, 6 Home Runs, 37 RBI, 42 Stolen Bases
He didn't show the power expected in '86 by those who thought he was the second coming of Ryne Sandberg. On the other hand, he's almost as clean-cut as Ryno, and he does steal bases. A consistent, productive second baseman, Doran may someday hit those 25 home runs that people expect, and justify the inflated price he commands these days. $25.

**MARIANO DUNCAN.**  .229 BA, 8 Home Runs, 30 RBI, 48 Stolen Bases
Originally drafted in Rotisseball on the basis of pedigree alone—he's a Dominican shortstop from San Pedro de Macorís—Duncan's speed and occasional power have made him a hot commodity. So what if he's no Tony Fernandez with the glove, as long as he stays in the lineup. Duncan may steal 80 bases one of these years, and that makes him a catch. $15–$18.

**SHAWON DUNSTON.**  .250 BA, 17 Home Runs, 68 RBI, 13 Stolen Bases
Almost worth the price—any price—just to have that howitzer of an arm on your club, even if it doesn't add any points. Fortunately, this model also comes equipped with offense. And he's only 23. Years old, that is. But if he continues to develop, that will soon be his price. $16.

**TIM FLANNERY.**  .280 BA, 3 Home Runs, 28 RBI, 3 Stolen Bases
The lefty half of the Padres' second-base platoon that bumped Bip. Flannery has no speed or power to speak of, but he's made himself into a decent slap hitter with a future as a spare part. $1.

**TOM HERR.**  .252 BA, 2 Home Runs, 61 RBI, 22 Stolen Bases
As Herr's owner you might not care if Willie McGee hits .250 or .350—but you should. In 1985, McGee was MVP and Herr drove in 110 runs, hitting .302 behind him. In '86 McGee hit the skids and the numbers above are partly the result. He's a .280

lifetime hitter, though, and he can motor again after surgery in '83. But at 31, he may have had his best years. $12.

**GLENN HUBBARD.** .230 BA, 4 Home Runs, 36 RBI, 3 Stolen Bases

Always sold short—and it's true, he's only 5'8"—but he's averaged 7 home runs and 40 RBI a year over nine major league seasons. Beware, though, if the Braves finally put Ken Oberkfell at second, where he's always belonged. $3–$4.

**STEVE JELTZ.** .219 BA, 0 Home Runs, 36 RBI, 6 Stolen Bases

What do you call a Rotisserie shortstop with a decent glove who hits .220 with lots of at-bats but without speed or power? In general, you call him a $1 player; in this case, though his given first name is Larry, you call him Steve.

**BARRY LARKIN.** .283 BA, 3 Home Runs, 19 RBI, 8 Stolen Bases

The Reds' *new* shortstop of the future (see Kurt Stillwell) made the long jump from Double A and took over the job. If he can hit and run the way he did in '86, he may also be the Reds' new leadoff man. $4–$5.

**VANCE LAW.** .225 BA, 5 Home Runs, 44 RBI, 3 Stolen Bases

He led the Expos' pitching staff with a 2.25 ERA, easily the best part of his '86 performance. Personal problems might explain his falloff from the 27 home runs he hit over the two preceding years. If your fellow owners believe that Law is no better than the player we saw last year, he might be a steal at the draft. $10.

**RON OESTER.** .258 BA, 8 Home Runs, 44 RBI, 9 Stolen Bases

Looking for what you'd call an average Rotisserie League second baseman? Look no farther. His career average going into '86 was .267, which is about what your team will hit if you're wise and lucky. If Oester played all his games on the carpet, where he hits .300, he'd be a star. But, thank heaven, even Rotisseball is sometimes played on grass. $6–$8.

**RAFAEL RAMIREZ.** .240 BA, 8 Home Runs, 33 RBI, 19 Stolen Bases

The enlightened world is divided between those who believe

Ramirez is a disaster at short and those who will come to believe it, given time. Pressed back into action when Andres Thomas flopped, Ramirez continued a four-year slide in his batting average (.297, .266, .248, .240). Give him points for consistency, though—he did lead the league in errors five straight years. You can see why the Braves want to shed him—and probably will. $2.

**JOHNNY RAY.**   .301 BA, 7 Home Runs, 78 RBI, 6 Stolen Bases
Give this guy a major league lineup to hit around and he could be truly dangerous. Meanwhile, with the Pirates, all he does on average over the past five years is hit over .285 with seven home runs and more than 65 RBI. Have a heart. Give the guy (and yourself) a break and let him play on your team. $15.

**CRAIG REYNOLDS.**   .249 BA, 6 Home Runs, 41 RBI, 3 Stolen Bases
Half of Houston's shortstop platoon, with Dickie Thon, Reynolds is just another glass of milk—a workmanlike shortstop whom you'll probably overlook unless you're smart enough to own him. He usually goes for a song and pays off like a Pavarotti. Try to steal him. $3.

**JERRY ROYSTER.**   .257 BA, 5 Home Runs, 26 RBI, 3 Stolen Bases
Half of the Padres' second-base platoon, with Tim Flannery, he has more power but less chance to use it. At 35, his future is, as they say, behind him. $1.

**JUAN SAMUEL.**   .266 BA, 16 Home Runs, 78 RBI, 42 Stolen Bases
The fact that Samuel's middle name is Milton should in no way diminish his value. Where else, this side of Ryne Sandberg, can you find this kind of speed and power from a second baseman? All the Juanderful One does is hit 15–20 home runs a year, drive in 70–80 runs, and steal 40–60 bases. Just 26 years old, he's capable of a year that makes even those numbers look modest. $30–$35.

**RYNE SANDBERG.**   .284 BA, 14 Home Runs, 76 RBI, 34 Stolen Bases
The top of the line. A legitimate four-category man at a notoriously unproductive position. They say he had a career year

as MVP in 1984, then he came back with perhaps a better all-around year in '85. 1986 was an off year, but does anyone care to bet on '87? You'll have to, because he'll fetch at least $40 in virtually any draft.

**RAFAEL SANTANA.**  .218 BA, 1 Home Run, 28 RBI, 0 Stolen Bases

This guy's a Dominican shortstop and he's not even from San Pedro de Macorís, so how much can you really expect from him? If he goes to the plate 500 times, a guy like this can really hurt. $1.

**STEVE SAX.**  .332 BA, 6 Home Runs, 56 RBI, 40 Stolen Bases

As an offensive-minded owner, you've got to *love* leadoff men—guys with speed who hit for average and whose Rotissestats are relatively independent of the big league lineup in which they play. Sax is just such a love object. He's not a Raines or a Henderson, granted, but he does hit first and *produce,* and he's in his prime at 27 years of age. All of which your fellow owners won't fail to notice. He won't come cheap. $18.

**OZZIE SMITH.**  .280 BA, 0 Home Runs, 54 RBI, 31 Stolen Bases

The best defensive shortstop ever to play the game has always been worth the millions Gussie Busch pays him. But Osborne Earl Smith has only begun to realize his Rotisserie earning power in the past few years. In '86 he didn't show the surprising power he had the year before (6 home runs), but he hits for average and steals bases and drives in about 50 runs a year. That's three categories—count 'em, three. Which puts him high on the list of the most productive men at his position. $18.

**KURT STILLWELL.**  .229 BA, 0 Home Runs, 26 RBI, 6 Stolen Bases

The erstwhile Reds' shortstop of the future never hit much in the minors and didn't break form in his rookie stint. He's the kind of middle infielder you can pick up cheap and just hope he surprises you. $1.

**GARRY TEMPLETON.**  .247 BA, 2 Home Runs, 44 RBI, 10 Stolen Bases

When he was traded for Ozzie Smith in 1982, it seemed fair

enough. Just try to make that deal now. Templeton can't steal 30 bases a year anymore, and last season was one long slump at the plate. Once the top-priced Rotisserie shortstop, he will come cheap this year. But will he be worth it? $7.

**TIM TEUFEL.** .247 BA, 4 Home Runs, 31 RBI, 1 Stolen Base

A good second half in '86 suggested that he's a better hitter than his season's overall stats suggest. And he's got more pop than your average second baseman (he hit 24 home runs in the two years before he came to the Mets' platoon). With a year of National League hitting under his belt, he could make an owner look real smart—if he gets to play. $6.

**ANDRES THOMAS.** .251 BA, 6 Home Runs, 32 RBI, 4 Stolen Bases

Great glove, hot stick, quick feet, and, at 23, Atlanta's shortstop of the future—or so the Braves had hoped until he started swinging at everything and doing his lackadaisical macho strut on defense. If he wins back the job he had and lost, he could be a good one. $5.

**ROB THOMPSON.** .271 BA, 7 Home Runs, 47 RBI, 12 Stolen Bases

There is a serious question among right-thinking people whether you can trust a grown man (even a young man of 25) who calls himself Robbie. But after Thompson's great second half rescued his rookie year, a wise owner would call him Robbie *gladly*. $8.

**DICKIE THON.** .248 BA, 3 Home Runs, 21 RBI, 6 Stolen Bases

What can you say about a 25-year-old MVP candidate who . . . oh, never mind. Prebeaning, in 1983, he was among the very best players in the game (.286, 20, 79). Now he platoons against left-handed pitching and hangs tough. Rumors of his demise were clearly premature. But can he ever even approach his earlier form? $4.

**JOSÉ URIBE.** .223 BA, 3 Home Runs, 43 RBI, 22 Stolen Bases

You'll love his speed, you'll hate his average, you'll wish desperately that he didn't hit eighth. And you'll never confuse him with all those José Gonzaleses out there. $4.

# *In the Outfield*

If you're not a died-in-the-wool believer in the innate superiority of the Senior Circuit, you've got to admit that the American League seems to have pretty close to a monopoly on the exciting outfield sluggers who put big numbers on the boards. There may not be any young player quite like Eric Davis over in the AL, and Dave Parker can hold his head up with anybody, but you can think of a dozen names, young and old, in the Junior Circuit with numbers better, for example, than Darryl Strawberry's.

The reasons for this can be debated endlessly, and the fact that it's true doesn't necessarily make the AL the better league, but it does affect Rotisserie League drafting strategy, and that's the main thing that matters here. The question is, how high do you bid on intrinsic worth, how high do you bid on need? On worth alone, there are few NL outfielders who deserve a salary much over $30. If you're following a pitching/speed strategy especially, you might want to set aside your big ticket purchases for top relief pitchers, starters, and speed merchants. But *demand* will probably drive the salaries of Murphy, Parker, and a couple of others well into the $40s. Do you go along? Can you do without the power numbers they can give you, or get it elsewhere, cheaper? Such are the thoughts of which Rotisserie Nights are made.

**KEVIN BASS.**   .311 BA, 20 Home Runs, 79 RBI, 22 Stolen Bases

He's the only ex-Brewer left from the trade that popped Don Sutton from Houston, and still it was a terrific deal for the Astros. He hits for average, hits for power, runs, swims, cooks, and plays tenor sax. $25–$30.

**BARRY BONDS.**   .223 BA, 16 Home Runs, 48 RBI, 36 Stolen Bases

He may never hit for average, but he walks often enough to get a lot of base-stealing opportunities (which he usually converts), and his power is undeniable. You may have to shell out $33 for him, and that would be exactly his father's price in the inaugural Rotisserie draft back in 1980.

**VINCENT COLEMAN.**   .232 BA, 0 Home Runs, 29 RBI, 107 Stolen Bases

Last March, during the Rotisserie Spring Training Expedition to Clearwater Beach, First Furrier Lee Eisenberg confided, "He can't hit. The league's gonna catch up to him. The guy's a bum." He was right: Coleman can't hit, but he gets on base anyway, and that makes him $45, if a penny.

**JOSÉ CRUZ.**   .278 BA, 10 Home Runs, 72 RBI, 3 Stolen Bases
Throughout his career, so famously underrated he was overrated. By now, though, approaching his 60th birthday, José just can't put up the numbers. His contemporary value is $8, and most of that is sentimental.

**KAL DANIELS.**   .320 BA, 6 Home Runs, 23 RBI, 15 Stolen Bases
His given name is Kalvoski. With Ericstein Davis and Tracichevsky Jones, makes an impressive young outfield. $17.

**CHILI DAVIS.**   .278 BA, 13 Home Runs, 70 RBI, 16 Stolen Bases
See Jeff Leonard. Insisted last year that he be called "Emice de Boeuf au Purée des Tomates et Flageolets." He doesn't run the way he used to, but he hits just as well. $20.

**ERIC DAVIS.**   .277 BA, 27 Home Runs, 71 RBI, 80 Stolen Bases
Last year, the Stein Brenners had him—*and* Vince Coleman—at $10 each. If his summer of '86 meant anything at all, Eric's the most valuable Rotisserie commodity alive today: Henderson's speed, Gwynn's batting eye, Murphy's power. Take what you'd pay for the three of them, add the numbers together, divide by 5.5, and add 23. (Somewhere around $40.)

**ANDRÉ DAWSON.**   .284 BA, 20 Home Runs, 78 RBI, 18 Stolen Bases
If your strategy is to win in 1982, break the bank. If you're aware that 1982 was five years ago, don't go higher than $18 for the earthbound Hawk.

**BOB DERNIER.**   .225 BA, 4 Home Runs, 18 RBI, 27 Stolen Bases
In any ranking of National League outfielders, he's the most aptly named, if you get our French. He'll kick your batting average and knock in about three runs a month, but if you think his stolen-base total is worth it, then go ahead and waste your money. $8.

**LEN DYKSTRA.** .295 BA, 8 Home Runs, 45 RBI, 31 Stolen Bases

Speed, batting average, occasional power (his slugging average much of last year was higher than Dale Murphy's or Dave Parker's)—Lenny merits $20.

**DAN GLADDEN.** .276 BA, 4 Home Runs, 29 RBI, 27 Stolen Bases

The creator of Rotissehistory's greatest half season (1984). You, too, can finish sixth with Dan Gladden, whose speed is the only thing that keeps his price in double figures. $14.

**KEN GRIFFEY.** .308 BA, 12 Home Runs, 32 RBI, 12 Stolen Bases

Seemed to be at the end of the line when he was still with the Yankees; when the Braves traded for him, that made it certain. But then he hits .308 with 12 homers in half a season. $8–$16, depending on whether he's washed up.

**TONY GWYNN.** .329 BA, 14 Home Runs, 59 RBI, 37 Stolen Bases

On batting average and speed alone, he's worth $20. This year—you heard it here first—he's also going to hit 25 home runs. $32.

**TERRY HARPER.** .257 BA, 8 Home Runs, 30 RBI, 3 Stolen Bases

Might be a sleeper. Expect him to enter the season as an extra man, then slowly win his way back into the lineup around late May or early June and have the kind of year he had in '85. A steal at the $6 you'll have to pay for him.

**BILLY HATCHER.** .258 BA, 6 Home Runs, 36 RBI, 38 Stolen Bases

One of the base-stealing elite, with nearly one stolen base per 10 at-bats. Expert risk in '87. $18–$20.

**VON HAYES.** .305 BA, 19 Home Runs, 98 RBI, 24 Stolen Bases

With his speed, his ability to hit for average, his skill at drawing walks, the man would be worth $33 as a leadoff hitter, which is what he ought to be. But as no one in the Phillies' front office can imagine a 6'5" leadoff man with power, Von's stuck at a solid $28–$30.

**TRACY JONES.** .349 BA, 2 Home Runs, 10 RBI, 7 Stolen Bases
Where do the Reds find all these talented outfielders? And,
having found them, why can't they win? $13.

**JOHN KRUK.** .309 BA, 4 Home Runs, 38 RBI, 2 Stolen Bases
Will the Padres find a regular spot for him in the lineup? $6.

**KEN LANDREAUX.** .261 BA, 4 Home Runs, 29 RBI, 10 Stolen
Bases
The Dodgers are unlikely to give him playing time if one of
their overrated rookie outfielders can make it in center field. $4.

**JEFF LEONARD.** .279 BA, 6 Home Runs, 42 RBI, 16 Stolen
Bases
Insisted last year that he be called "Jeffrey" instead of "Jeff."
In the process, his nickname changed from "Penitentiary Face" to
"Correctional Facility Face." Ballplayer wit, sounds like. Defi-
nitely on the decline, but still worth around $22.

**DAVEY LOPES.** .275 BA, 7 Home Runs, 35 RBI, 25 Stolen
Bases
Since he stole 47 bases at 39, maybe he'll steal 50 at fifty—
after all these years, he's still the single best major leaguer from
Rhode Island. Also, being a mediocre fielder at many different
positions, he manages to get a lot of playing time. $9.

**CANDY MALDONADO.** .252 BA, 18 Home Runs, 85 RBI, 4
Stolen Bases
Al Campanis' biggest mistake he might be, but there's no way
Candy will be as productive a pinch hitter in '87 as he was in '86.
As he's death in the outfield, don't expect the Giants to make him
a regular, either. An extremely good fifth outfielder, if you can
afford $7 for a fifth outfielder.

**MIKE MARSHALL.** .233 BA, 19 Home Runs, 53 RBI, 4 Stolen
Bases
He went 3 for 56 during one stretch last July and August, but
as most Marshall seasons also contain a stretch when he hits about
7 homers a day, the value's still there. One hedge: His back
probably will limit him to 120–30 game, at best. $29.

**CARMELO MARTINEZ.** .238 BA, 9 Home Runs, 25 RBI, 1 Stolen Base

No residual value, unless Steve Garvey runs for Senator this year. $4.

**GARY MATTHEWS.** .259 BA, 21 Home Runs, 46 RBI, 3 Stolen Bases

Despite his second-half explosion last year, it's time to bust Sarge down to corporal. $4.

**WILLIE McGEE.** .256 BA, 7 Home Runs, 48 RBI, 19 Stolen Bases

Was the MVP of '85 the real McGee? Is the Pope Hasidic? Figure him for a .280 hitter, 5 taters, 50 RBIs, 40 steals, two terms on the DL, $27.

**KEVIN McREYNOLDS.** .287 BA, 26 Home Runs, 96 RBI, 8 Stolen Bases

It's bright lights, big city time for the Arkansas Traveler, who, depending upon how he handles things—and how he hits in the Mets No. 6 spot—could be as popular in New York as Reggie Jackson, or, alternatively, as George Foster. $16.

**EDDIE MILNER.** .259 BA, 15 Home Runs, 47 RBI, 18 Stolen Bases

With over 400 at-bats in '86, he got more playing time than expected in the Reds' crowded outfield. He's worth $10 for the speed and the occasional power.

**KEVIN MITCHELL.** .277 BA, 12 Home Runs, 43 RBI, 3 Stolen Bases

Sort of the K-Mart version of Tony Gwynn—not quite as much power, not quite as much speed, not quite so lofty a batting average, not quite as short and fat (although he comes awfully close in this last category). After a winter trade, he's expected to be playing third base in his old home town. $14.

**KEITH MORELAND.** .271 BA, 12 Home Runs, 79 RBI, 3 Stolen Bases

The man can hit. The man can't run. The Cubs are lousy. Put

Keith's RBI bat behind some people who can get on base and he's worth $22; keep him on the Cubs, you can cut that to $16.

**OMAR MORENO.**  .234 BA, 4 Home Runs, 27 RBI, 17 Stolen Bases

Overpriced six years ago, when he could still run. He'll last until mid-June and the return of Andy Pafko. $3.

**JERRY MUMPHREY.**  .304 BA, 5 Home Runs, 32 RBI, 2 Stolen Bases

The answer to the question Who did the Cubs get when they traded Billy Hatcher? $1.

**DALE MURPHY.**  .265 BA, 29 Home Runs, 83 RBI, 7 Stolen Bases

A terrific hitter, a decent base stealer if his manager lets him run, a 162-games-a-year man, a great American—and he's so humble that not a single NL beat reporter has yet learned that Dale has a Ph.D. in particle physics and writes Schoenbergian twelve-tone choral music in the off-season. $43.

**JOE ORSULAK.**  .249 BA, 2 Home Runs, 19 RBI, 24 Stolen Bases

The least valuable base stealer in the league. Does nothing else. Won't do anything for long. Sorry, Joe. $10.

**DAVE PARKER.**  .273 BA, 31 Home Runs, 116 RBI, 1 Stolen Base

A stand-up guy who has put up MVP numbers two straight years. Welcome back, Big Dave. $30–$33.

**TIM RAINES.**  .334 BA, 9 Home Runs, 62 RBI, 70 Stolen Bases

As a leadoff hitter, when he can rack up his 70 nabs as well as 8–12 bumps, he's worth $38; batting third, where the stolen bases drop a bit but the ribbies surge, the value of the sublime Raines plummets to, oh, $37.

**GARY REDUS.**  .247 BA, 11 Home Runs, 33 RBI, 25 Stolen Bases

Several years ago, Percival Everett wrote a fine novel called *Suder*, about a Hamlet-like Seattle third baseman. "Suder," of course, is "Redus" spelled backward. (Just thought you might want to know.) I'd pay six bucks for Suder, no more than twice to three times that much for Redus, who has always shown promise as a complete Rotisserie player—second only to Eric Davis in the NL—but has never fulfilled it.

**R. J. REYNOLDS.** .269 BA, 9 Home Runs, 48 RBI, 16 Stolen Bases

Doubles don't count. A four-category player for teams that want to finish fifth. $13.

**JEFF STONE.** .277 BA, 6 Home Runs, 19 RBI, 19 Stolen Bases

He runs like crazy, but expect him to do it as some AL team's DH. In the AL, as a full-timer, $33; in the NL, commuting between Portland and the Vet, $15.

**DARRYL STRAWBERRY.** .259 BA, 27 Home Runs, 93 RBI, 26 Stolen Bases

One of these years, he'll be the $40 player everyone thought he'd be. For the moment, $33.

**FRANKLIN STUBBS.** .226 BA, 23 Home Runs, 58 RBI, 7 Stolen Bases

Stubbs had the chance to make his mark in '86 when Guerrero went down, but he tailed off in futility during the second half of the season. When will the Dodgers run out of patience? $16.

**ANDY VAN SLYKE.** .270 BA, 13 Home Runs, 61 RBI, 21 Stolen Bases

The man has great speed, which he mostly uses to get tagged out *very quickly* on steal attempts. Reduced to platooning with Tito Landrum, and to a value in the area of $14.

**MITCH WEBSTER.** .290 BA, 8 Home Runs, 49 RBI, 36 Stolen Bases

A few National League partisans got their noses out of joint when a guy who couldn't stick as a Blue Jays reserve became a regular on Canada's NL club. $15 for those stolen bases.

**REGGIE WILLIAMS.** .277 BA, 4 Home Runs, 32 RBI, 9 Stolen Bases

He's a lot better than Ralph Bryant, Ed Amelung, Cecil Espy, and Terry Whitfield. $7.

**GLENN WILSON.**   .271 BA, 15 Home Runs, 84 RBI, 5 Stolen Bases

Have you heard Glenn Wilson talk? This is what Max Headroom would sound like if he came from Buda, Texas. $14.

**MOOKIE WILSON.**   .289 BA, 9 Home Runs, 45 RBI, 25 Stolen Bases

Two things have to happen for this guy's value to get up where it used to be: He needs to be traded to a team that'll play him every day, and he needs to stop using a nickname that is terribly unbecoming for a thirty-year-old. With the Mets, speed alone puts him around $17; as someone else's regular center fielder, $30. Let him get 600 AB in a better hitter's park than Shea, and he'll hit 15–20 taters to go with his steals.

**MARVELL WYNNE.**   .264 BA, 7 Home Runs, 37 RBI, 11 Stolen Bases

Probably the worst everyday outfielder in the league, now that Herm Winningham is a bench-sitter. $7.

## Off the Bench

It used to be when a manager needed a run in the late innings he would call down to the far end of the dugout and from out of the murky darkness would lumber guys like Walt "Moose" Moryn, George "The Judge, Big Daddy" Crowe, Forrest "Smokey" Burgess, Harry "Peanuts" Lowrey, James "Dusty" Rhodes, William "Gates" Brown, and Jerry "Jerry" Lynch. They were called pinch hitters, and they barely exist today.

These were men with substance. Men with presence. Men with nicknames. They tried to hit the ball out of the park and then, no matter what happened, return to the nether regions of the bench. For if they got on base, they would have to leave for a pinch runner. And if they didn't end the game in the ninth, a defensive replacement was mandatory. They couldn't run, they couldn't field—they were pinch hitters, that's all.

Now we've got 24-man rosters and designated hitters. And instead of Moryn and Crowe there're Lawless and Youngblood. These guys can play four positions. They can run the bases. They can advance runners. They just can't hit. They're technocrats, not pinch hitters.

For Rotisserians, the demise of the pinch hitter has made it all the more difficult to put together a squad of productive Rotissere-serves. Still, the right ones can make a difference: An extra 10 home runs or a dozen stolen bases are nothing to laugh at. So don't snort when Enos Cabell's name comes up as the draft drags on to its dreary end—he could be the next "Candy" Maldonado. These are your basic $1 ballplayers—and some could be heroes at that price.

**MIKE ALDRETE.**   .250 BA, 2 Home Runs, 25 RBI, 1 Stolen Base
See Randy Kutcher.

**BRUCE BOCHY.**   .252 BA, 8 Home Runs, 22 RBI, 1 Stolen Base
Bochy fills two bills—he's cheap and he's a catcher. With an untested rookie probably getting the nod, he could see extra action.

**THAD BOSLEY.**   .275 BA, 1 Home Run, 9 RBI, 3 Stolen Bases
Bosley cracked seven home runs in the friendly confines in 1985. Informed that many Rotisserians are willing to pay a buck per home run, he responded by hitting one home run last year.

**ENOS CABELL.**   .256 BA, 2 Home Runs, 29 RBI, 10 Stolen Bases
With the Dodgers' love for the DL well established, you can bet Cabell will get a chance to drive in 25–30 runs and steal 10 bases.

**MIKE DIAZ.**   .268 BA, 12 Home Runs, 36 RBI, 0 Stolen Bases
Playing part-time, Mike hit more home runs than Bo and Carlos combined. In fact, this backup catcher and outfielder hit more round-trippers than Tony Pena and Junior Ortiz combined. Diaz is good. You'll probably have to go more than $1 to get him, but grab him and hope Pena gets dealt after the draft.

**TOM FOLEY.**   .266 BA, 1 Home Run, 23 RBI, 10 Stolen Bases
If you're stuck for a middle infielder with only $1 to spend at the end of the draft, Foley can bail you out. Just don't count on much more.

**CURT FORD.**   .248 BA, 2 Home Runs, 29 RBI, 13 Stolen Bases
Ford's batting average and on-base percentage are nearly 20 points higher than Vince Coleman's. Granted, Ford steals 100 fewer bases, but other than that, why isn't he leading off for the Redbirds? Ford's stolen bases give him the edge over Tito Landrum among the Cardinals' bench-warmers.

**DANNY HEEP.**   .282 BA, 5 Home Runs, 33 RBI, 1 Stolen Base

Some great pickups started on the Mets' bench—Len Dykstra and Kevin Mitchell, for example. But Heep is the only one who has stayed on the bench year after year to help Rotisserians more than the Mets. Though not in '87, he has vowed.

**RANDY KUTCHER.**   .237 BA, 7 Home Runs, 16 RBI, 6 Stolen Bases

Couldn't think of anything to say about Aldrete. Kutcher, either.

**TITO LANDRUM.**   .210 BA, 2 Home Runs, 17 RBI, 3 Stolen Bases

See Curt Ford.

**RON ROENICKE.**   .247 BA, 5 Home Runs, 42 RBI, 2 Stolen Bases

Roenicke went on a tear last year while Gary Redus was hurt and Milt Thompson went back to Triple A. It's unlikely he'll see much action in '87, but if he does, he could be well worth your last buck.

**TED SIMMONS.**   .252 BA, 4 Home Runs, 25 RBI, 1 Stolen Base

There's enough pop in Simmons' bat to give you a few home runs and with his bad knees you won't have to worry that he'll end up starting and killing your average.

**TONY WALKER.**   .222 BA, 2 Home Runs, 10 RBI, 11 Stolen Bases

For a few stolen bases more.

**JOEL YOUNGBLOOD.**   .255 BA, 5 Home Runs, 28 RBI, 1 Stolen Base

See Randy Kutcher.

# THE LITTLEFIELD EFFECT—REDUX

*In the great order of things, there are certain natural forces and phenomena so powerful and omnipresent in our lives that their names become common coin in the language. The Doppler Effect. The Heisenburg Uncertainty Principle. Newton's First Law of Thermodynamics. The Pythagorean Theorem. The Littlefield Effect.*

*Recognized immediately upon publication in 1984 of* Rotisserie League Baseball *as a profound and subtle insight into baseball life (and life in general), the Littlefield Effect soon gained legendary stature. It is reprinted as follows, revised and updated, for your edification.*

It is an immutable fact of Rotisserie League life that yesterday's box scores unreasonably influence today's roster decisions. Whether it be September roster expansion time, or earlier on, when you're looking for a third baseman to replace Chris Brown when he convalesces (again!), even veteran owners tend to be mesmerized by recent performance, to lean too hard on the age-old question, What have you done for me lately? No matter that a journeyman's career is a flawless model of mediocrity; if he's 10 for his last 32 with 2 HR, 7 RBI, and 3 steals, this suddenly looks very much like the year when he'll surpass all reasonable expectations.

Every owner, no matter how shrewd, eventually falls into the trap. Call it myopia. Call it romance. We call it the Littlefield Effect. In the physics of Rotisseball, the Littlefield Effect is a force as basic as gravity—and about as easy to escape. The day the apple dropped was the occasion of the second annual player draft in 1981, when John Littlefield—a young San Diego bullpen hand with a modest past and a future in middle relief—became the object of spirited bidding that inflated his price to bullpen ace levels. What bamboozled owners of such high intelligence was the fact that Littlefield had notched two saves in two appearances in the first few days of the major league season that preceded the draft. Two saves in two games! In a market where stoppers are scarce, he looked like the second coming of the Goose.

Sure, there was every reason to believe it was merely a fluke (considering Littlefield's lifetime stats and stiff competition in the Padres' pen), but the promise implicit in yesterday's box scores, the chance for a miraculous season, was too powerful to resist. John Littlefield went for $15 to the Eisenberg Furriers. Six months later, at season's end, Littlefield was 2–3, with an ERA of 3.66, a ratio of 1.156—and two saves.

*It should be noted that while the legend of the Littlefield Effect grew, Littlefield (the pitcher) didn't. John Littlefield did not play major league baseball beyond the 1981 season. His lifetime stats are 7 Wins, 8 losses, 3.39 ERA, 1.323 Ratio, and 11 saves. Which doesn't begin to measure his Effect on the game.*

# American League

## Warmup

Rattle the fences! Rain base hits like coconuts dropping in a Fiji typhoon! Welcome to the American League, land of the big bangers and the shell-shocked pitching corps. In the National League they pitch from mounds; in the Junior Circuit there's talk of letting the pitchers toss them up from trenches. League President Dr. Bobby Brown soon will propose new rules to reshape AL baseball along the lines of volleyball—first team to score 15 runs wins the game, but you have to win by 2.

All kidding aside, folks, there *is* a difference between the two leagues, most certainly from a Rotissepoint of view, and if you're a National League expert who's putting a toe into the American League pond—as were some of the original Rotisserians who went into the Junior League—it helps to learn that difference in some other school than Hard Knocks. If you estimate batting, home run, and RBI numbers that would put you at the top of those categories in a NL Rotisserie race, you'd end up in the middle of the pack in an AL league. Think Big, AL Rotisserians! Guys who hit 20 home runs in the NL are coveted sluggers, in the AL they're lucky to get off the bench. Draft a starter with a 4.00 ERA in the NL and you're ready to think about next year; in the AL he's likely to be an ace of your staff.

These facts of life require a different, and perhaps more complex, strategy in planning for AL Rotissedrafts. The big hitters are likely to go for big numbers, and there are so many of them. The handful of top pitchers also draw high salaries, and there are fewer of the latter to go around. AL drafts are often more chaotic and chancy than NL drafts. Pennants can be won or lost in the final minutes of a draft, in the ugly, messy end game, after you've spent your big bucks and you're down to roster-filling. A little-known rookie or a guy coming off a terrible year who will turn out a candidate for Comeback Player of the Year, available in the $1–$5 scrambling at the end, could be the make-or-break factor. Will that last one-buck pitcher give you a ratio of 1.300 or 1.900? Is there another Rob Deer out there, waiting for a patient manager—and a savvy (or lucky) RL owner—to make him a star?

Damage Control as a theory of Rotisserie League drafting is too tame for the gunslingers who play the American League brand of Rotisseball. Better to be safe than sorry does not win Junior League pennants. You're gonna get damaged, and you're going to be sorry a lot of the time you open the morning paper and read the pitching lines. Go for the Bobby Witts of this world! You can be like the genius who knew Sandy Koufax would be great even before he found his control. And the 1991 championship is a lock.

## On the Mound

They thought the ball was livelier last year, but in truth, the arms were deader. American League pitching is the pits. You know it's bad when you begin to covet your neighbor's Ken Schrom. With few exceptions, there are two types of pitchers in the AL: those who couldn't get their fast balls arrested in a school zone, and those who need Rand McNally (Dave's brother) to find the plate.

This doesn't mean the Rotisserian should neglect his AL pitching. *Au contraire*, this means he can get a sizable jump on his adversaries by judicious selection. Just remember, after the Top 25 starters and the Top 10 relievers, talent falls off like the Continental Shelf. Get three of the latter and two of the former and then go bargain-hunting.

**JOAQUIN ANDUJAR.**   12 Wins, 1 Save, 3.82 ERA, 1.256 Ratio

The operational word here, as every Joaquin-watcher knows, is youneverknow. He hurt himself last year taking batting practice just in case the AL owners decided to overturn the DH in midseason. *Muy loco*, but the guess here is that he needed the year off after pitching 1,021 ⅔ innings in the four previous seasons. Hails from San Pedro de Macorís, Dominican Republic, the Norway, Iowa, of the Caribbean. $10.

**FLOYD BANNISTER.**   10 Wins, 0 Saves, 3.54 ERA, 1.270 Ratio

There's an axiom in baseball that you should never give up on a left-hander before he's 32. Bannister will be 32 this year. $5.

**JIM BEATTIE.**   0 Wins, 0 Saves, 6.02 ERA, 1.762 Ratio

This Portland, Maine, high school product will benefit from the year off. We like him because he's bald, he went to Dartmouth (inspiration for the greatest movie of all time), and his nickname is "Zelmo." Actually, Beattie could turn out to be the Dennis Leonard of '87. See Joe Johnson and Billy Swift. $1.

**BERT BLYLEVEN.**   17 Wins, 0 Saves, 4.01 ERA, 1.178 Ratio

This is what will happen in the first two or three months of the season. You will curse him, you will shudder when coming into contact with anything remotely Dutch, you will think of trading him for Bill Mooneyham. Then in June, the clouds will break, Bert will run off 10 complete games, and you will start eating Edam cheese. Speaking of cheese, Blyleven wears a T-shirt that says, I LOVE TO FART. $15.

**MIKE BODDICKER.**   14 Wins, 0 Saves, 4.70 ERA, 1.319 Ratio

The consummate pitcher, as opposed to thrower. He'll get knocked around occasionally, but try not to worry, because he'll pay off in the end. Hails from Norway, Iowa, the San Pedro de Marcorís of the Corn Belt. $14.

**OIL CAN BOYD.**   16 Wins, 0 Saves, 3.78 ERA, 1.246 Ratio

Do you want to endorse any player who walks out on his ball club in the middle of a pennant race? Still, Oil Can can pitch. It's an ethical dilemma that's up to you. Do you want a crazed deserter with an 18-inch waist winning 15 games for your team? Probably. $8.

**JOHN BUTCHER.**　1 Win, 0 Saves, 6.56 ERA, 1.698 Ratio

If you even think of drafting him, start playing for next year. Perhaps the most amazing thing about John's butcherlike season is that his one victory came in a shutout. $1.

**JOHN CANDELARIA.**　10 Wins, 0 Saves, 2.55 ERA, 1.025 Ratio

Tender is the elbow. Uneasy lies the head of his owner. Nice ratio, though, and great lifetime ERA. A risk at $11.

**TOM CANDIOTTI.**　16 Wins, 0 Saves, 3.57 ERA, 1.348 Ratio

Tom unleashed a knuckle ball and saved a remarkably mediocre career. 16 wins is nothing to sneeze at. $5.

**STEVE CARLTON.**　4 Wins, 0 Saves, 3.69 ERA, 1.311 Ratio

You could see it in the pitching lines: Even though Lefty was getting knocked around, he was racking up the old strikeouts. The two good moves the Hawk made last year were picking up José DeLeon and Carlton. He still has something left. $3.

**JOHN CERUTTI.**　9 Wins, 1 Save, 4.15 ERA, 1.359 Ratio

The only major leaguer who went to Amherst, not counting Milwaukee GM Harry Dalton. Now, if you play your cards right and get Codiroli, Candiotti, and Cerutti, buy a bottle of Chianti, and order a canolli to celebrate, *capice*? $5.

**JIM CLANCY.**　14 Wins, 0 Saves, 3.94 ERA, 1.208 Ratio

Nothing exciting about Clancy, except that he once pitched for Jersey City. He did win 14 last year, he won't hurt you, and you could end up with another 14. $10.

**ROGER CLEMENS.**　24 Wins, 0 Saves, 2.48 ERA, 0.969 Ratio

Pray nightly that his arm is sound. If it is, he will be that rarest of pitchers, the Cy Young Award winner who doesn't go down the toidy. Twenty-four wins. A 2.48 ERA. An 0.969 ratio. Brown hair and green eyes. By the way, the Mets originally drafted him in 1981, so imagine him in the same rotation with Dwight Gooden. Now stop imagining. Stop. $30.

**CHRIS CODIROLI.**　5 Wins, 0 Saves, 4.03 ERA, 1.407 Ratio

Chris is a skilled auto mechanic, in case your team hits the skids or runs out of gas or fails in the clutch. $5.

**EDWIN CORREA.**  12 Wins, 0 Saves, 4.23 ERA, 1.448 Ratio

He's going to be very, very good. It may take another year, but he's a solid investment. You loved his work with Weather Report. $3.

**JOE COWLEY.**  11 Wins, 0 Saves, 3.88 ERA, 1.331 Ratio

You have to love anybody who tells Billy Martin, "Good move, Skip," when the manager goes to the mound to take him out. But you don't have to love him that much. $2.

**JOSÉ DELEON.**  4 Wins, 0 Saves, 2.96 ERA, 1.152 Ratio

Until he came to the AL, he had the best stuff with the worst results in the history of baseball. It's true: His 2–19 record for the Pirates in '85 was the worst record since Warren Harding was in the White House. The inside word is that he was tentative about throwing inside on hitters. If he busts AL hitters inside, pounce on DeLeon. $4.

**KEN DIXON.**  11 Wins, 0 Saves, 4.58 ERA, 1.369 Ratio

He averaged one home run every 5.75 innings last year, which is not what Earl had in mind when he ordered up Dr. Longball. $1.

**RICHARD DOTSON.**  10 Wins, 0 Saves, 5.48 ERA, 1.497 Ratio

He showed signs of returning to form at the end of last season, and he's only 28. Balked at changing his name to Nissan, though. $4.

**DOUG DRABEK.**  7 Wins, 0 Saves, 4.10 ERA, 1.336 Ratio

A good arm, but he made a lot of mistakes last season. He could turn out to be a sleeper. $1.

**MIKE FLANAGAN.**  7 Wins, 0 Saves, 4.24 ERA, 1.424 Ratio

Flanagan has wits, guts, and class, none of which are factors in the Rotisserie League. Come to think of it, maybe the RL should have a chemistry quotient. Anyway, he occasionally shows flashes of his Cy Young form. Money well spent. $5.

**RON GUIDRY.**  9 Wins, 0 Saves, 3.98 ERA, 1.248 Ratio

This may be much too low a ranking for the Gator, especially considering he's an on-again, off-again, and last year was an off-year. Still capable of a $30 year, but don't spend that much. $12.

**JOSÉ GUZMAN.** 9 Wins, 0 Saves, 4.54 ERA, 1.503 Ratio

Of the Rangers' two Puerto Rican starters (see Edwin Correa), Guzman is the safer pick, but he probably won't get much better. $3.

**MOOSE HAAS.** 7 Wins, 0 Saves, 2.74 ERA, 1.065 Ratio

The only pitcher in baseball who bears the name of his owner. For what it's worth, he's also an amateur magician. He made himself disappear last summer after a promising start. $3.

**NEAL HEATON.** 7 Wins, 1 Save, 4.08 ERA, 1.434 Ratio

If you have a weakness for young left-handers who have never lived up to their potential, Neal just might be the guy for you. $2.

**TEDDY HIGUERA.** 20 Wins, 0 Saves, 2.79 ERA, 1.208 Ratio

How can you resist a Mexican left-hander with the middle name of Valenzuela? The Brewers are a team on the rise, so he should be picking up *muchas victorias*. His 5-year-old son, Teddy, Jr., can imitate every Brewer, so you might want to draft him for your farm system. Just hope the kid doesn't imitate Jamie Cocanower. $20.

**CHARLIE HOUGH.** 17 Wins, 0 Saves, 3.79 ERA, 1.203 Ratio

He's not going to win 20, but he'll give you a guaranteed 15 if he doesn't break the pinky finger of his pitching hand shaking hands with a judge, which is what he did last year. He's 39, but as you know, knuckle-ballers go on forever, and besides, his ratio is excellent. $15.

**BRUCE HURST.** 13 Wins, 0 Saves, 2.99 ERA, 1.256 Ratio

Mel Parnell may not like this, but the trouble with Hurst is that he's a left-hander in Fenway Park. It's a tired cliché, but it's the truth, and Bruce will never win more than 13 games as a Red Sox. On the other hand, if he's traded (see John Tudor, Bob Ojeda), double his value. $10.

**DANNY JACKSON.** 11 Wins, 1 Save, 3.20 ERA, 1.379 Ratio

He should have had a breakthrough year in '86, but he suffered the malaise that affected the whole KC staff. Lefties are almost always worth taking a chance on. $4.

**JOE JOHNSON.**   7 Wins, 0 Saves, 3.89 ERA, 1.318 Ratio

The best stat we heard last year came from *The Elias Baseball Analyst* and concerned this Portland, Maine, high school product: "Believe it or not, he is the first Joe Johnson to play major league baseball." See Billy Swift and Jim Beattie. $2.

**JIMMY KEY.**   14 Wins, 0 Saves, 3.57 ERA, 1.276 Ratio

His 1986 statistics were spoiled by some truly horrendous early outings. Just make sure that he doesn't let it happen again. Jimmy's hobbies, by the way, are hunting and fishing. $10.

**ERIC KING.**   11 Wins, 3 Saves, 3.51 ERA, 1.236 Ratio

If his control improves, he could be very, very special. The San Francisco Giants traded him—and this will tell you a little something about baseball scouting—because he hurt himself in the minors riding a motorcycle. $10.

**MARK LANGSTON.**   12 Wins, 0 Saves, 4.85 ERA, 1.492 Ratio

Forewarned is forearmed. There will be periods when his presence among the Probable Pitchers will make your day, and other times when it will cause you to lose sleep. Just to let you know what kind of stuff he has, neither Wade Boggs nor Don Mattingly can hit him. $10.

**TIM LEARY.**   12 Wins, 0 Saves, 4.21 ERA, 1.429 Ratio

The Brewers didn't have a rotation last year, and he managed to fall out of it. $1.

**CHARLIE LEIBRANDT.**   14 Wins, 0 Saves, 4.09 ERA, 1.301 Ratio

Just when people were learning how to spell his name, he became eminently hittable. This may or may not turn out to be a permanent condition. His stock was once so low that the Reds traded him for a pitcher from Princeton, and two years later he won 17 games. Who knows? $3.

**DENNIS LEONARD.**   8 Wins, 0 Saves, 4.44 ERA, 1.339 Ratio

Out of sentiment last year, a Junior Circuit owner drafted Leonard for $1. Two hours later, he pitched a one-hitter. Two months later, the same owner had a chance to trade Leonard straight up for Bert Blyleven, but again out of sentiment, he kept him. Leonard began throwing baseballs the size of 16-inch Clinchers. The morale of this story: Sentiment lasts only once around the league. $2.

**MIKE LOYND.**   2 Wins, 1 Save, 5.36 ERA, 1.619 Ratio
Excitable college star who will never be at a loss for a shoe contract. His father is the president of Converse. Unless he throws in a pair of Chuck Taylors, bid no more than $1.

**KIRK McCASKILL.**   17 Wins, 0 Saves, 3.36 ERA, 1.214 Ratio
Now known as "Mr. McK." Wonderful stuff. A fine collegiate hockey player—his father, Ted, was a Red Wing—Kirk can probably pull the shirt over the head of anyone in baseball. The real reason he gave up hockey was that he was just too good-looking. $15.

**SCOTT McGREGOR.**   11 Wins, 0 Saves, 4.52 ERA, 1.345 Ratio
Would you be willing to bet that McGregor and Frank Tanana have never been seen in the same place at the same time? $2.

**MIKE MOORE.**   11 Wins, 1 Save, 4.30 ERA, 1.402 Ratio
The rich and glorious history of the Mariners is filled with pitchers of great promise who lose it all of a sudden. Moore lost it. In fact, he lost it 13 times last year. Will Mike Moore become the next Mike Parrot? Stay tuned. $7.

**MIKE MORGAN.**   11 Wins, 1 Save, 4.53 ERA, 1.521 Ratio
Somehow he won 11 games last year with a ratio of over 1.50 and an ERA of 4.53. Come to think of it, an ERA of 4.53 is good in the American League. $1.

**JACK MORRIS.**   21 Wins, 0 Saves, 3.27 ERA, 1.165 Ratio
The one constant of the 1980s, he has averaged 17 wins a year for the past seven years. He'll occasionally go through bad spells, but resist the temptation to trade him. He can be petulant, but what do you care? It's not likely you'll meet him. $25.

**JOE NIEKRO.**   9 Wins, 0 Saves, 4.87 ERA, 1.607 Ratio
Awful last year, but he may have a good season or two left. Knuckle-ball pitchers are very reliant on their catchers, and the Yankees' messy situation behind the plate did not help Niekro. $3.

**PHIL NIEKRO.**   11 Wins, 0 Saves, 4.32 ERA, 1.598 Ratio

You have to love the guy, you really do, and maybe hope he throws his knuckler down Steinbrenner's throat. But he must be starting to wonder which Dick Schofield he's pitching to. Besides, his ratio is terrible. $2.

**JUAN NIEVES.**   11 Wins, 0 Saves, 4.97 ERA, 1.630 Ratio

Not just another Avon Old Farms graduate from Puerto Rico. His numbers weren't all that impressive, but he's young and he's a winner. $8.

**AL NIPPER.**   10 Wins, 0 Saves, 5.38 ERA, 1.465 Ratio

This is the pitcher the adjective "gutty" was coined for. That may be one reason he has an ulcer condition. $3.

**DAN PETRY.**   5 Wins, 0 Saves, 4.66 ERA, 1.509 Ratio

*Sports Illustrated* went so bold as to predict Petry would win the Cy Young Award. Went so stupid, too. Actually, Petry blew out an elbow. Here's an anatomical rule of thumb: Elbow injuries are easier to come back from than shoulder injuries because doctors know a lot more about elbows. Only $7, because not everyone knows that rule.

**MARK PORTUGAL.**   6 Wins, 1 Save, 4.31 ERA, 1.437 Ratio

The newest member of *The Baseball Encyclopedia*'s League of Nations: Ossie France, Germany Schaefer, Frank Brazil, Al Holland, Tim Ireland, Buck Jordan, Chili Davis, Hugh Poland, and Edwin (South) Correa. $1.

**DENNIS RASMUSSEN.**   18 Wins, 0 Saves, 3.88 ERA, 1.158 Ratio

The one knock against him—and this will tell you a little more about baseball scouting—was that he spent too much time in front of the mirror. Mirror, mirror, on the wall, who's the best AL southpaw of all? Maybe it's not Dennis, but he's right up there. $10.

**BRET SABERHAGEN.**   7 Wins, 0 Saves, 4.15 ERA, 1.244 Ratio

A victim of the Cy Young curse, the darling of '85 became just another long reliever. This could be very temporary. Then again, it might not. Does the name Pete Vuckovich ring a bell? $4.

**KEN SCHROM.** 14 Wins, 0 Saves, 4.54 ERA, 1.291 Ratio

Like Vernon Law, Ken comes from Idaho. Resemblance ends there. It's hard to believe he won 14 games, and his ERA must be a misprint. $4.

**TOM SEAVER.** 7 Wins, 0 Saves, 4.03 ERA, 1.339 Ratio

He can't go on forever, unless they grant a major league franchise to Cos Cob, Connecticut. Still worth a shot, if only to see him get his knee dirty. $5.

**MIKE SMITHSON.** 13 Wins, 0 Saves, 4.77 ERA, 1.470 Ratio

Mr. BP. Once dressed up as Vanna White for a *Wheel of Fortune* promotion in the Humpdome. $4.

**DAVE STEWART.** 9 Wins, 0 Saves, 3.74 ERA, 1.353 Ratio

Does the name Lucille mean anything to you? If it does, you won't want to mention it to Dave, an expert in martial arts. His career has been wasted as a reliever. He turned out to be a much better starter. $4 if the other owners remember him best as a reliever, $9 if they were awake during the second half of the 1986 season.

**DAVE STIEB.** 7 Wins, 1 Save, 4.74 ERA, 1.590 Ratio

His book was titled *Tomorrow, I'll Be Perfect*. The sequel will be *Yesterday, I Stunk Up Exhibition Stadium*. It'll be a mystery: How did one of the best pitchers in the league turn into Dave Lemanczyk? Seriously, folks, take a flyer on him. $9, and he could be worth $29.

**DON SUTTON.** 15 Wins, 0 Saves, 3.74 ERA, 1.164 Ratio

Cunning, crafty, artful, wily, sly, insidious, shifty, cagey, and 42 on Opening Day. If they take away his grade 50 sandpaper, he's in trouble. $4.

**BILLY SWIFT.** 2 Wins, 0 Saves, 5.46 ERA, 1.761 Ratio

This Portland, Maine, high school product is one of 15 children. See Joe Johnson and Jim Beattie. $2.

**GREG SWINDELL.** 5 Wins, 0 Saves, 4.23 ERA, 1.167 Ratio

Nicknamed "Flounder" after the character in perhaps the greatest movie of all time, *Animal House*. Swindell's moniker is derived from his fishlike body. Just remember this: The University of Texas has produced such out-of-shape pitchers as Roger Clements, Calvin Schiraldi, and now Swindell. $2.

**FRANK TANANA.**   12 Wins, 0 Saves, 4.16 ERA, 1.386 Ratio
See Scott McGregor.

**WALT TERRELL.**   15 Wins, 0 Saves, 4.56 ERA, 1.367 Ratio
Why is it that you can't read anything about this guy without having the description "bulldog" thrown in? It's hard to like bulldogs. They drool and cling to your leg. $2.

**FRANK VIOLA.**   16 Wins, 0 Saves, 4.51 ERA, 1.384 Ratio
Once thought to be the best young left-hander in the league, opposing hitters now play Viola like Yo Yo Ma. He'll get you wins, though, so if you're looking for an 18-game winner with an ERA of over 4.00, here's your man. $9.

**BILL WEGMAN.**   5 Wins, 0 Saves, 5.13 ERA, 1.311 Ratio
A better pitcher than his abysmal record, but he suffered from whiplash—32 dingers in less than 200 innings. $1.

**BOBBY WITT.**   11 Wins, 0 Saves, 5.48 ERA, 1.731 Ratio
This arm is unbelievable. At one point last year, he had pitched 9 innings against the Brewers with this line: 2 hits; 2 runs, both earned; 15 walks; and 19 strikeouts. If you can absorb this ratio, you might want to take the chance he finds the plate this year. $2.

**MIKE WITT.**   18 Wins, 0 Saves, 2.84 ERA, 1.082 Ratio
One of these days, he'll win 20 games. That day is at hand. He has such a good curve ball that it has been said his and catcher Bob Boone's idea of a "perfect game" would be to go an entire game throwing nothing but curves. He did throw a real *perfecto* on the last day of the '84 season, and he'll get you into the seventh every time. $25.

# IT'S ONLY A GAME, HOWARD

The following item appeared one afternoon last summer in the sports pages of the *New York Post,* a tabloid owned by press baron Ruppert Murdoch that is infamous for its lurid sensationalism:

## *Armed and very dangerous*

With the amount of time **Jim Fregosi** has spent yanking his White Sox pitchers lately, it's a wonder the manager doesn't have a sore arm.

In a recent four-game stretch, the Sox starters—**Joel Davis, Richard Dotson, Floyd Bannister** and **Joe Cowley**—pitched a combined total of five innings and gave up 27 hits and 23 earned runs for an ERA of 38.84. "In 26 years, I've never seen four guys give up runs like that," said Jim.

Tell it to Howard Neu, founding owner of the Bruce Louis All-Stars of the Junior League. His starting rotation at the time consisted of—you guessed it—Davis, Dotson, Bannister, and Cowley. Not only that, three of his mound aces had recently been acquired in trades. Only Dotson was an original All-Star; the others he actively pursued after the season started.

"What could I do with those guys?" recalls Neu. "I fired my pitching coach—that's me—and started thinking about next year. It was that or find a hit man who would accept a four-man contract."

# *Out of the Bullpen*

Right up there with cliff-diving in Acapulco, racing at LeMans, and tiger-hunting in India is the dangerous pursuit of relief pitching. Pound for pound, relief pitchers command the highest salaries in the Rotisserie League, yet they are notoriously unreliable and erratic. The most consistent one of all, Dan Quisenberry, went for $50 in the Junior Circuit and spit up 12 saves, or about $4 per. For $49 less, somebody picked up Dan Plesac and got 12 saves. So knowing your second-line relievers helps. Knowing the voodoo secrets of Haiti will help even more.

**DON AASE.**   6 Wins, 34 Saves, 2.98 ERA, 1.212 Ratio

Aase did a great job last year, saving 34 games. But his arm began to bother him toward the end, and he wasn't effective enough to keep the Orioles out of the cellar. He will be very expensive if he's available in the draft, and he will not be worth it. Of course, we could be wrong. [Editor's note: The guy who wrote this traded Kirby Puckett for Tony Phillips before the start of last season.] $25.

**KEITH ATHERTON.**   6 Wins, 10 Saves, 4.08 ERA, 1.505 Ratio

Any Number One man in a bullpen is worth this much. However, if the Twins wake up and decide to find a real reliever, this estimate will become like the sign in a restaurant coatroom *not responsible for any articles lost or stolen.* $12.

**BUD BLACK.**   5 Wins, 9 Saves, 3.20 ERA, 1.182 Ratio

He doesn't like relieving, and he's perfectly justified in feeling that way because two years ago he looked like the best young left-hander in the league. Let's put it this way: If the Royals announced tomorrow that they were putting him back in the rotation, bid at least $10 for him. As is, sitting in the bullpen, he's worth $5.

**RICH BORDI.**   6 Wins, 3 Saves, 4.46 ERA, 1.364 Ratio

Big deal, you say, three saves. But Aase's arm may go south of the Bordi, so to speak, and who else can the O's turn to? At least you'll be getting a lot of innings for your money. $2.

**ERNIE CAMACHO.**   3 Wins, 19 Saves, 4.08 ERA, 1.588 Ratio

One of the game's great flakes, Ernie likes to keep the bone chips from his elbow operation in a jar in his locker. His fast ball is so good that whenever he throws a curve, manager Pat Corrales storms out to the mound and starts jabbing him in the chest. The Indians are no longer a joke, so Ernie might begin racking up serious save numbers. $15.

**BILL CAMPBELL.**   3 Wins, 3 Saves, 3.88 ERA, 1.203 Ratio

Soup is just about finished, but he might have a save or three left in him. He's a great guy, and the game will be lessened by his passing. So will the Tigers' ERA. $1.

**BILL CAUDILL.** 2 Wins, 2 Saves, 6.19 ERA, 1.460 Ratio

So, what happened? The Jays put him on a shelf, with just cause. In 36⅓ innings, Caudill gave up 25 runs and 6 homers. But he also had 32 strikeouts, so his arm isn't dead. He might be worth taking a chance on, especially if you don't believe in the miracle of Henkehorn. $1.

**MARK CLEAR.** 5 Wins, 16 Saves, 2.20 ERA, 1.208 Ratio

He pitched very well last year, partly because he no longer felt the pressure of Boston. As long as the Brewers continue to play .500 ball and their fans continue to stay home, Mark will be fine. $12.

**MARK EICHHORN.** 14 Wins, 10 Saves, 1.72 ERA, .0970 Ratio

See Tom Henke.

**STEVE FARR.** 8 Wins, 8 Saves, 3.13 ERA, 1.180 Ratio

A great setup man, and if the Royals decide to ignore Quisenberry altogether, he'll be their main man. The Clevelands released him for no apparent reason other than stupidity, and KC picked him up only after a sportswriter, Tracy Ringolsby, touted him to the GM, John Schuerholz. See, sportswriters are good for something. $10.

**BRIAN FISHER.** 9 Wins, 6 Saves, 4.93 ERA, 1.468 Ratio

There is no truth to the rumor that he was the one responsible for all those fires in the Bronx last year. He does have a live arm, so maybe it wasn't his fault. Maybe he listened to one too many Yankee pitching coaches. $3.

**GEORGE FRAZIER.** 1 Win, 6 Saves, 4.39 ERA, 1.461 Ratio

Harry Caray called him "the most inept pitcher I've ever seen." Of course, that was before Harry had a chance to see the guy Frazier was traded for, Ron Davis. When *USA Today* asked George what he would do if he were commissioner, we half-expected him to say, "Make walks five balls and strikeouts two strikes. . . ." All kidding aside, don't trust this guy with any kind of a lead, but the Twins did, and he saved six games at the end of the season. There's also this to consider: His competition for the short job is Keith Atherton. $5.

**GREG HARRIS.**  10 Wins, 20 Saves, 2.83 ERA, 1.303 Ratio

Still a bit of a secret. With the rise of the Rangers, he'll be getting even more saves. Ideally, you would want a thoroughbred like Righetti and a plowhorse like Harris for your save needs, but forget it, because you're not going to get both of them. Harris is ambidextrous, so Mizuno made him a glove that goes both ways— the Glenn Burke Autograph Model? $20.

**TOM HENKE.**  9 Wins, 27 Saves, 3.35 ERA, 1.041 Ratio

Henke and Mark Eichhorn are a quiniela. Eichhorn was sensational last year but Henke lapped up 17 more saves. It would be nice to have both these former rejects, but if you must choose, consider this: Henke's wife's maiden name is Swoboda. By the way, whatever happened to Bill Caudill and Gary Lavelle? $20 each, or as a special offer, $38 for the pair.

**WILLIE HERNANDEZ.**  8 Wins, 24 saves, 3.55 ERA, 1.218 Ratio

In his two "off-years" following his 1984 MVP, Hernandez has racked up 31 and 24 saves. Not many people know this, but Hernandez, who is from Puerto Rico, spent part of his formative years in Cambridge, Massachusetts. It's true, as Paul Harvey would say, he speaks English with both a Puerto Rican and a Boston accent. Strangest thing you've ever heard. $30.

**JAY HOWELL.**  3 Wins, 16 Saves, 3.38 ERA, 1.426 Ratio

Worry about his arm. In fact, whatever you do, don't draft him. [Another editor's note: The guy writing this is in dire need of relief pitching this year, so he is probably warning you off this pitcher in the belief that the other members of his Junior Circuit will be reading this, and thus he will be able to pick up Howell at a reasonable price.] $15.

**BOB JAMES.**  5 Wins, 14 Saves, 5.25 ERA, 1.441 Ratio

The club's nominal stopper suffered from bad knees and a soaring ERA last year. He still scares the daylights out of hitters. A big risk, though. Our guess is that he will come cheap because of Bobby Thigpen. $15.

**JOHN HENRY JOHNSON.**  2 Wins, 1 Save, 2.66 ERA, 1.205 Ratio

What an incredible story! Twenty years ago the guy was mowing down tacklers for the Steelers, and now he's setting 'em up for Clear and Plesac. $1.

**PETE LADD.**   8 Wins, 6 Saves, 3.82 ERA, 1.231 Ratio

You have to like Pete's head, his heart, and his feet. You'll notice that doesn't include his arm. Still, with Seattle's bullpen, it is quite literally anybody's ball game. $3.

**GARY LUCAS.**   4 Wins, 2 Saves, 3.15 ERA, 1.116 Ratio

Not so very long ago, Lucas was a front-line reliever for the Padres. Excellent insurance in case Moore goes down. Noses out teammate Urbano Lugo alphabetically in *The Baseball Register*. $5.

**TIPPY MARTINEZ.**   0 Wins, 1 Save, 5.63 ERA, 1.875 Ratio

If he makes their club, go ahead, put him on yours. He was a gamer not too long ago. $1.

**DALE MOHORCIC.**   2 Wins, 7 Saves, 2.51 ERA, 1.278 Ratio

A sort of rummage sale pitcher with, apparently, a rubber arm, Mohorcic tied Mike Marshall's record for consecutive appearances last season and picked up 7 saves. When Mohorcic belonged to the Pirates, Chuck Tanner had to tell him, "Sorry, Lefty, we're sending you down." Mohorcic is right-handed. $5.

**BILL MOONEYHAM.**   4 Wins, 2 Saves, 4.52 ERA, 1.705 Ratio

He lives up to his nickname. His nickname is Wild Bill. No, not because he's holding aces and eights. $1.

**DONNIE MOORE.**   4 Wins, 21 Saves, 2.97 ERA, 1.128 Ratio

You've got to like a right-hander whose nickname is "Lefty." He wasn't as good last year as he was in '85, but he came back from arm problems and pitched pretty well the second half. He's also a terrible fielder, but what the hey? $30.

**EDWIN NUNEZ.**   1 Win, 0 Saves, 5.82 ERA, 1.382 Ratio

A serious *cabeza* case. But Don Mattingly says the most fun he ever had was when he and Nunez went at it, *mano a mano*, fast ball after fast ball. Mattingly ended up popping up and sent a beer over to the Mariner clubhouse in tribute to Nunez. But that was two years ago. Worth a shot. $1.

**STEVE ONTIVEROS.**   2 Wins, 10 Saves, 4.71 ERA, 1.334 Ratio

Not to be confused with the Steve Ontiveros who played a bad third base for the Giants and Cubs and later for the Hiroshima Carp, or whoever. What a strange world we live in, when two Steve Ontiverosi make the majors, and only one Joe Johnson. Sorry, you wanted a real scouting report on Ontiveros: Not all the returns are in on this youngster, but if his arm is sound, he could supplant Howell. $10.

**FRANK PASTORE.**   3 Wins, 2 Saves, 4.01 ERA, 1.582 Ratio

He has a heavy burden to bear. The Twins put him Number Three behind Keith Atherton and George Frazier. $1.

**DAN PLESAC.**   10 Wins, 14 Saves, 2.97 ERA, 1.209 Ratio

Whoever had the idea of turning this left-hander with just one relief appearance in three years in the minors into a short man in the bullpen deserves a lot of credit. Half of the answer to the trivia question Name two major leaguer relievers who played basketball for NC State in the Final Four. The other half is Tim Stoddard, and this is the last time he'll be mentioned here. $10.

**DAN QUISENBERRY.**   3 Wins, 12 Saves, 2.77 ERA, 1.427 Ratio

The Quiz didn't pitch all that well last year, but he was the victim of mismanagement, or at least mispitching-coachment. The Royals were so impatient that they never allowed him to get into a groove, and as a consequence, the whole staff was screwed up. To give you some idea of the Royals' thinking, Quisenberry was told to pitch the last innings of the Hall of Fame game in Cooperstown, a game that was such a joke that Ranger coaches were playing in the field. Well, the Quiz decided to throw overhand for the first time. When he got back to the dugout, pitching coach Gary Blaylock told him, "Show a little professionalism out there." Professionalism? Blaylock owns a 4–6 major league record with no saves. Quisenberry is 47–42 with 229 saves. Anyway, he'll be devalued and a bargain. $25.

**DAVE RIGHETTI.** 8 Wins, 46 Saves, 2.45 ERA, 1.153 Ratio

The riches of Rags are many. Not only will you be getting an outstanding arm, but also a big heart. This man did not let the infantile ravings of his owner detract from his performance. The only danger is if (1) George hands the team over to his son Hank, or (2) Billy Martin becomes the manager for, what is it, the sixth time? Hank and Billy want to make a starter out of Righetti. $40.

**JOE SAMBITO.** 2 Wins, 12 Saves, 4.84 ERA, 1.566 Ratio

Still another of baseball's noblemen. Joe picked up 12 saves as the Bosox' left-handed short man, but he couldn't get anybody out after July. This year, they'll probably leave Schiraldi in to face the lefties. $2.

**CALVIN SCHIRALDI.** 4 Wins, 9 Saves, 1.41 ERA, 1.000 Ratio

The Bosox could not have won their division without him. He arrived much too late to rack up big numbers, but given the unreliability of Bob Stanley, he will go into the season as the stopper. Schiraldi was originally drafted by the Mets on a supplemental pick awarded to them for the loss of free agent Pete Falcone to the Braves. Pete's a minister now, by the way. $30.

**DAVE SCHMIDT.** 3 Wins, 8 Saves, 3.31 ERA, 1.311 Ratio

A decent pitcher, but he'll have to scavenge for saves between James and Thigpen. $1.

**ROD SCURRY.** 1 Win, 2 Saves, 3.66 ERA, 1.527 Ratio

It's getting a little tiring hearing about his great curve ball. In six years, he has a total of 37 saves. Not even to mention the . . . oops, you almost wheedled it out. $1.

**BOB STANLEY.** 6 Wins, 16 Saves, 4.37 ERA, 1.592 Ratio

A good guy to keep in mind, especially if Schiraldi turns out to be a mirage. He could probably do with a change of scene—he is no longer a popular guy in Boston—so if he's traded, jack up his ranking. $10.

**BOBBY THIGPEN.** 2 Wins, 7 Saves, 1.77 ERA, 1.064 Ratio

The club's phenomenal stopper the last few weeks of the season, he was unbeatable, untied, and virtually unscored-upon.

You can think of him as this year's Todd Worrell—or this year's Edwin Nunez. $15.

**MARK THURMOND.**   4 Wins, 3 Saves, 1.92 ERA, 1.180 Ratio
What you would be doing here is taking out a policy on Willie Hernandez. You would also be hoping the Tigers don't get the bright idea of reverting Thurmond to starterhood. $1.

**TOM WADDELL.**   (Did not play in 1986)
He was absent from the '86 campaign, but he had a note from his doctor. He was born in Scotland, which automatically gives him that character trait most appreciated in relief pitchers—stinginess. $1.

**MITCH WILLIAMS.**   8 Wins, 8 Saves, 3.58 ERA, 1.510 Ratio
Did a very nice job for the Rangers, despite 79 walks in 98 innings. If you think the left-hander was wild last year, consider that prior to his major league debut, Williams had 479 walks in 504⅔ minor league innings. He also had 537 strikeouts in the minors. Watch out for more than his ratio: The Rangers also have a pitcher named Matt Williams, who's a mediocre right-hander. $8.

**FRANK WILLS.**   3 Wins, 4 Saves, 4.91 ERA, 1.464 Ratio
Once the fair-haired pitcher of the Royals organization, he fell upon mediocrity. He became a gypsy, traveling from the Royals to the Mets to the Mariners and now to the Indians. Will he finally find contentment and a spot in Cleveland's spider-infested bullpen? $2 says he will.

**MATT YOUNG.**   8 Wins, 13 Saves, 3.82 ERA, 1.475 Ratio
The Mariners are trying to make a Dave Righetti out of Young. In this case, they are making a mistake, because as bad as their relief pitching is, their starting is even worse. But you might as well play along with them. $12.

## Behind the Plate

In what some still misguidedly call "real" baseball, teams need two catchers, one to play, the other not to play so he can be available if the Number One catcher gets injured or thrown out of the game for bad-mouthing the umpire. Some even carry three catchers so there's always somebody in the bullpen to play catch with the odd-man-outfielder between innings. The Rotisserie League's Founding Fathers decreed in their wisdom that Rotisseball should resemble the "real" thing as much as possible, meaning that every Rotisserie League team must carry two catchers, even if *that* means spending good money for guys whose role is pretty much to sit and spit.

Catcher is probably the one position where Rotissedraft strategies vary most widely. Because even starting catchers are likely to get fewer at-bats than field position players, and because their numbers are likely to suffer when they *do* get more at-bats, some RL drafters practice Damage Control with a vengeance, leaving the catching slots to the end and picking up their catchers in the $1–$5 range. That, of course, disqualifies them for the Rich Gedmans of the world—and a power-hitting catcher who drives in runs is almost sure to cost less than a cornerman or outfielder with comparable numbers. The All-Time purchase price for the catching position is probably the $54 the NL Wulfgang franchise spent one year on Gary Carter and Terry Kennedy. So buckle on the tools of ignorance and pick your strategy.

**ANDY ALLANSON.** .225 BA, 1 Home Run, 29 RBI, 10 Stolen Bases

**CHRIS BANDO.** .268 BA, 2 Home Runs, 28 RBI, 0 Stolen Bases
These two pretty well divided the Indians' catching chores in '86, and it's anybody's guess who will be behind the plate in Municipal Stadium in '87. Allanson's stolen bases may deserve a look where little else does. $1, take your pick.

**BOB BOONE.** .222 BA, 7 Home Runs, 49 RBI, 1 Stolen Base
This distinguished elderly gentleman is 39 years old and has long since extinguished the rap against his throwing arm that the Phillies laid on him when they sold him to the Angels. But what does his brilliant defense do for you, Rotisserie GM? $4.

**SCOTT BRADLEY.** .300 BA, 5 Home Runs, 28 RBI, 1 Stolen Base
The catcher of the Mariners' future, or a platoon player with 250 at-bats? Roll the dice . . . if he's a regular, $6 might buy a lot of good offensive numbers.

**RICK CERONE.** .259 BA, 4 Home Runs, 18 RBI, 1 Stolen Base
Hasn't driven in more than 28 runs in a season since his all-star year in 1980. $1.

**RICK DEMPSEY.**  .208 BA, 13 Home Runs, 29 RBI, 1 Stolen Base

He'll be entertaining fans during rain delays somewhere else besides Baltimore. $1.

**CARLTON FISK.**  .221 BA, 14 Home Runs, 63 RBI, 2 Stolen Bases

Was it the Hawk's mind games or 39 years of age that made '86 a misery? $7 for sentimentalists who remember '75.

**RICH GEDMAN.**  .258 BA, 16 Home Runs, 65 RBI, 1 Stolen Base

Postseason exposure will raise his price. $14.

**RON HASSEY.**  .323 BA, 9 Home Runs, 49 RBI, 1 Stolen Base

Back in pinstripes again in '87? $8.

**BOB KEARNEY.**  .240 BA, 6 Home Runs, 26 RBI, 0 Stolen Bases

Stole seven bases in 1984. $1.

**TERRY KENNEDY.**  .264 BA, 12 Home Runs, 57 RBI, 0 Stolen Bases

Did the Orioles know what they were getting? A hitter whose production has tailed off, a catcher whose defense is barely mediocre. The Orioles don't need more designated hitters. $17.

**TIM LAUDNER.**  .244 BA, 10 Home Runs, 29 RBI, 1 Stolen Base

Hit home runs in his first two major league games. $3.

**CHARLIE MOORE.**  .260 BA, 3 Home Runs, 39 RBI, 5 Stolen Bases

Also plays the outfield. $2.

**LANCE PARRISH.**  .257 BA, 22 Home Runs, 62 RBI, 0 Stolen Bases

He may see more action at DH or first base than as catcher. His power numbers in '86 are brilliant considering only 327 at-bats because of injury. $24.

**MARK SALAS.**  .233 BA, 8 Home Runs, 33 RBI, 3 Stolen Bases
In 1986 he slipped from his rookie season numbers, and it looks like the Twins don't want to give him the regular job. $2.

**JOEL SKINNER.**  .232 BA, 5 Home Runs, 37 RBI, 1 Stolen Base
Might be a starter somewhere, if not New York. $3.

**DON SLAUGHT.**  .264 BA, 13 Home Runs, 46 RBI, 3 Stolen Bases
Coming into his prime years with the Rangers. Optimists may bid him over $10.

**JIM SUNDBERG.**  .212 BA, 12 Home Runs, 42 RBI, 1 Stolen Base
A superior defensive catcher whose playing time will hurt your batting average. $5.

**MICKEY TETTLETON.**  .204 BA, 10 Home Runs, 35 RBI, 7 Stolen Bases
They walked him intentionally 8 times in Double A in '84. Must have feared his power. An extra buck for that. $2.

**ERNIE WHITT.**  .268 BA, 16 Home Runs, 56 RBI, 0 Stolen Bases
Left-handed power in the Exhibition Stadium wind tunnel. $9.

## At the Corners

Perhaps more than at any other position, what you're looking for at these positions mirrors the needs of major league teams. Muscle. Crunch. Dingers and ribbies, and more dingers and ribbies. Even Phil Rizzuto knows that teams need Schwartzenegger-like power at first and third. Middle infielders can thrive in Rotisserie League Baseball with Willie Randolph-type stats: a .276 average, 5 home runs, 50 RBIs, and 15 stolen bases. Let them happily take their wimpy $8–$12 salaries back to their wives in the burbs. Catchers— largely due to injury and durability problems—should come cheaper than Bowery wine. And even a couple of your outfielders can get away with being one- or two-category players, albeit expensive ones (Gary Pettis, Cangelosi, Dave Collins, the Kingman-Gorman crowd, *et al.*). But first and third are your opportunities, particularly in the American League, to get hairy-backed beasts who can help you in three, sometimes four categories. Junior Circuit cornermen are the kinds of guys you want to bring home to grope your sister, get drunk with in a red-checkered-tablecloth saloon, and give you a character reference after you're caught in a major drug bust with some speedy outfielder who's named after a synthetic fabric.

*None* of the following players will come cheap. If you wind up with a cornerman for under $5, the chances are you'll be lookin' at the second division, unless you're playing in something called the Figgy Pudding League with a bunch of guys whose middle names are Boghurst and Fenton. A few of these guys are worth $40 and up. Several are worth paying over $30 for. You get the right one for $18 and it'll be the best bargain you've had since you stole your grandmother's good silver while she was having an asthma attack.

**STEVE BALBONI.** .229 BA, 29 Home Runs, 88 RBI, 0 Stolen Bases

Okay, he doesn't look good even when he keeps his hat on, and he's going to drag your average down, but he won't hit as low as he did in '86 and he *will* hit around 30 HRs. But don't pay a dollar a dinger. Try $27.

**WADE BOGGS.** .357 BA, 8 Home Runs, 71 RBI, 0 Stolen Bases

He may not hit .400 but he *will* hit. .350. This year. Next year. The year after. And every year, as long as he stays in Fenway Park and Frank Perdue stays in business. Boggs is certainly capable of getting 600 at-bats and hitting .360–.370, which means you'd have to have the drafting ability of Curly Howard not to get at least 11 points in batting average. This guy is also capable, by 1988, of hitting 15 home runs a year and driving in at least 75 runs. $42.

**GEORGE BRETT.** .290 BA, 16 Home Runs, 73 RBI, 1 Stolen Base

A gamble. A great player. *Great.* But his stats were down in '86 and, while they will probably improve in '87, he ain't going to have a Mattingly year anymore and he no longer runs. But it sure is nice to have George Brett on your team. If you can get him for $33, don't hesitate. If the auction gets up to $36, sigh and let him go.

**BILL BUCKNER.** .267 BA, 18 Home Runs, 102 RBI, 6 Stolen Bases

Sometimes guys just get old. It ain't pretty but nobody told you the Rotisserie League was a rose garden. Pick Bill Bucks up cheap, you might have the bargain of the year. Pay over $20 for him, you might make the Mike Torrez of October 1978 look like a happy guy. Try $12.

**BUECHELE, BOCHTE, MULLINIKS/IORG, COLES.**

(Steve Buechele, .243 BA, 18 Home Runs, 54 RBI, 5 Stolen Bases; Bruce Bochte, .256 BA, 6 Home Runs, 43 RBI, 3 Stolen Bases; Darnell Coles, .273 BA, 20 Home Runs, 86 RBI, 6 Stolen Bases)

Flip a coin. Coles has a decent shot at being the Tigers' third baseman on the strength of his 1986 first half. Mulliniks is good, but he's got a funny middle name (his first name is actually Steve), and he just can't be as good as his past three years' worth of stats. Buechele's a journeyman bum, and Bochte's Bochte, and if they start for their respective teams in 1987, then Charlton Heston really *should* be the next President of the United States. Your pick for $7.

**AL DAVIS.** .271 BA, 18 Home Runs, 72 RBI, 0 Stolen Bases

Kind of a surprise choice in this exalted range, but this is a sweet-swinging guy. In a full season with Dick Williams on his case, he'll have the same year as Hrbek. Look for him to dial 8 at least 30 times in '87 and cost $35.

**DOUG DECINCES.** .256 BA, 26 Home Runs, 96 RBI, 2 Stolen Bases

As usual, he could be a steal, he could be a disaster. Take a long look at Jack Howell in spring training and the first week of the season. You can forget about any more 26 HR, 96 RBI seasons from Doug, but he wants to show Gene Mauch a thing or two. If free agency means anything, he'll prove you *can* go home again, if a hot corner in Baltimore is home. Could be a bargain at $13.

**DARRELL EVANS.** .241 BA, 29 Home Runs, 85 RBI, 3 Stolen Bases

One night in 1986 Sparky Anderson started right-handed-hitting Dave Engel against a right-handed pitcher, in Yankee Stadium, while a healthy Darrell Evans sat on the bench. Engel had never played first base before, but who knows, maybe he was a natural. That's the way Sparky thinks, if you call that thinking. But why not? Sparky had said in spring training that Evans (the 1985 American League home-run clean-up) was over the hill and couldn't hit anymore. Which he can't, of course, unless he plays. How much will he be worth in 1987? Ask Sparky. Or $13.

**GARY GAETTI.** .287 BA, 34 Home Runs, 108 RBI, 14 Stolen Bases

He can't hurt you at this price because let's say he falls to 22 homers and 75 RBIs and .248, which is certainly possible, he'll still have 13–15 steals. You'll be surprised, but look at the bottom line and he's a $29 ballplayer.

**KENT HRBEK.** .267 BA, 29 Home Runs, 91 RBI, 2 Stolen Bases

A mini-Mattingly/Murray who weighs more than both combined. Lucky for Kent, we don't have fielding stats in RLB, so he's worth almost as much money. He will hit around .270, with 29 home runs and 90 RBIs. He's the perfect guy to keep for half a season, get some tremendous numbers, then trade for relief or speed, because he'll go for so much money he'll almost always be put back in the draft—and then go for just as much money again. $37.

**GARTH IORG.** .260 BA, 3 Home Runs, 44 RBI, 3 Stolen Bases

See Buechele *et al*.

**BROOK JACOBY.** .288 BA, 17 Home Runs, 80 RBI, 2 Stolen Bases

Bargain time. He probably won't be with Cleveland by the time you read this, and the coming of Cory Snyder depressed his numbers in 1986. But Jacoby is a player. You think Atlanta would like to have him and Brett Butler back? $23.

**WALLY JOYNER.**   .290 BA, 22 Home Runs, 100 RBI, 5 Stolen Bases

Say this one over and over again: "I'm a believer in Wally World. But do I believe in $35 for a sophomore who's never hit with the kind of power he showed in '86? No! I'm a believer in Wally World. But do I . . ." So only go to $34.

**CARNEY LANSFORD.**   .284 BA, 19 Home Runs, 72 RBI, 16 Stolen Bases

Doesn't run anymore. Will hit .280–.295 with 14–16 taters and 70–75 RBI. And, miracle of miracles, he actually played a season without a sojourn on the disabled list. $20–$25, depending on your faith in his health.

**DON MATTINGLY.**   .352 BA, 31 Home Runs, 113 RBI, 0 Stolen Bases

Time to admit it, although it still doesn't make sense since he does everything so easily and unspectacularly . . . but he's probably the best player in baseball and, except for Rickey Henderson, the most valuable offensive player in Rotisserie League Baseball. Want to know what Stan Musial would have cost in Rotis-dollars? Take a look at what you'd pay for Don the Man. $45.

**PAUL MOLITOR.**   .281 BA, 9 Home Runs, 55 RBI, 20 Stolen Bases

You'll get him cheap this year because he pulled a hamstring every other day in '86 and couldn't run. He won't steal 40 anymore, maybe not 30. But in '87 he's capable of stealing 20, hitting 8–10 home runs, and batting .280. Go up to $22.

**RANCE MULLINIKS.**   .259 BA, 11 Home Runs, 45 RBI, 1 Stolen Base

See Buechele *et al*.

**EDDIE MURRAY.**   .305 BA, 17 Home Runs, 84 RBI, 3 Stolen Bases

Money in the bank. When big Ed is elected to the Hall of Fame, an entire nation is going to gasp in shock as they realize he went through a brilliant career without winning an MVP award. He didn't quite have his year-in, year-out 30 HR, 110 RBI season in 1986 because of injuries, so you may get lucky and get him a few dollars cheaper than he would normally be. Get him. Play him. Every day. Name him captain. Trade Edward Bennett Williams. $43.

**PETE O'BRIEN.** .290 BA, 23 Home Runs, 90 RBI, 4 Stolen Bases

A bit of surprise in this stratosphere, but look at the numbers. He could be a .290 hitter with 18 dingers and 85 RBIs for a long time to come. He's the kind of player who could have an MVP season under Bobby Valentine. Everyone tends to ignore him. You might sneak in and get him cheap. Open him early, while everyone's waiting for Mattingly. $30.

**MIKE PAGLIARULO.** .238 BA, 28 Home Runs, 71 RBI, 4 Stolen Bases

For some reason, he's one of these guys where you want to say, "I was smart enough to pick him up for $14 and he had a $33 year." He definitely has the potential to have a $33 year—in fact, he just had one. But because he plays for Boss George and he had never done it before and not *everybody* can repeat two years in a row (or Joltin' Joe Charboneau might still have normal hair and be playing for Cleveland), Pags just might have a $14 year in '87. But think of paying $32 because the pessimists might be wrong.

**JIM PRESLEY.** .265 BA, 27 Home Runs, 107 RBI, 0 Stolen Bases

If you think you're going to get an Elvis gag here, forget it! Go buy some cheap book without Rotisserie class! One of these days, Seattle's going to win. And Mike Moore will pitch up to his potential. And Al Davis will become a superstar. And Jim Presley will hit 42 homers. . . . Until then, $28.

**PAT TABLER.** .326 BA, 6 Home Runs, 48 RBI, 3 Stolen Bases

Be very, very careful, unless you have a side bet on BA with the bases loaded. May not play all that much in '87. Solid hitter but doesn't seem to belong in the big leagues. You don't want him, but if you screw up and don't get any of the guys above, you could do worse for $12.

**WILLIE UPSHAW.** .251 BA, 9 Home Runs, 60 RBI, 23 Stolen Bases

See Gary Gaetti, 1984, under "LOST: ONE HOME-RUN

SWING." Okay, raise your hand if you knew Willie had any speed. How many of you thought he was Willie Aikens? How much money could we all have made if we had a Rotisserie convention in Vegas and we all put up $100 and bet that Upshaw would have more steals than home runs in '86? *A LOT OF MONEY!* Pay $21 and show him the right-field fence.

**GREG WALKER.** .277 BA, 13 Home Runs, 51 RBI, 1 Stolen Base

Every so often, there's a guy who you just *know* is going to hit .300 and have 35 home runs and drive in 100 runs. So every year you pay too much for him. Not $38, but $28, because even though that *sounds* expensive, you *know* he's going to do it. He gets hurt, or he can't hit left-handers, or the manager doesn't like him, or he can't field. . . . Are you listening, Greg?! $22.

## Up the Middle

The best thing you can say about American League middle infielders is that you have to have three of them. Most of these little banjo players don't run much faster than the guy chasing the bicycle in *The Bicycle Thief*, and most don't have any more power than a young, fit Wally Cox (who should never be confused with Wally Pipp—or even Wally Cleaver, for that matter).

If you don't get Trammell or Ripken or Whitaker or Fernandez or . . . okay, so some of these mugs can play. But don't break the bank. Keep in mind at all times that Dave Henderson at 8 bucks'll give as many, if not more, RBIs than Marty Barrett at 15. Let MI stand for Medium Income.

**MARTY BARRETT.** .286 BA, 4 Home Runs, 60 RBI, 15 Stolen Bases

Very nice numbers and seems to be consistent. Expect all Red Sox except Boggs to fall from their '86 seasons; however, try to get Marty for $8. Go as high as $10. After that, draft Dave Stapleton at a buck and pray for some form of serious bone injury.

**TONY BERNAZARD.** .301 BA, 17 Home Runs, 73 RBI, 17 Stolen Bases

We don't believe his 1986 power or his RBI total, but he's still one of the better Rotiss second sackers. (By the way: If any of you Rotisserians out there aren't sending monthly newsletters to each other, you're missing one of the world's great joys— actually getting to write the words "second sackers.") You could do a lot worse than have the entire Cleveland offense. Just don't get confused and draft the entire Cleveland pitching staff. $15.

**BUDDY BIANCALANA.** .242 BA, 2 Home Runs, 8 RBI, 5 Stolen Bases

He ain't the new Paul Schaffer. And he ain't even Angel Salazar. $1.

**JUAN BONILLA/JACKIE GUTIERREZ.** .243/.186 BA, 1/0 Home Runs, 18/4 RBI, 0/3 Stolen Bases

And people wonder why Weaver retired? One Junior Leaguer arrogantly drafted Gutierrez for one smacker last season, positive he'd steal 15 bases and put his team over the top in that category. The same owner also once believed Sparky about Chris Pittaro. $1—if possible, 50 cents apiece.

**JULIO CRUZ.** .215 BA, 0 Home Runs, 19 RBI, 7 Stolen Bases

He should get no playing time in 1987, but we stuck him in here for sentimental reasons. At one time (remember when Julio could get on base enough to steal 50+ bases?) he was the best buy in the Junior League. He's also been (remember the past few seasons?) the worst. Leave him in the schoolyard. $1.

**TONY FERNANDEZ.** .310 BA, 10 Home Runs, 65 RBI, 25 Stolen Bases

He may turn out to be the best shortstop of the 1980s, which is going some. Imagine Ozzie Smith winning the batting crown and hitting 15 home runs—because that's what Fernandez is going to do before the decade's over. $18–$20.

**SCOTT FLETCHER.** .300 BA, 3 Home Runs, 50 RBI, 12 Stolen Bases

Serious Rotisserians always knew Fletcher could hit .300. Unfortunately, many of us paid for this knowledge in every year but 1986. Count on .280 and 50 ribbies. $8.

**JULIO FRANCO.** .306 BA, 10 Home Runs, 74 RBI, 10 Stolen Bases

For some reason he's stopped running, but he still goes on an occasional walkabout. Julio's the real thing, though. He'll keep you up worrying at night, he'll slump ferociously, he might disappear for a day or two, but he's worth every dollar of the $16 you should pay for him.

**GREG GAGNE.** .250 BA, 12 Home Runs, 54 RBI, 12 Stolen Bases

Gagne means "win" in French, something Greg's not going to do in Minnesota. But he will hit a few dingers. About $10.

**JIM GANTNER.** .274 BA, 7 Home Runs, 38 RBI, 13 Stolen Bases

Starting to fade but still a pro. $8.

**DAMASO GARCIA.** .281 BA, 6 Home Runs, 46 RBI, 9 Stolen Bases

Every year some wise Rotisserian writes Garcia off, saying he's got a bad attitude, he can't run anymore, he'll be in the National League, etc. And every year he keeps his job and plays like one of the better middle infielders in the league. But in 1987, it'll be official. Write Garcia off! He's got a bad attitude, he can't run anymore, and he'll be in the National League. $8.

**ALFREDO GRIFFIN.** .285 BA, 4 Home Runs, 50 RBI, 33 Stolen Bases

He'll never have another '85. But who will? He's still worth $14 for the 30+ steals.

**OZZIE GUILLEN.** .250 BA, 2 Home Runs, 47 RBI, 8 Stolen Bases

Picture Ozzie Smith, except he can't hit, run, or field as well. He *can* do all three of those things better than Ozzie Nelson, however, raising his price to a lofty $5.

**TIM HULETT.** .231 BA, 17 Home Runs, 44 RBI, 4 Stolen Bases

The White Sox are a team going nowhere fast. But you can't go wrong spending $11 for Hulett's power. He'd go for more if his low BA and high at-bats weren't so risky.

**STEVE LOMBARDOZZI.** .227 BA, 8 Home Runs, 33 RBI, 3 Stolen Bases

He might actually get beaten out by Chris Pittaro, the greatest rookie prospect Sparky ever managed. That ought to tell you something. $5.

**SPIKE OWEN.** .231 BA, 1 Home Run, 45 RBI, 4 Stolen Bases

You gotta love someone with the name Spike. You also have to hesitate before inviting his parents over for a Salade Niçoise and a chilled rosé, but that's another matter. Expect the Spikeroo to hit .250–.260 in Fenway and pay $4 or $5 for him.

**TONY PHILLIPS.** .256 BA, 5 Home Runs, 52 RBI, 15 Stolen Bases

Also worth $8–$10. One day this kid'll have a $17 year. Trust us.

**RAY QUINONES.** .218 BA, 2 Home Runs, 22 RBI, 4 Stolen Bases

Except for the fact that he can't run, see Harold Reynolds. So what if he has a safecracker's hands? This is baseball. $1.

**WILLIE RANDOLPH.** .276 BA, 5 Home Runs, 50 RBI, 15 Stolen Bases

The Yanks should have traded him two years ago. Now it's too late to get real value—at least until Ken Harrelson gets another GM job. Willie had a good season in '86 but age and all the years of Steinbrenner have to be wearing him down. $8.

**HAROLD REYNOLDS.** .222 BA, 1 Home Run, 25 RBI, 30 Stolen Bases

Dick Williams left the Padres for this??? Okay, so Reynolds can run. Let's all rise and repeat together: "You can't steal first base. . . . You can't steal first base. . . ." $8 if he hits enough to play enough to steal second and third enough.

**NELSON RILES.** .254 BA, 9 Home Runs, 47 RBI, 7 Stolen Bases

Ah, for the good old days when Yount was in the infield. Riles is okay, but 1986 is what you should get in 1987. The Brewers are a team to watch, however—they have the horses to play in the

East. So add a couple of bucks to Riles' salary, figuring he'll respond to a pennant race. $8–$9.

**CAL RIPKEN.** .282 BA, 25 Home Runs, 81 RBI, 4 Stolen Bases

Maybe Dad'll rest him every 300 innings or so. Doesn't matter. Cal Jr.'s a blue chipper through and through. The season he had in '86 is the exact same one he'll have in '87 and '88 and probably '89. A likely Hall of Famer and, if he ran, he'd be worth over 30 Belangers. As is, $25–$27.

**ANGEL SALAZAR.** .245 BA, 0 Home Runs, 24 RBI, 1 Stolen Base

What gives? He played a decent short and he hit okay (at least he hit better than Buddy) and then he sat a lot! Here's a little True/False Quiz: Did the owner writing this chapter own Salazar or not? If you need the answer, play golf. $1–$2.

**DICK SCHOFIELD.** .249 BA, 13 Home Runs, 57 RBI, 23 Stolen Bases

It seemed impossible two years ago, but Schofield will be a legitimate star. His 1987 stats will read: .260 BA, 16 HR, 60 RBIs, 28 SBs. That's a $14–$16 year, though spend less if possible.

**WAYNE TOLLESON.** .265 BA, 3 Home Runs, 43 RBI, 17 Stolen Bases

Anyone who thinks Tolleson will still be the Yankees' starting shortstop by the All-Star Game, please call. We've got a uranium mine in Asbury Park we want to sell you. $3.

**ALAN TRAMMELL.** .277 BA, 21 Home Runs, 75 RBI, 25 Stolen Bases

The Tram is back! His second half of '86 was a joy to behold, especially if you owned him and got to revel in his daily box scores. He hit, he hit for power, he ran. The most valuable Rotiss middle infielder in the American League. $23–$25.

**LOU WHITAKER.** .269 BA, 20 Home Runs, 73 RBI, 13 Stolen Bases

This Lou is truly sweet. We wonder how many Lous have had the nickname "Sweet"? Johnson . . . Piniella . . . Costello . . . Pay $18–$20 for Sweet Lou Whitaker.

**FRANK WHITE.**  .272 BA, 22 Home Runs, 84 RBI, 4 Stolen Bases

He's just as sweet as Whitaker and he's worth exactly the same price. One of these days, though, he's *got* to get old. If he has a really fast April/May/June, get rid of him while the gettin's good. $18–$20.

**ROB WILFONG.**  .219 BA, 3 Home Runs, 33 RBI, 1 Stolen Base

You can do worse for $1. If you don't do better for $2, start playing for next year. And if Mark McClemore isn't ready, the Angels can start playing dead.

**CURTIS WILKERSON.**  .237 BA, 0 Home Runs, 15 RBI, 9 Stolen Bases

Bobby "My Funny" Valentine better hope that Jeff Kunkel gets a lot better. And fast! $1.

## In the Outfield

Over in the National League, let some outfielder amass 15 home runs and maybe 70 runs batted in and they're sure to tout him as MVP material; in the Junior Circuit, those are the numbers of your average platoon hitter who grumbles that he never sees right-handed pitching. Whatever theory you prefer—weaker pitching in the American League, the dingerdomes in Seattle and Minnesota and bandbox ball parks elsewhere, or simply an awesome new supply of fearsome hitting talent—there are a plethora of big-number, three- and even four-category outfielders to choose among, and since you need five of 'em, you have to watch out that macho zeal to rack up some humongous hitting numbers doesn't leave you dollars short when it's time to pick the pitchers, and you end up with a humongous ERA and ratio, too.

**TONY ARMAS.**  .264 BA, 11 Home Runs, 58 RBI, 0 Stolen Bases

Injuries have reduced the league's leader in homers (43) and RBIs (123) of 1984 to the power equivalent of your basic shortstop. He's not much for average—.250 lifetime, .260s the last couple of years—and he's nothing for speed, and maybe at 33 the great years are behind him. If he's around for the '87 draft, be a genius and predict his comeback, or be cautious. Some sentimentalist will pay $10 for him.

**HAROLD BAINES.** .296 BA, 21 Home Runs, 88 RBI, 2 Stolen Bases

An ornament for any team. This is a man who quietly puts up All-Star numbers year after year without the hype that attends lesser figures elsewhere. You can be sure as long as he's on your club he'll produce a .300 season with 20-some homers and around 100 RBIs, though he's basically not running at all anymore. At 28, he'll just be coming into his prime in '87. Figure $35–$40, maybe more if he gets a press agent.

**JESSE BARFIELD.** .289 BA, 40 Home Runs, 108 RBI, 8 Stolen Bases

**GEORGE BELL.** .309 BA, 31 Home Runs, 108 RBI, 7 Stolen Bases

Let's take the Killer B's as an entry. You can't afford them both, for sure, but you can't go wrong with either. Both are now annual MVP candidates, and at 27 they are only going to get better for at least a year or two more. Each will give you .300-plus average, 30-plus home runs, and 100-plus RBIs, though neither is stealing bases as in past years. Bell's personality problems—the chance that he'll talk himself into an umpire's suspension or an injury-producing brawl—may make Barfield the preference. Either way, they're in the $40-and-up category.

**DARYL BOSTON.** .266 BA, 5 Home Runs, 22 RBI, 9 Stolen Bases

Don't take your eye off this kid. He was a first-round draft pick, he's only 24, and he hasn't yet had a full year in the majors. In late '86 he was hitting for average and stealing some bases, though he hasn't shown much signs of power. Still, average and especially speed are at a premium in the AL, and if the bidding stops at around $10, take a flyer.

**PHIL BRADLEY.** .310 BA, 12 Home Runs, 50 RBI, 21 Stolen Bases

Another one of the 27/28-year-old sluggers so bountiful in the American League—or is it only that all their names begin with B? He went from no homers in '84 to 26 in '85, though his power production was down considerably in '86. Consistent .300 hitter, more than a dozen stolen bases, Bradley could help a team a lot in the $25–$30 range.

**TOM BRUNANSKY.**  .256 BA, 23 Home Runs, 75 RBI, 12 Stolen Bases

He breaks the mold—he's only 26. Bruno has put together some big years already, with 20 or more homers in five successive seasons. Last year his run production was down but his average was up, and he started to steal some bases. Hard to know which way Bruno is going—if it's toward superstardom, grab him on the moderate side at around $30–$35.

**BRETT BUTLER.**  .278 BA, 4 Home Runs, 51 RBI, 32 Stolen Bases

Talk about not knowing where people are going. A preseason injury may have been the cause of Butler's '86 falloff in average and stolen bases, which is what you want him for, since he has no power and his run production is negligible. Is his starting role in jeopardy? Time will tell, and maybe '87 will be a comeback year, but it's unlikely he'll command the price he once did. Dreamers and those desperate for stolen bases may put him in the lower $20 range.

**JOHN CANGELOSI.**  .235 BA, 2 Home Runs, 32 RBI, 50 Stolen Bases

An inspiration to little guys. At 5'8" and 150 pounds, on base he looks like a midget next to your average 6'2", 200-pound first baseman. But can he scoot. He's the only guy on the horizon likely to give Rickey Henderson a challenge for the stolen base title. No average, no power, but hey, everybody needs speed. Somebody will bid him into the $20s.

**JOSÉ CANSECO.**  .240 BA, 33 Home Runs, 117 RBI, 15 Stolen Bases

José, can you see? Often not, because he's on his way to setting new planet records for strikeouts. But oh, what a powerful slugger when he connects! Still only 22, if he adjusts to pitchers faster than they adjust to him, he'll be among league leaders in home runs and RBIs for years to come. And he runs a little. And his average is as likely to go up as go down. Mortgage the furniture, latch on to the Babe Ruth of our time, only $45–$50 or so.

**JOE CARTER.**  .302 BA, 29 Home Runs, 121 RBI, 29 Stolen Bases

We're running out of superlatives, and we're only in the C's!

Carter will probably end up on first base instead of the outfield, but take him where you find him after his first full-time injury-free season in '86 proved that his champions when he languished in the Cub farm system were not wrong—to your basic .300 average, 25-plus homers, 100 RBIs add better-than-good stolen-base numbers. A genuine four-category star. 'Round about $45.

**DAVE COLLINS.** .270 BA, 1 Home Run, 27 RBI, 27 Stolen Bases

How much longer can this man run? He's 35, and in your basic Butler-Cangelosi class, with a respectable average, still respectable speed, and no power production. If some team thinks he can make things happen, he'll get his 30 or so stolen bases, and that gives him value at around $12–$15.

**MIKE DAVIS.** .268 BA, 19 Home Runs, 55 RBI, 27 Stolen Bases

Another of the bumper crop born in 1959, this member of baseball's Davis team had a great year in '85 and a mysterious one last year. As they say, the jury is still out. He runs, but basically he has moderate power, inconsistent run production, and an average average. Will this year be different? Try him in the $18–$22 range.

**ROB DEER.** .232 BA, 33 Home Runs, 86 RBI, 5 Stolen Bases

The Giants didn't believe his minor league numbers, or looked too hard at his Canseco-style strikeouts. Who else but Bambi saw he was a Gorman Thomas clone? So he'll be a home run champion and drive in lots of runs and hit around .230 and steal a base every other month. How long will he let his hair grow? Take him for $25–$30 if you can.

**BRIAN DOWNING.** .267 BA, 20 Home Runs, 95 RBI, 4 Stolen Bases

A fine, consistent hitter for nearly a decade, will this 36-year-old be around to do it again in '87? Last year saw a falloff in homers, but he was still hitting in the .260 range and drives in runs among the best of them. No speed. A $15–$20 ballplayer these days.

**DWIGHT EVANS.** .259 BA, 26 Home Runs, 97 RBI, 3 Stolen Bases

Now we're in the old pros part of the alphabet. Dewey has

had solid year after solid year, no less so in '86. Do you believe that 35 is a mellow age for ballplayers? Can he crank out another 20-plus homers, 80-plus RBIs, hit .260? (He doesn't run, needless to say.) If your answers are yes, you'll spend $25 or so, let's hope not for old times' sake.

**KIRK GIBSON.** .268 BA, 28 Home Runs, 86 RBI, 34 Stolen Bases

Gibson's injury threw '86 into a cocked hat. Or did it? Proportionate to his fewer at-bats, he had about the same homer and RBI production, a little lower average, and even more stolen bases. A healthy Gibson is still one of the league's great superstars, and batting average is the only category he needs to bring up before he challenges the all-time Rotisserie bid records (see HENDERSON, R.). Grab him while you can at around $45.

**MEL HALL.** .296 BA, 18 Home Runs, 77 RBI, 6 Stolen Bases

The other half of the Rick Who? trade (with Joe Carter) kept healthy in '86 and produced the kind of year people were waiting for from him. But he was benched a lot after a slow start and it's not clear that the Indians see him as a full-time player, especially with all the ace outfielders in their farm system. Maybe $15–$20 is just about right for him.

**DAVE HENDERSON.** .265 BA, 15 Home Runs, 47 RBI, 2 Stolen Bases

Did he buy a new lease on life with the Red Sox? More playing time, more men on base in front of him may make him a more valuable player than he has proved so far. He has been one of your basic middle-middle players, with average homers, RBIs, and average, and no speed. Rotisserie teams need journeymen just like all others, just so you don't pay too much for them. $10–$12 could be a deal.

**RICKEY HENDERSON.** .263 BA, 28 Home Runs, 74 RBI, 87 Stolen Bases

Go to your dictionary, and look up "Four-Category Player." There you will find the name that explains it all. If you want Henderson, the thing you have to worry about is, Will he cost me so much that I can't get enough other good players to have a contender? He hasn't led the Yankees to any titles, has he? In '86, his batting average tailed off a bit. Maybe that will give you a chance to grab him at only $50 or so.

**PETE INCAVIGLIA.**   .250 BA, 30 Home Runs, 88 RBI, 3 Stolen Bases

Whoops, there goes Canseco's strikeout record! That's the only category where Incaviglia challenges Canseco, but hey, give him time, he never swung at a professional pitch before his first major league game. His numbers ain't bad the first time around. Check out Mike Schmidt's first full season, they always say (.198, 18, 52 in 367 at-bats). No speed. Maybe $25 will be enough.

**RUPPERT JONES.**   .229 BA, 17 Home Runs, 49 RBI, 10 Stolen Bases

Hard to believe he's only 32. Seems like he's Methuselah. Been knocking around since he was a mere 21, bounced to the minors, bounced back up. Will he escape Mike Port's housecleaning? If Ruppert's around in '87, see what he can give you—15 or so home runs, more than the occasional stolen base, here and there an RBI. He's the kind of guy who's overlooked in the draft and may go for a song at the end, and if you can get him for under $10, you've got a bargain.

**LEE LACY.**   .287 BA, 11 Home Runs, 47 RBI, 4 Stolen Bases

The oldest outfielder in the American League (he turns 38 soon after opening day '87) continues to have Lee Lacy–type years. Only he doesn't run as much as he did in the National League; in fact, he hardly runs anymore at all. That tends to make him an admirable but not so valuable Rotisserie player. He's in the Ruppert Jones class—at $10 he'd be a grab.

**CHET LEMON.**   .251 BA, 12 Home Runs, 53 RBI, 2 Stolen Bases

He had his one big year with the White Sox in '79, and he's been a consistent ballplayer for a long time, always steady with decent average, homers, and run production, though no speed. Last year was a bad year. He's 32, and which way is he going? Pick him for a comeback and you may be prognosticator of the year, but don't spend more than $8–$10 if you can help it.

**FRED LYNN.** .287 BA, 23 Home Runs, 67 RBI, 2 Stolen Bases
Another old-man consistency with the numbers. Although his at-bats were down last year, his average was up, and he's had 20 or more homers and 60 or more RBIs for five straight years. No speed. He's 35 now, and who knows what the future holds? Check him out at around $15.

**ODDIBE McDOWELL.** .266 BA, 18 Home Runs, 49 RBI, 33 Stolen Bases
Oddibe's an apprentice four-category star. His around 30 stolen bases a year rank him with speedsters like Collins and Butler, but he hits with power and is building up his average. Run production is the only area where Henderson-type numbers don't yet seem in the cards. With that drawback, maybe $30–$35 will take him away.

**LLOYD MOSEBY.** .253 BA, 21 Home Runs, 86 RBI, 32 Stolen Bases
The Shaker is an authentic four-category star. In the past couple of years he has tended to be overshadowed by his team-mates the Killer B's, but don't let that fool you. He's just a little bit behind them in average, homers, and RBI—but unlike them he's still a major threat on the base paths. He'll go for $35–$40 south of the border, but in Toronto, where they know him better, add $5—and not just for the exchange rate.

**JOHN MOSES.** .256 BA, 3 Home Runs, 34 RBI, 25 Stolen Bases
Another little guy who got his chance to play in '86 and turned out a speedster. His stolen bases make him worth a look even though he has zero power, not much more run production, and no fancy batting average. Grab him at draft dregs time for no more than $6.

**DWAYNE MURPHY.** .252 BA, 9 Home Runs, 39 RBI, 3 Stolen Bases
Murphy has been among the league's elite in homers and run production for much of the 1980s, but '85 showed a slippage and '86 was a disaster. He doesn't hit for average and he stopped running a few years ago, and even his great glove—make no mind, Rotisserie GMs—hasn't kept him in the lineup every day. At 32 in '87, Murphy is a big If. Gamblers should find him in the under-$5 bin.

**DAN PASQUA.** .293 BA, 16 Home Runs, 45 RBI, 2 Stolen Bases

With George's boys you never know—they could be in Columbus, they could be in a triple-left-handed platoon. On pure ability, Pasqua could put big numbers on the board if he got the at-bats. Per plate appearance his homer and RBI totals are outstanding, and he can hit around .300, though he doesn't steal. But as the philosopher Andujar reminds us, youneverknow. Still, he'll go $20–$25 on potential alone.

**GARY PETTIS.** .258 BA, 5 Home Runs, 58 RBI, 50 Stolen Bases

No one has ever won a Rotisserie League championship with defense. Pettis offers nothing in average and even less in power, but he does run-run-run, and he'll probably end up in the top three in the stolen base race for years to come. That alone for a steal-starved Rotisserie clubowner is likely to boost his salary into the $25–$30 range.

**KIRBY PUCKETT.** .328 BA, 31 Home Runs, 98 RBI, 20 Stolen Bases

What a name, what a man! The pride of Triton College hit no homers in '84 and a mere 4 in his first 1,200 major league at-bats, but last year he discovered the magic pine tar. And he steals a few bases. Break the piggy bank, grab the rent money, shell out maybe $45 for Kirby the Great.

**JIM RICE.** .324 BA, 20 Home Runs, 110 RBI, 0 Stolen Bases

The American League's sterling home-run hitter and run producer of the past decade decided last year that he was hitting into too many double plays and stopped swinging for the Green Monster. His homers fell by about half, he drove home a couple of dozen fewer runs, but he raised his average by about 20 points from his usual .300. And he stopped running altogether. Some may think that, at 34, Rice has descended from the Olympian heights and is now merely a great player. That may drop his price into the $35–$40 range.

**JOHN SHELBY.** .228 BA, 11 Home Runs, 49 RBI, 18 Stolen Bases

You think Shelby has the talent to be a regular. You imagine he might be the kind of guy you want on your team. And then you look at the numbers: low average, little power, minimal run production. The one thing he's started to do is steal some bases. When you're filling up your roster at the end of the draft, picking from among the also-rans, those stolen bases may make him worth picking off the under-$5 table.

**RUBEN SIERRA.**  .264 BA, 16 Home Runs, 55 RBI, 7 Stolen Bases

All those hittin' people, where do they all come from? This one's from Puerto Rico, he's the youngest outfielder in the league at 21, and after coming up during '86 he showed the kind of power and speed that could make him somebody very special for a long time to come. Grab him at $10–$15 before he has a chance to put some big numbers on the board.

**LONNIE SMITH.**  .287 BA, 8 Home Runs, 44 RBI, 26 Stolen Bases

Smith showed signs of slowing down in '86. He's 31, and his principal allure has been those 50–60 stolen bases, since he has little power and run production, and his batting average in the American League has not matched his hitting in the National. Still, 25–30 stolen bases make him a commodity, and somebody will pay for them at around $12–$15.

**CORY SNYDER.**  .272 BA, 24 Home Runs, 69 RBI, 2 Stolen Bases

His middle name would be Awesome if it weren't already Cory. The All-American boy from Brigham Young and the U.S. Olympic team might endanger that old brick yard by Lake Erie with his home-run power. His batting average and run production are not yet in the same Gee Whiz! class, and he doesn't steal bases, but the Cleveland fans—and you find them everywhere—won't let him get away for under $35.

**DAN TARTABULL.**  .270 BA, 25 Home Runs, 96 RBI, 4 Stolen Bases

Were those 43 home runs he was alleged to have hit at Calgary in '85 a Canadian typographical error? No way, says Father José. In his first regular major league season he produced the kind of numbers to put him among the league's elite. Lack of speed is the only drawback to keep him in the $25–$30 range.

**GARY WARD.**   .316 BA, 5 Home Runs, 51 RBI, 12 Stolen Bases
     This old pro decided in '85 to be a base stealer, which he never was before. This old pro decided in '86 to hit over .300, which he never had before. What will this old pro decide to do in '87? Well, it may be that he won't produce the homers and RBI that he did a few years ago, but in his early 30s he contributes as a four-category player even more than before. Somewhere, someway, he's likely to help a team. $25–$30.

**WILLIE WILSON.**   .269 BA, 9 Home Runs, 44 RBI, 34 Stolen Bases
     Last season was not a standout year for Wilson. His batting average and stolen bases, the two categories that made him a star, were both down. Lacking power and run production, at 31 he will still be valuable for 25–30 stolen bases but not a luxury item for 50–60. Unless you foresee a comeback year, look in the $15–$20 range.

**DAVE WINFIELD.**   .262 BA, 24 Home Runs, 104 RBI, 6 Stolen Bases
     Owners may peak at 28 or so, but some players just keep on getting better—so they say. Winfield's '86 numbers were not quite up to past triumphs, his average was down, and he stole fewer bases. But he's still a force to be reckoned with, assuming he can turn his attention from Yankee mind games to ball games. $35 should do it.

**ROBIN YOUNT.**   .312 BA, 9 Home Runs, 46 RBI, 14 Stolen Bases
     From an offensive viewpoint—the only Rotisserie viewpoint—Yount was a great shortstop but is only an average outfielder. His homers and run production in '86 were way down from his peak years. He brought his batting average back up over .300, and he contributed some stolen bases. Great as he was, you can't afford to buy memories: $15–$20 tops.

## Designated Hitters

Anyone playing with a full deck of baseball cards loves to watch Don Baylor batting with the game on the line. Hal McRae stroking a double to right center with runners in scoring position, and

Reggie admiring another flare as it soars over the right-field fence. Nonetheless, the Founding Fathers of Rotisserie League Baseball collectively and individually agree with American League President Bobby Brown: The designated hitter stinks.

(At least that's the way *Dr.* Bobby Brown felt about the DH before he got his current job.)

But the DH is a fact of American League life, so a smart Rotisserie League GM won't waste time whining about loss of purity but will recognize that an important strategic question is involved in filling that position on Draft Day.

Because a lot of hitters qualify at DH, you'll never have to worry about scraping the bottom of the barrel (at least not to the same degree you will in finding a second catcher or third middle infielder). On the other hand, a handful of thumpers—Baylor, Easler, Kingman—qualify *only* at DH, so teams that pick them up won't be able to juggle their lineups later in the draft and reenter the DH-bidding when a bargain appears.

What this means is that it's possible to hang back and, with a little bit of luck, pick up a Cliff Johnson for a song—or, better still, for a buck, as the Junior League's Stevie Wunders did in 1986. Rule of thumb: Don't fill the DH position until at least midway through the draft.

**DON BAYLOR.**   .238 BA, 31 Home Runs, 94 RBI, 3 Stolen Bases

Okay, okay, he's a *great* clubhouse leader. Problem is, most Rotisserie League teams don't have clubhouses. Too bad, because Baylor is all class. More to the Rotissepoint, the power output was wonderful last season, but the .238 scares us. His bat has to slow down a little this year . . . doesn't it? He'll fetch $25, and this could be the first season someone regrets paying it.

**CECIL COOPER.**   .258 BA, 12 Home Runs, 75 RBI, 1 Stolen Base

He's 37, but a young 37. Problem is, Billy Joe Robidoux is a young 23. If Robidoux comes back strong from knee surgery, look for Cooper to DH. He won't like it, but youth is going to be served in Milwaukee, so help us Harry Dalton. $14 if he gets his cuts.

**MIKE EASLER.**   .320 BA, 14 Home Runs, 78 RBI, 3 Stolen Bases

Repeat after George Steinbrenner: "This was a good trade for the Yankees." And, for once, he's right (which just goes to show that even a blind chicken will pick up a piece of corn every now and then). If Baylor had continued to call Yankee Stadium home (an eerie thought), his home run total would have been a lot nearer Easler's 14 than the 31 he posted out of Fenway. Easler's RBI-per-at-bat ratio was better than Baylor's, and those 64 batting-average points could mean the difference in a close Rotisserie League race. A solid $19.

**CARLTON FISK.** .221 BA, 14 Home Runs, 63 RBI, 2 Stolen Bases

*If* he is the White Sox DH (and that depends on Ron Hassey's knees and Ron Karkovice's bat), and *if* he stays healthy, and *if* the Sox have any kind of season at all, and *if* he doesn't waste energy pining for the rocks and rills of New Hampshire, Pudge could have a 1987 somewhere between 1986 and 1985 (.238, 37, 107, 17, in case you've forgotten). So buy him for somewhere between $12 and $20.

**REGGIE JACKSON.** .241 BA, 18 Home Runs, 58 RBI, 1 Stolen Base

Pride and muscle will produce another 16–18 dingers and 50–60 RBI—if he finds a place to swing the bat. You'll know for sure by the time you read this, but one guess is that Reggie will be taking his cuts at Comiskey Park this year. $11–$14, depending on the park where Reggie ends up hanging his hat.

**CLIFF JOHNSON.** .250 BA, 15 Home Runs, 55 RBI, 0 Stolen Bases

Imagine a game with Mike Hargrove, George Foster, and Cliff Johnson batting 1-2-3, and Carlton Fisk behind the plate for the other team. You'd never get out of the top half of the first. But hey, if you were as old as Cliff, you'd take your time getting to the plate and savor every swing. Hit like him, too, and you'd be a steal at $9.

**DAVE KINGMAN.** .210 BA, 35 Home Runs, 94 RBI, 3 Stolen Bases

What's a nice guy like him doing in a rough game like this? He'll go for a song—always does—because half the owners in your league wouldn't have him on their teams at any price. If you're in the other half, you'll only have to pay a fraction of what his numbers are worth—say, $15 for Mr. Warmth.

**RON KITTLE.** .218 BA, 21 Home Runs, 60 RBI, 4 Stolen Bases
Funny, he doesn't *look* like Dave Kingman. $10.

**HAL McRAE.** .252 BA, 7 Home Runs, 37 RBI, 0 Stolen Bases
You gotta hope that son Brian has the tools to make it fast so that Hal can realize his dream of playing ball with his boy, and then retire gracefully. In the Royals' pennant year (1985, in case you've forgotten; and if you paid much attention to the Royals last year, you might well have), McRae came on strong in the second half and reminded you why he's always been the quintessential DH. Last year he was flat the whole season. Is this the end? We hope not, but we're not going to risk big bucks that it isn't. Pick him up at $1 or not at all.

**JORGE ORTA.** .277 BA, 9 Home Runs, 46 RBI, 0 Stolen Bases
The other half of the Royals' DH semiplatoon (McRae continued to hit against some right-handers last year) could see more action this season. And, if he does, count on him to deliver. He's a dead-solid hitter, designated or otherwise, with a lifetime BA of .279 to prove it. Figure $2 if McRae comes back, $5 if somebody else handles the righty side of the platoon.

**LARRY PARRISH.** .276 BA, 28 Home Runs, 94 RBI, 3 Stolen Bases
Until Cory Snyder came along to make Brook Jacoby expendable, Parrish led the league in name-most-often-mentioned-in-trade-rumors. Think for a minute of just how tough the Rangers would be today if they had traded Buddy Bell when they should have—four years ago. Instead of nothing (his name was Duane Walker), they would now have a seasoned starting pitcher who could get the ball over the plate (Bob Welch?), a quality second baseman (Steve Sax?)—and Parrish at third. All that 1986 production in only 464 at-bats. $26, and worth every penny of it.

**KEN PHELPS.** .247 BA, 24 Home Runs, 64 RBI, 2 Stolen Bases
Who's the bigger butcher at first base, Phelps or Alvin Davis? As soon as Dick Williams decides, the other becomes the full-time DH, and a doggone good one at that. We think it will be Phelps,

who has a super home-run/at-bat ratio (one per 13.2 at-bats if you count 1984 and 1986, when he hit 48 in 634 appearances—and ignore 1985, when Chuck Cottier apparently decided he wasn't much of a hitter). Unless he turns out to be an even-year-only hitter, he'll be worth $19 in 1987 but go for less. Who knows from Seattle?

**LARRY SHEETS.** .272 BA, 18 Home Runs, 60 RBI, 2 Stolen Bases

Earl Weaver with a Mennonite as his DH? It couldn't last. Look for Sheets to have a huge year under Cal Ripken, Sr. The youngest DH in the league, he can play a little outfield, and there was talk late in the season of teaching him to catch. At $17, he'll deliver.

**ROY SMALLEY.** .246 BA, 20 Home Runs, 57 RBI, 1 Stolen Base

Gene Mauch's nephew gets no respect. He can play third, he can play first, he can hit homers from the left side, and he's a stand-up guy (he proved that in New York). And still people dismiss him. Maybe it's the name—"Smalley" doesn't sound like a power hitter's monicker. Wait around and you'll get him for cheap—$11 or so.

**GORMAN THOMAS.** .187 BA, 16 Home Runs, 36 RBI, 3 Stolen Bases

We *know* the Brewers gave him his unconditional release last October. Whatdya think, we don't read the Transactions report in the morning paper? No matter, we want to take this opportunity for a final (?) tip of the Rotissecap to Stormin' Gorman. He made many a Rotisserie League owner proud and happy to own him. We particularly remember one July night game against the Yankees, with Gorman talking mighty cuts against Dave LaRoche's blooper pitch, and the Brewers' bench collapsing with laughter, and . . . But, hell, *everyone* has a great Gorman memory. This guy is who Joe Garagiola is talking about when he talks about "good old country hard ball." How do you put a dollar sign on a heart like his? Easy: $0 unless he hooks up somewhere, $2 if somewhere is Minnesota.

**ANDRÉ THORNTON.** .229 BA, 17 Home Runs, 66 RBI, 4 Stolen Bases

The patron saint of Cleveland has been a Charlie Abel Baker

in the Junior League for almost as long as he's been an Indian. The Bakers drafted him five seasons ago for $1 (see note above on waiting until late in the auction to go for a DH), then signed him to a three-year contract in his option year for $11. This season he becomes a free agent (in Rotisseball, that is) and may well have to take a salary cut to $8.

**SPARKY TIGER.**
The Maestro in Detroit gave a lot of guys a shot at DH last season. Some did well (Johnny Grubb, Darrell Evans), some didn't, and some had no business whatsoever filling what should be a run-producing slot (Dave Collins was supposed to lead off and steal 60 bases; Sparky said so in spring training). Who's it going to be this year? Probably the best of Sparky's four catchers, the one with the muscles and bad back. But who knows for sure? Certainly not Sparky.

## Off the Bench

The concept of "bench" probably means less in the American League right now than at any time in major league history. With DH taking care of the guys who are slow and can't field, with no need for pinch hitters for pitchers, with some teams religiously platooning, the idea of a team having half a dozen reserves who pinch-hit, spot-start, and play a clearly defined strategic role is almost obsolete. In the days of the 25-man roster the Blue Jays decided the 25th man was superfluous and used that spot for rookies left unprotected, whom they snatched from other teams' minor league rosters. Their lack of a bench cost them a pennant, but never mind. What matters to a Rotisserie drafter is whether anybody cheap and good is available among the reserves, or are you simply going to pay money to rent somebody's pine time? Among the extra men, however, there may be somebody—a Billy Beane? a Bo Jackson?—who takes it upon himself to become a star in '87.

**DUSTY BAKER.**   .240 BA, 4 Home Runs, 19 RBI, 0 Stolen Bases
Was '86 the swan-song year for the 37-year-old Baker? $1.

**BILLY BEANE.**   .213 BA, 3 Home Runs, 15 RBI, 2 Stolen Bases
Once he was a first-round draft pick. Will '87 be the year that that promise gets translated into big league numbers? $3.

**JUAN BENIQUEZ.** .300 BA, 6 Home Runs, 36 RBI, 2 Stolen Bases

Hits for good average, but otherwise not much help for an RL team. $1.

**GLENN BRAGGS.** .237 BA, 4 Home Runs, 18 RBI, 1 Stolen Base
Might be the year he cracks the Brewer lineup. $2.

**RANDY BUSH.** .269 BA, 7 Home Runs, 45 RBI, 5 Stolen Bases
Doesn't look like there's much room for him among all the Twins' sweet swingers. $2.

**CARMEN CASTILLO.** .278 BA, 8 Home Runs, 32 RBI, 2 Stolen Bases

From San *Francisco* de Macorís. $1.

**JOHN GRUBB.** .333 BA, 13 Home Runs, 51 RBI, 0 Stolen Bases

All in 210 at-bats! $5.

**MICKEY HATCHER.** .278 BA, 3 Home Runs, 32 RBI, 3 Stolen Bases

Less playing time, no power. $1.

**GEORGE HENDRICK.** .272 BA, 14 Home Runs, 47 RBI, 1 Stolen Base

No Comment. $5.

**LARRY HERNDON.** .247 BA, 8 Home Runs, 37 RBI, 2 Stolen Bases

No longer a regular. $2.

**BO JACKSON.** .207 BA, 2 Home Runs, 9 RBI, 3 Stolen Bases
Why not on-the-job training in the bigs? $6.

**MIKE KINGERY.** .258 BA, 3 Home Runs, 14 RBI, 7 Stolen Bases

Maybe Jackson's taking the job he applied for. $1.

**RUDY LAW.** .261 BA, 1 Home Run, 36 RBI, 14 Stolen Bases
See Mike Kingery. $2.

**RICK LEACH.**   .309 BA, 5 Home Runs, 39 RBI, 0 Stolen Bases
Go Blue! $2.

**RICK MANNING.**   .254 BA, 8 Home Runs, 27 RBI, 5 Stolen
Bases
Great glove. $1.

**BEN OGLIVIE.**   .283 BA, 5 Home Runs, 53 RBI, 1 Stolen Base
Superseded by the Brewers' youth movement. $4.

**FLOYD RAYFORD.**   .176 BA, 8 Home Runs, 19 RBI, 0 Stolen
Bases
After an excellent '85, a disastrous '86 puts his big league
career in jeopardy. $1.

**PAT SHERIDAN.**   .237 BA, 6 Home Runs, 19 RBI, 9 Stolen
Bases
He *does* run. $1.

**JIM TRABER.**   .255 BA, 13 Home Runs, 44 RBI, 0 Stolen Bases
In 212 at-bats. Expect more in '87. $12.

**MIKE YOUNG.**   .252 BA, 9 Home Runs, 42 RBI, 3 Stolen Bases
Like Rayford, another budding star came crashing down in
'86. $6 says it rises again in '87.

## THE POOR MAN'S GUIDE TO WINNING
## ROTISSERIE BASEBALL

Let's say you're cheap. Let's say you adhere to the philosophy
of Calvin Griffith, which, in Rotisserie terms, means you refuse to
pay more than $5 for a ballplayer. Let's say your plane from
Acapulco was delayed and you arrive two hours late for the Draft,
after all the expensive players have been taken. Let's say you're
poor. Do any of the conditions listed above prevent you from
becoming a winner at Rotisserie League Baseball?

Of course not! You just have to be smarter than all the others
in your league. Simply refuse to bid on all the high-priced players
in the first few hours of the draft. It'll drive your competitors
crazy! Then pick up all the good players whom they have ignored,
inexpensively.

Here's a test. The following team was assembled using actual salaries of players drafted in the Original Rotisserie League in the 1986 draft or as holdovers from previous drafts. Only players with salaries of $5 or less were eligible. See how this team would have done during the 1986 season.

## THE ALL-CHEAPO ROTISSERIE LEAGUE ALL-STARS

| Pitchers | Sal. | Wins | Saves | ERA | Ratio |
|---|---|---|---|---|---|
| Mike Krukow | $3 | 20 | 0 | 3.05 | 1.057 |
| Bob Knepper | $5 | 17 | 0 | 3.14 | 1.140 |
| Bob Forsch | $1 | 14 | 0 | 3.25 | 1.213 |
| Danny Cox | $3 | 12 | 0 | 2.90 | 1.132 |
| David Palmer | $1 | 11 | 0 | 3.65 | 1.350 |
| Ron Robinson | $1 | 10 | 14 | 3.24 | 1.311 |
| Dave Dravecky | $4 | 9 | 0 | 3.07 | 1.259 |
| Gene Garber | $1 | 5 | 24 | 2.54 | 1.231 |
| Dave Smith | $2 | 4 | 33 | 2.73 | 1.089 |
| PITCHING TOTALS | $21 | 102 | 71 | 3.15 | 1.190 |

| | Batters | Sal. | BA | Home Runs | RBI | Stolen Bases |
|---|---|---|---|---|---|---|
| C | Alan Ashby | $3 | .257 | 7 | 38 | 1 |
| C | Bruce Bochy | $1 | .252 | 8 | 22 | 1 |
| 1B | Enos Cabell | $1 | .256 | 2 | 29 | 10 |
| 2B | Rob Thompson | $4 | .277 | 7 | 47 | 12 |
| SS | Craig Reynolds | $2 | .249 | 6 | 41 | 3 |
| 3B | Jim Morrison | $2 | .274 | 23 | 88 | 9 |
| CR | Denny Walling | $3 | .312 | 13 | 58 | 1 |
| IF | Wally Backman | $5 | .320 | 1 | 27 | 13 |
| OF | Eddie Milner | $2 | .259 | 15 | 47 | 18 |
| OF | Kevin Bass | $4 | .311 | 20 | 79 | 22 |
| OF | Gary Matthews | $3 | .259 | 21 | 46 | 3 |
| OF | Davey Lopes | $5 | .275 | 7 | 35 | 25 |
| OF | Nick Esasky | $5 | .230 | 12 | 41 | 0 |
| UT | Tim Flannery | $1 | .280 | 3 | 28 | 3 |
| | BATTING TOTALS | $41 | .280 | 145 | 626 | 121 |

Total cost of this team, $62. Pitchers, obviously, are the best cheap pickups—pitchers coming back from bad seasons or bum arms, wild-throwing rookies whom you think will find the plate. It's harder to find batting production cheap: Only three of the thirteen offensive players had more than 500 at-bats. Solution? Load your team with great cheap pitchers and trade for offense. Or keep the team you drafted. This one, if it had played the 1986 season in the Original Rotisserie League, would have finished 2nd in wins, 2nd in saves, 2nd in ERA, and 1st in ratio—a cool 37 points in pitching alone. It would have been 1st in BA, 4th in home runs, 7th in RBI, and 9th in stolen bases—the latter a commodity that seldom goes overlooked. Not bad, 60 points for $62 and third place, a half point out of second. Cheapos of the world, play the end game!

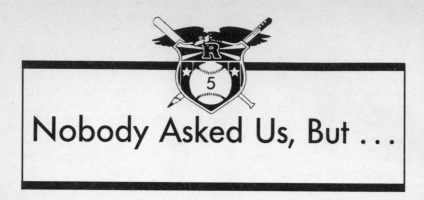

# Nobody Asked Us, But . . .

## What Every Major League Team *Must* Do by Opening Day

It's not easy being a major league GM these days. You've got to deal with crafty agents, fickle fans, the Players Association, arbitrary owners, smart-ass reporters, long-term contracts, the Basic Agreement, objective arbitrators, incentive clauses, bottom lines, lawyers out the gazoo, and enough pampered prima donnas with gold chains around their necks to stock a debutante ball. You've got to deal with all that before you can even think of dealing with your own kind, with that small fraternity of shrewd, experienced baseball men who would change their teams' composition as often as civilians change their socks. Would if they could, that is.

Hey, guys, we know where you're coming from. We traded baseball cards when we were kids. We still pore over all the annuals and magazines and baseball previews that flood the newsstands every March, trying to figure out what to do about our/your starting rotation. We've sat on a lot of hard seats in a lot of ball parks, sat there thinking, we oughta trade that bum to the Mammoths while he still has value. Or, that kid will take over at short if we give him the chance, and we can move so-and-so with the big contract. Or, that skinny guy with the funny motion is going to win 16–18 games, mark my words, and we won't trade him for nothing

. . . unless they would be willing to throw in that lefty reliever they got in Triple A, plus a middle infielder with a little speed. We've been there, which is why we're here.

Yeah, sure, wheeling and dealing has gotten tough in modern-day baseball. But, guys, it's not as tough as you make it out to be. Come on, lighten up. Stockbrokers show more swash and buckle than you've shown lately; look at Ivan Boesky. *Dentists* take more chances than you do, for Frank Lane's sake. You've gotten to the top of the heap, there are only 26 guys with your job in the whole world, and you've gone cautious on us.

Enough already. Get on the phone and make a move. Wheel. Deal. Shake things up. Go with the kids. Take a chance on a veteran having one more good season in him. Roll the dice. Have some fun.

And just in case you're not 100% sure just what it is you ought to do (some of you have obviously forgotten), we're only too happy to tell you.

# NATIONAL LEAGUE

## Summer Reruns

### ATLANTA BRAVES

The Braves ought to can it with America's Team and accept the fact that the Superstation will always be a third-rate local station as long as it relies on a bunch of lead-assed clumpers, not to mention *The Return of Leave It to Beaver*. Like, where's the entertainment, Ted? What America really needs is some good old-fashioned hard ball, mean and nasty. So break ranks and sign Tim Raines and his gimpy sidekick André Dawson, who'll blossom again on God's good earth. Let Bob Horner go to the Cubs, where he can play first or third and hit fifty big ones at the you-know-what Confines. Then take a nap and have lunch. After that, trade Rafael Ramirez for the best starting pitcher available; and send Ozzie Virgil, Brad Kominsk, and Andrew Denson to the Pirates for Tony Pena. Return Ken Oberkfell to second base, and get a thumper for third. Like Nick Esasky, who can be yours fairly cheap: Jeff Dedmon and a couple of prospects. Put Gerald Perry at first, where he is ready (trust us) to play every day. And bring up Tom Glavine for the rotation. On opening day it should look like this:

## OPENING DAY LINEUP

| Raines | LF | Perry | 1B |
|---|---|---|---|
| Oberkfell | 2B | Pena | C |
| Murphy | CF | Esasky | 3B |
| Dawson | RF | Thomas | SS |
| | | Smith | P |

In other words, power *and* speed. Ain't that what it's all about, Ted?

# Wait 'til Next Year ... Next Year ... Next Year

### CHICAGO CUBS

Everyone wails about the collapse of their pitching. And let's face it, it was awful (last in the league, in fact). But the reality is, this team stunk because it's old and tired and slow (13–28 on the rug; 16–32 at night). And even if Dallas Green were willing to trade his pricey pitching staff at the bottom of their market, who would want them?

The sad fact is that what the Cubs really need to do is radically overhaul the team Gene Michaele (or whoever) puts on the field every day, and pretty much stick with at least three of their top four starters, if "top" is a word that can be used to refer to guys with ERAs higher than the prime interest rate.

Put it this way: The only guys who ought to be shopping for houses in Chicago are Ryne Sandberg, Shawn Dunston, and Jody Davis up the middle, along with Leon Durham and Lee Smith. All other bets are off.

First, look for a third baseman to replace the statue who's been there since the Dodgers broke up their dream infield. Maybe they could get this kid Esasky from Cincinnati for a song. They could give the Reds some power for their bench and the experienced veteran a contender needs (tee-hee). Take Gary Matthews. Take Jerry Mumphrey. Take Ron Cey. Please.

Next, a real center fielder. Bob Dernier just ain't it. (Rotisserie League scouts recognized that four years ago during their annual spring training trip; one look at White Lightning at the plate, and he fetched only $8 in the draft. Okay, he was worth more than that—one year.) If they could pry Mookie Wilson away from the Mets, along with one of those hot young arms Frank Cashen has stacked up in Tidewater and Lynchburg, it might be worth giving up Keith Moreland, who could play third in New York and drive in 125 runs in Davey Johnson's lineup. But the really big New York deal—a long shot, but so was Manhattan for $24—might take place in the House that Ruth Built. Coming off a big year—his last, the way we figure it—Matthews is perfect sucker bait for Boss of Bosses Steinbrenner. Give him Steve Trout and the Sarge, Dernier— all the spare parts—and hope he'll do something rash and stupid, like give up Dave Winfield. It wouldn't be George's first bad deal.

But if the trades don't work out, and they probably won't (Dallas Green is no alchemist, after all), then go to the free agent market—and let the embargo be damned. André Dawson has got to want to play in the Friendly Confines—lifetime, he's hit 50 points higher in daylight than at night. Besides, the grass would be easy on his knees, and that ivy in left would be ever so close for him.

And let the kids play: Rafael Palmiero in left, Dave Martinez in center, Brian Dayett off the bench. Youth must be served, even if it's to the lions in the bleachers.

## OPENING DAY LINEUP

| Martinez | CF | Davis | C |
|---|---|---|---|
| Sandberg | 2B | Palmiero | LF |
| Dawson | RF | Esasky | 3B |
| Durham | 1B | Dunston | SS |
| | | Sutcliffe | P |

# No Dogs Allowed

## CINCINNATI REDS

True to the form she established in handling her baseball personnel, Marge Schott—in one of her last acts as principal owner of the Reds—charged her players $50 apiece for the cases of autographed baseballs they each used to get free at the end of the season. It only added insult to injury when the players learned that the cost to her was $37 per case.

We say balls to Marge.

And we say it's time to forget what everyone thinks of as the Schotzzie Era. From this day on, no dogs on this ball club (although the club—and baseball—will miss Doggie). No mascots at all, in fact.

On the field, a club that has seemed ancient for the past few years is in fact brimming with young blood. All that's really needed is a move to shore up the pitching staff and add a couple of big sticks to back up all that young speed.

Then—instant contender.

The eight positions players we'd put on the field every day are set: Dave Parker moves to first, leaving Kal Daniels, Eric Davis, and Eddie Milner in the outfield (and young Tracy Jones as the fourth man); Barry Larkin and Ron Oester up the middle; Bo Diaz behind the plate; and a reborn Buddy Bell at third.

Much as it pains us, Mario Soto must go. We know just how much he's lost, and we have to get some value back before there's no one left who will take a chance on him. Package him with John Kurt Stillwell—Larkin has made him expendable—or Nick Esasky, and maybe one of the kids everyone loves from Indy, Paul O'Neill or Wade Rowden. We're looking toward San Diego, where they need what we've got and want to unload what we need—Jimmy Jones, the pitcher taken in the draft before Dwight Gooden, and the Goose, who's out of there anyway. And we figure to pick up some bench power in the deal (maybe the slow kid with the fast bat, Carmelo Martinez).

That would give us a rotation of Tom Browning, Bill Gullickson, Jones, Ron Robinson (in from the bullpen), and John Denny (unless we can dump him, too). With Ted Power as a spot starter and prime long man and Rob Murphy setting up the Goose and John Franco, we'd have as good a pen as anyone in the National League west of Manhattan.

## OPENING DAY LINEUP

| | | | |
|---|---|---|---|
| Milner | CF | Daniels | RF |
| Larkin | SS | Bell | 3B |
| Davis | LF | Diaz | C |
| Parker | 1B | Oester | 2B |
| | | Gullickson | P |

# Mission Control

## HOUSTON ASTROS

The Astros have arrived. And as GM of the little-known Houstons, your task is at once more elementary than that facing most of your counterparts—and infinitely more complex. Having gotten to within half a whisker of the gonfallon in 1986, you've got to do all those little somethings that put you over the top without upsetting the delicate balance that got you so near.

It is, oddly enough, essentially the same challenge met by Frank Cashen at the close of the 1985 season, the one he met with the Bobby Ojeda and Tim Teufel deals, providing the Mets with (a) another solid lefty starter to complement El Sid and (b) a decent right-handed bat at second, so that Wally Backman could go back to being the terrific platoon player he was born to be.

In the Astros' case, however, the last pieces of the jigsaw will not be so easily found. For one thing, the club's most obvious need, the one that cost them the league championship—a strong left arm out of the bullpen to go with Dave Smith and Charlie Kerfeld—is an extraordinarily rare commodity, more highly prized in baseball precincts even than Dominican shortstops who hit 1.7 times their weight.

There are, to be precise (if you don't count Mark Davis, and who does?), at the moment only two such beings in the entire National League: Jesse Orosco and John Franco. Each of whom, alas, happens to be the property of a club that would sooner welcome back Marvin Miller than help Houston along to a pennant. Nor are pickings much better over in the AL, where only Dave Righetti, presumably untouchable, and Willie Hernandez, presumably in decline, fit the bill. Ultimately, your best bet here is to try to pull a schiraldi (a.k.a. a worrell or a mccullers) and convert a hard-throwing minor league prospect into a stopper. Moreover, you have an obvious candidate: Rob Mallicoat.

Which, by the way, makes sense in another way—because the melancholy truth happens to be that unlike, say, the Mets over the past few years, you have precious few quality players you can afford to give up in the trade. A Carter deal, even an Ojeda deal, is pretty much out of the question. You're certainly not going to rip apart that pitching staff. You're not going to touch Glenn Davis at first, or Bill Doran at second, or Kevin Bass or Billy Hatcher in the outfield. And at 38, coming off a so-so year, sentimental favorite José Cruz, even if you *dared* to move him, probably wouldn't bring much. Nor will Ty Gainey, the perennial minor league phenom, who, in any case, you want to keep around as Cheo's eventual replacement.

No, facts are facts. What you must continue to do is precisely what the Astros' front office has done so brilliantly of late—scavenge. For the team's surge in 1986 was built not only on revived veterans (Mike Scott, Nolan Ryan) and formidable home-grown talent (Doren, Davis, Kerfeld) but also on an uncanny ability to make judicious use of retreads (Davey Lopes, Aurelio Lopez) and, even more so, to pick up, gift-wrapped, generally in exchange for aging veterans, terrific ballplayers drastically undervalued by other clubs. Remember that Bass came as part of the package for Don Sutton; Billy Hatcher for Jerry Mumphrey; and Jim Deshaies, astonishingly enough, for Joe Niekro.

So be flexible and stouthearted, keep your eyes and ears open. You could, remember, use a catcher with more pop. Someone might give you one for Jim Pankovits. But forget trying to find a quality third baseman to replace the Garner-Walling platoon; you don't have enough to give.

So this is a year for tinkering—and hoping. Save the blueprints for a major overhaul until Ryan *and* Cruz start playing their age.

## OPENING DAY LINEUP

| Hatcher | RF | Bass | CF |
|---------|----|------|-----|
| Doran | 2B | Garner-Walling | 3B |
| Cruz | LF | Reynolds | SS |
| Davis | 1B | Ashby | C |
| | | Ryan | P |

# O'Malley in the Wilderness

## LOS ANGELES DODGERS

Face it. It's all over for the Dodgers. All these years since Brooklyn they've had this incredible boffo run in LA, amassing a fortune in downtown real estate, cleaning up on all that club-owned parking, drawing $2.5 million per year, winning pennants. Then last year struck, a year of locusts and fire and pestilence and open sores with hideous green yuk leaking out. Enough to make John Carpenter puke.

This is terminal, friends, and don't bother seeking a second opinion. The biblical plagues lasted only seven years at a pop. But the Dodgers, who had previously survived even Billy Grabarkewitz and Len Gabrielson, are overdue. They've been in LA nearly three decades, fat and lucky, and now they've got three decades of penance to pay, thirty years (or so) to wander in the desert (the Mojave, presumably). By the time the Dodgers are good again, Tommy Lasorda will look like an Italian Haystack Calhoun, and he'll be getting clubhouse visits from Adrienne Barbeau's grandchildren.

Consider: Last year the Dodgers had four of the best arms in the National League in their rotation. They had in major league uniforms some of the most coveted talent to blossom in the minors in half a decade—Stubbs, Bryant, Gonzalez. Mike Marshall isn't 30 yet. Steve Sax had a virtual MVP year. There aren't five catchers in baseball better than Mike Scioscia. Tommy Lasorda does know a thing or two about the game. And still LA was lucky to finish ahead of Atlanta.

Our recommendation: divestment. Announce that the 1987 season will be played by a volunteer group of Vegas comics (a subtle blend of headliners and lounge acts), and cast the entire 24-man roster to the winds. Send Fernando to the Padres, so he'll be closer to home. Welch to St. Louis, so Whitey doesn't have to start four lefties. Honeycutt and Hershiser to Philadelphia, so the Mets won't repeat. Guerrero to Fenway Park, where he'll hit 50 home runs. Sax to coach baseball at Stanford, so he can be called Palo Alto Sax. Stubbs to the Cubs, just because it sounds right.

Finally, send Lasorda to the Disney people to be frozen alongside Uncle Walt, so that when the Dodgers come back in a generation or so, he'll be ready to lead them to glory.

| | | | |
|---|---|---|---|
| Don Rickles | 2B | Jan Murray | 1B |
| Shecky Greene | SS | Corbett Monica | RF |
| Dan Rowan | LF | Monti Rock III | 3B |
| Buddy Hackett | C | Marty Allen | CF |
| | | Jackie Mason | P |

# When It Raines . . .

## MONTREAL EXPOS

We're at a disadvantage here. You already know what happened to Tim Raines this off-season, and we don't. Trying to tell the Montreal front office what to do without knowing Rock's status is like setting out to fly the Atlantic without knowing if there is any gas in the tanks. So, two options here.

*Scenario One: The Bronfman family decides to sell off a hunk of Dupont and meet Raines' contract demands.* That's a smart start, because the pitching staff of a bona fide contender is already in place (if Joe Hesketh returns to form, that is). But the franchise needs some new playmates.

The tradeable value here is Tim Wallach. Think of the teams who could use Eli's bat, his glove, his consistency. The Padres, say, or the Orioles. The Cubs (but what would they give?), the Braves, the Astros. Sure, the Mets. (Funny, except for the Orioles, American League clubs seem to be set at third.)

Think of Fred Lynn playing in the outfield with Mitch Webster and Raines. Smile, then move Hubie back to third, trade minor league slugger Mike Hocutt for golden glover Pete Macoris at short, and deal Andy McGaffigan for some bench strength. *Au revoir*, Jim Wohlford, *toutes les Montréal* will miss you.

Andre Dawson? If signing the Hawk is the only way to keep Raines, sign him. But come May, send Dawson to Wrigley (where he deserves to finish out his great career) for a Cub pitcher (somebody has to throw BP) and Rafael Palmiero, the left-handed bat (he's a lot better than Hocutt) the Expos need to platoon with Andres the Giant at first.

*Scenario Two: The Bronfmans, preoccupied with the promotion of wine coolers, let Raines escape.* Simple. Put John McHale at first, Jim Fanning at second, Board Chairman Charles Bronfman at third, any single Montreal Canadiens line in the outfield, Buck Rodgers behind the plate, and Original Expo/current broadcaster Claude "Frenchy" Raymond on the mound.

Funny, why has no American-born pitcher in Montreal ever been nicknamed "L'Anglaise"?

## OPENING DAY LINEUP

| | | | |
|---|---|---|---|
| Raines | LF | Lynn | CF |
| Webster | RF | Law | 2B |
| Brooks | 3B | Fitzgerald | C |
| Galarraga | 1B | Macoris | SS |
| | | Youmans | P |

# Lights—Camera—Action!

### NEW YORK METS

"Lights" was one of the printable things Gary Carter's Expo teammates used to call him, because of the Kid's love of publicity. Not much has changed on the old interpersonal relationship front in New York (which, the last time we looked, has a few more TV cameras than Montreal), but that World Championship ring sparkling on his finger may make Carter's colleagues on the Mets a little more accepting in 1987. Hell, some of them may even be looking to sign Gary as their press agent.

How much do you tinker with a team that's just won 108 regular season games, the pennant, and the World Series? That dominated the rest of the league in every phase of the game? You've already swung a beauty—Kevin McReynolds for a good chunk of your Farm System. Should you do more? But as overlord of the Mets, your watchword must be CAUTION: Given the disposition of New York fans, a major screwup is likely to do more than simply get you canned. Like, for instance, imagine getting ripped up so the animals can take home pieces of *you* as souvenirs.

First things first. You will not tamper with that starting rotation. They're still babies—average age on opening day '87, 26—and babies have a habit of maturing. Ditto right-handed relief ace Roger McDowell, 26.

But lefty Jesse Orosco is another story. To wit: Thirty years old and coming off two seasons of recurrent shoulder trouble is enough to scare you even if he was unhittable in the World Series. And you've got Randy Myers, reputedly the best left arm in the organization, waiting in the wings.

Though the wishing list is a short one, Jesse must be spent wisely:

- Do you spring for a strong backup to Carter, perhaps allowing the Kid to rest that knee in the outfield a bit more frequently? But, hey, you've already got Ed Hearn and John Gibbons, both of whom looked more than adequate in '86.
- How about something more productive—not to mention more colorful—at short? Then, again, Rafael Santana does seem to get the job done. How'd you like to be stuck with the other Raffy, the one over in Atlanta, instead? Anyway, you have Gregg Jefferies on the verge, so you may not even need Santana a whole season.
- Maybe you want to replenish the farm system you robbed to get McReynolds. The two men you'll have to replace in years to come are Carter and Keith Hernandez, so you might wait to get a future catcher and first sacker.

Nah, the place to make your move is where the Mets have needed help since the dawn of recorded time, 1962. How many bodies have done time at third by now, 760? Sure, it could be that Howard Johnson is an everyday third baseman, or that Dave Magadan is ready. But Frank Cashen has got to feel that—coming over from Minnesota for Orosco, Johnson, and outfielder Marcus Lawton (the Twins, who have never stopped kicking themselves for surrendering Jesse in the first place, need *everything*)—Gary Gaetti is going to look spectacular in a Mets uniform.

## OPENING DAY LINEUP

| | | | |
|---|---|---|---|
| Dykstra | CF | Strawberry | RF |
| Backman | 2B | Gaetti | 3B |
| Hernandez | 1B | McReynolds | LF |
| Carter | C | Santana | SS |
| | | Gooden | P |

# Less Philling

## PHILADELPHIA PHILLIES

The Phillies are perennially their own worst enemy (and that's saying a lot, considering the Phillies' fans): The front office runs from arrogant, to impatient, to petulant, to hey, let's have another round. (For a revealing view of the way the Philadelphia "Brain Trust" operates, takes a look at *A Baseball Winter*, edited by Terry Pluto and Jeffrey Neuman. Astonishing. Makes you wonder.)

The order of the day, guys, is simple: Make out a list and stick to it. You need a left-handed reliever if Don Carman is going to stay in the rotation, as indeed he should; you need a decent defensive catcher (Bertrand Russell would be better than John); you need to stay calm and give your rotation a chance (Rawley, Carman, Gross, Ruffin, and Starvin' Marvin are better than they sound); and—most of all—you need a batting order that makes sense.

Hitting Juan Samuel second does *not* make sense: He can't take a pitch (unless it's a pitchout, and even then we're never sure), thus neutralizing the speed of Milt Thompson or Gary Redus in the leadoff slot. Hitting him sixth makes even less sense; from all appearances, he's allergic to it. Consider this: Lead off with Thompson, follow with Von Hayes (who is finally, *finally* reaching his promise), and put Sammy in the third slot. The rest of the lineup you already know.

If Thompson can't hit enough to hold the leadoff spot (and we strongly believe he can), try Craig James up top. If James can't cut the mustard, bring down Whitey from the broadcast booth. At 60, Richie Ashburn is still certain to collect .290 worth of singles, and look classy doing it.

So who's the new catcher and where's the lefty reliever to back up Bedrosian? At the moment, in San Diego. Pull up a chair, Trader Jack. Jeff Stone, John Russell, and Rick Schu for Bruce Bochy and Craig Lefferts and minor league first baseman Tim Pyznarski, and the next round's on us.

## OPENING DAY LINEUP

| | | | | |
|---|---|---|---|---|
| Thompson | CF | Wilson | | RF |
| Hayes | 1B | Easler | | LF |
| Samuel | 2B | Bochy | | C |
| Schmidt | 3B | Jeltz | | SS |
| | | Rawley | | P |

# Steeltown Blues

## PITTSBURGH PIRATES

Oh, boy. Talk about thankless . . . The big question for the GM of the Pirates is where to start. Back in 1984, Pittsburgh actually led the league in team ERA and, thanks to miserable run production, still managed to finish last. In 1986, the hitting was there—the Pirates finished fifth in runs scored—but the pitching was a disaster area. Last again. What is going on here?

On the other hand, isn't this where Frank Cashen was five years ago? It's not like you're messing with a contender. After watching the team take a long-term lease on the National League East basement, the most diehard Pirate fan—rumor has it he does exist—will identify virtually any move as progress. Your hands are unbound, and your imagination ought to be.

First, though, let's examine the pluses—which, surprisingly enough, are not inconsiderable: some promising outfield talent, several live young arms, enough incipient power occasionally to send the mind skittering back to the Fam-alee. Then, too, getting down to cases, a couple of the bodies you are prepared to move that have definite trade value.

The first order of business, of course, is to straighten out the pitching. You begin by surprising everyone—and NOT trading Tony Pena. Catchers are so hard to come by that the Pirates should resist most efforts to get him. Besides, with a staff as young as the Pirates, the catching should not be trusted to a youngster. Indeed, in light of the character he displayed in '86, you give him the multiyear contract he's after and the big bucks he's worth. The veteran leader your young, talented staff needs is not named Reuschel. With time and a little luck, the kids—Bob Kipper, coming off a strong close in '86; rookie John Smiley, brilliant with the big club in September; and converted reliever Barry Jones—could soon have you back near to the top in team pitching numbers.

As for the bullpen, since Don Robinson has never quite measured up as a stopper, this year he'll serve merely as insurance in the event that Goose Gossage—picked up as a virtual throw-in from the Padres (who continue to bear a share of his hefty salary) in the deal sending R. J. Reynolds to San Diego—is unable to put it together one more time.

The right side of the infield is set: Johnny Ray is as underrated a second baseman as they come; Sid Bream is good and is going to get better. But you need lots of help on the left side, especially at short. You'll probably get it by replacing the anemic Belliard-Khalifa tandem with Garry Templeton, shadow-of-his-former-self and all, the other body in the Reynolds trade. You're okay with Jim Morrison at third, so long as you don't bank on a repeat of his 1986 power numbers.

In the outfield, look for improvement from Barry Bonds in center, and hope for it from Joe Orsulak and Bobby Bonilla. Aside from Bonds, the farm system is hardly producing like it once did, but there is a guy who went from Jim Leylard's doghouse to Triple A who should be given another chance: Mike Brown. Work with him on his outfield play, pep him up with praise—and give him a chance to prove that the second half of 1985 was no fluke.

### OPENING DAY LINEUP

| Orsulak | LF | Bream | 1B |
|---------|----|----|----|
| Ray | 2B | Brown | RF |
| Bonds | CF | Morrison | 3B |
| Pena | C | Templeton | SS |
| | | Reuschel | P |

# Experiments with the White Rat

## ST. LOUIS CARDINALS

Whitey Herzog couldn't hide from the Cardinals' utter collapse last season after the glory of 1985. Still, it's not time to push the panic button in St. Louis. The Redbirds finished strong, and the Mets can't be as good this season, and McGeeHerrClark can't be so utterly disappointing again—can they?

The Cardinals' problems—lack of punch and a major league catcher—could be solved through the free agent route. Bad back and all, Lance Parrish is worth the risk. The worst that can happen is that Parrish moves to first base after a while and Jack Clark goes back to the outfield. By the way, Whitey, be sure to resign Clark (but only to a one-year contract, of course).

Let's assume Parrish elects to stay in Detroit. Here's a radical proposal: Send Willie McGee and a spare lefty to power-laden but arm-lean Toronto for an outfielder with speed *and* power, probably Lloyd Moseby. With added power, the Redbirds can pass on Tony Pena and Jody Davis, whom they couldn't afford anyway short of trading Andy Van Slyke and a young starting pitcher like Greg Mathews.

What makes more sense is a minor deal for a receiver. There are two routes to pursue: an aging veteran or an unproven young talent. In other words, the White Sox' Carlton Fisk or the former Astros' starter Mark Bailey, a switch-hitter with power and a great arm who has been replaced on the Astros' roster by John Mizerock. The best bet here is Fisk. He can handle pitchers, he can still catch, and he has adequate relief in left-handed-hitting Mike La-Valliere. Again, the Cardinals have outfield talent (Curt Ford, John Morris) and a quality starter to deal. Sure it's a stopgap, but the Cards won in 1982 and 1985 with no offensive production from their receivers. What the Cards are missing on the field is leadership, and that's something Fisk can give.

The pitching? Don't touch it. Just don't work Todd Worrell to death.

## OPENING DAY LINEUP

| Coleman | LF | Van Slyke | RF |
|---------|----|-----------|----|
| Moseby | CF | Fisk | C |
| Herr | 2B | Pendleton | 3B |
| Clark | 1B | Ozzie | SS |
| | | Tudor | P |

# They Deserve a Break Today

### SAN DIEGO PADRES

Ever since Alan Wiggins went AWOL, and then on to Rochester via Baltimore, the Padres' greatest weakness has been the lack of a leadoff hitter. Last year's Bip Roberts experiment proved a bust, so it's time to get serious. Only someone with a Big Mac for brains wouldn't make signing Tim Raines the team's Number One priority. It's hard to imagine the numbers Raines could put up if he moved from the ice and Astroturf of Montreal to sunshine and natural grass. And think of the year Gwynn could have hitting with Raines on base all year. If Willie McGee can hit .353 behind Vince Coleman one year, what do you figure Gwynn could do under even more favorable circumstances?

Now that we've taken care of the Padres' chief need with a stroke of the pen, our next move is to replace Kevin McReynolds, delivered to the Mets for a whole bunch of future. The Blue Jays have a surplus of outfielders and a surfeit of pitching, so a simple but eloquent trade of Eric Show for Lloyd Moseby might be the ticket. Moseby would give the Pads added speed, if not as much punch as Big Mac, and liberals everywhere would applaud the deportation of the rightwinged Show to our neighbor to the North.

Since Steve Garvey might end up owning the team, we can't possibly trade him. He looks a little naked, though, standing there in the middle of the order, so in order to protect him, we make one more deal. Send Lance McCullers, the much-coveted reliever, to the Mariners for third baseman Jim Presley. The Mariners probably want to trade Presley before they have to start paying him what he's worth, and he would fit nicely in between Garvey and Kevin Mitchell, who we are moving to second base. Say what? Well, the Mets thought he could play shortstop, and the Padres once got the notion that Wiggins was a second baseman. The only shortcoming here is that Rich Gossage is left as the bullpen savior, but he does have a big heart—and mouth—and he can still throw it by some hitters.

## OPENING DAY LINEUP

| Raines | LF | Presley | 3B |
|---|---|---|---|
| Gwynn | RF | Mitchell | 2B |
| Moseby | CF | Santiago | C |
| Garvey | 1B | Templeton | SS |
| | | Dravecky | P |

# Candlestick

## SAN FRANCISCO GIANTS

Okay, Al Rosen, everybody gave you credit for what you built at Houston, and *any* move you might have made last year would have looked good in comparison with what went before. But if you don't want to wait until after you're long gone for a pennant to be ripped to tatters in the gales of Candlestick, it's time for bold action. First, a decision; then, a trade.

The decision, Al, involves something that Roger Craig doesn't seem to understand, namely a bullpen. Sometimes last season, it seemed as if "Hummm Babe" was Craigese for "time to change my bullpen strategy." Every time Rog uttered his magic incantation, somebody else got anointed as *Número Uno* in the corral. It didn't work, Al, if you get my Juan Berenguer. (He was the Giants' ace stopper for a long July weekend, wasn't he?)

So this year, hire a neurosurgeon to implant a microchip coded "Scott Garrelts" in Craig's noggin, in the corner of the lobe heretofore given over to "Hummm Babe." There Rog will be, come June, clapping his hands an inch in front of his incredible nose, exhorting his team, answering press questions, shouting at umpires, changing pitchers . . . and every time, he'll be saying "Scott Garrelts." It could mean the pennant.

Alternatively, Al, have Garrelts change his name to "Hummm Babe." Mr. Babe to you, of course.

Now, the trade. What have you got, Al? Outfielders, that's what. There's Mr. Davis, who slumped last year. There's Mr. Gladden, who isn't nearly as good as his rookie numbers of three years ago indicated. There's Mr. Leonard, Old Penitentiary Face, who has slipped a lot but still hits better than he publicly relates. And there's Mr. Maldonado, who no doubt surprised even Mrs. Maldonado last year.

So what do you do? Hold on to Chili, who will recover this year, unless you are absolutely blown away by an offer that includes two bona fide front-line starters. Hold on to Candy, so you won't hate yourself as much as Al Campanis does when he goes off and headlines somewhere else. And as for old Jailpuss, hold on to him, too, but move him to first, and trade Will Clark.

Yes, you heard right, trade the boy wonder with the sweet swing who jumped from Class A and looked like George Sisler for the early part of last year. The kid's value will never be higher, but he's not the franchise player your PR office is gearing up to tell the world he is. Move him now for the best young arms you can find (two should belong to pitchers, one to a catcher). Do it and you won't have to worry all spring that Vida Blue is Dorian Gray, or that the 1986 first-half Mike LaCoss was but a sham, the second-half LaCoss the real depressing thing. And if you land a catcher (the Red Sox have a live one named John Marzano), you could kiss

Bob Brenly good-bye, sending him and Mikes Aldrete and LaCoss off to Baltimore for the best available outfielder (Mike Young?) and a spare part or two.

With Young (or even Ken Gerhardt, if Hank Peters is stingy), you could still leave Calaboose-head at first and let Candy Maldonado become . . . we got it! A pinch hitter!

### OPENING DAY LINEUP

| | | | |
|---|---|---|---|
| Gladden | CF | Lynn | RF |
| Thompson | 2B | Brown | 3B |
| Davis | LF | Melvin (if Marzano isn't ready) | C |
| Leonard | 1B | Uribe | SS |
| | | Krukow | P |

# AMERICAN LEAGUE

## Bye-Bye, Birdies

### BALTIMORE ORIOLES

No wonder Earl Weaver threw in the towel. How can a team win with no second baseman, no third baseman, no catcher, a one-man bullpen, and a starting rotation whose biggest winner had a 4.70 ERA? Only rarely, that's how.

This season may be worse. Storm Davis for Terry Kennedy gives Baltimore the third-best offensive catcher in the American League (after Lance Parrish and Rich Gedman), but it also removes the one starting pitcher most likely to bounce back and have a good year. (The fact that Kennedy is lousy on defense doesn't matter much more in the American League, where a lot of teams don't run at all, than it does in the Rotisserie League.) A farmhand or two (Jim Traber, Ken Gerhart) might be for real, but the minor league cupboard is pretty bare. And what else do the Orioles have to deal?

How about a franchise ballplayer who's disenchanted with the franchise, a bona fide blue-chipper who would fetch a handful of quality players in exchange? We're talking Eddie Murray, of course, and we're just pleased to be talking here and not on the streets of Baltimore. But think for a minute what Baltimore might get in return: Bob Welch, Rick Honeycutt, Franklin Stubbs, and an outfielder (Reggie Williams? Ralph Bryant? Both?) from the Dodgers . . . Nick Esasky, Kal Daniels, Eddie Milner, Kurt Stillwell, and a warm arm from the Reds . . . Joaquin Andujar, Tony Phillips, and a prospect (Mark McGwire?) from the A's. Don't forget, the trial balloon went up last season.

Partisans of the Conspiracy Theory of History may well speculate that Edward Bennett Williams is so eager to move the Orioles out of Baltimore and closer to the Washington market that he won't let GM Hank Peters make the moves necessary to breathe life into a once-proud franchise. If the O's continue to stink up Memorial Stadium, the argument goes, attendance will drop far enough to "justify" following the Colts out of town.

We don't buy that. We believe the Orioles will make a lot of off-season moves to strengthen the club. Of course, we also believe that the Red Sox and Cubs will someday meet in the World Series—and play to a tie.

### OPENING DAY LINEUP

| Lacy | LF | Sheets | DH |
|------|----|--------|----|
| Lynn | RF | Traber | 1B |
| Ripken, Jr. | SS | Ripken, Sr.* | 2B |
| Kennedy | C | Milner | CF |
| Esasky | 3B | Boddicker | P |

*Who do they have that's better?

# "Groundball to Buckner..."

## BOSTON RED SOX

Will the Bosox recover from their sixth- and seventh-game folderoos? No way. Look for the team that was one strike away from a World Championship to finish fifth—behind the Blue Jays, Yanks, Tigers, and Indians (Cleveland Indians?!!! Yup.).

Bill Buckner will never be the same. Cut his RBI count by 20 to 25. Barrett will have the same year he had in '86. Spike Owen can hit a bit and run a bit but he looks a lot like a Little Leaguer in the field. He's a serious liability. Wade Boggs is magnificent. Rice is older but will hit .300 and drive in 95 runs. Evans is older but still solid. Dave Henderson may yet live up to his potential and be a .280, 25 HR, 90 RBI man. Gedman is probably the best catcher in the American League.

So far, so good. But now comes trouble.

The incredible Clemens will not win 24 again. Try 18–11. The Can will probably be pitching for Bellevue the second half of the season if he doesn't make the All-Star team. Nipper ain't any good. Hurst is an excellent pitcher. Give him 17 wins. After them, there's a fairly big dropoff. Decent starting pitching, if not awesome. But their pen will crumble in '87. You read it here first. Schiraldi will not be the same pitcher, not after his Series. Kiss Stanley good-bye (but not on the lips, please). After that you're left with a lot of guys who should be in Triple A.

The Sox should trade Schiraldi, Sambito, Crawford, Sellers, and Stanley (the whole pen has to go) to Oakland for Andujar, just so Joaquin and The Can can be on the same team. They should trade Nipper and first baseman Pat Dodson to Cincinnati for Kurt Stillwell. Then pray that Wes Gardner gets healthy and becomes their short man, which he should be able to do. They might want to try to put together a package around LaSchelle Tarver for a solid long relief man, too—something they need desperately. They can probably sucker the Pirates out of Brian Fisher for Spike Owen and Tarver. Put it all together and they just might be able to finish third without breaking any more hearts.

## OPENING DAY LINEUP

| | | | |
|---|---|---|---|
| Boggs | 3B | Evans | RF |
| Barrett | 2B | Henderson | CF |
| Buckner | 1B | Gedman | C |
| Rice | LF | Stillwell | SS |
| Baylor | DH | Clemens | P |

# Angels with Dirty Faces

## CALIFORNIA ANGELS

But kids they are mostly not. Doug (36) DeCinces, Brian (36) Downing, Bob (39) Boone, Don (42) Sutton, and maybe even Leon (53) Wagner will try once again to win one for Gene (75) Autry. Makes a body want to go lie down and rest, just thinking about it.

Hold on for a minute, though. Isn't Dick (24) Schofield already good and getting better? And isn't Devon (24) White supposed to be every bit as fast as Gary (29) Pettis, plus be able to hit with power? Mark (22) McLemore is ready to step in for Bobby (doesn't matter anymore) Grich, isn't he? And Ruppert (32) Jones has a young bat, don't you think? John (33) Candelaria has some years on him, but Mike (26) Witt and Kirk (25) McCaskill are just pups, right? And hey, we almost forgot—what about Wally (24 but he looks younger) Joyner? He's the best young player in the league, isn't he? (No, but he's plenty good.)

Fact is, the Angels are a strong, solid team, with a good balance of veterans and youngsters. They can hit, run, catch, and throw with any team in the AL West. True, they have to worry about Donnie (33) Moore's gimpy shoulder, and they don't have much to deal if it doesn't get better. And granted, if all of the back-nine-of-life guys get baseball-old together, the party's over. But if the Angels shore up the bench with a couple of medium-priced free agents, and if everyone stays healthy and plays young, they could win the pennant they were one strike away from winning in 1986.

Only they probably won't again, we figure, mainly because God ($\infty$) just flat out doesn't like Gene (61) Mauch.

## OPENING DAY LINEUP

| Pettis | CF | Jones | DH |
|---|---|---|---|
| White | RF | Schofield | SS |
| Joyner | 1B | Boone | C |
| DeCinces | 3B | McLemore | 2B |
| Downing | LF | Witt | P |

# Darning the Pale Hose

## CHICAGO WHITE SOX

The Hawk is gone, but he was only part of the problem. The Katzenjammer Kids, Eddie Einhorn and Jerry Reinsdorf, remain as owners, and until they learn to stay away from the front office and stop schmoozing with George Steinbrenner, the White Sox are destined for the mid-West. Besides discouraging the Sox from becoming a latter-day Kansas City A's—the team that used to feed the Yankees all its prospects—we have a radical solution: Trade Harold Baines.

What, you say, trade the heart and soul of the Chicago lineup? We know, the guy is a great ballplayer. But the White Sox are going nowhere with him, so what the heck. The one team that desperately wants him is Kansas City, which offered Danny Jackson and Mark Gubicza for him last year. The White Sox wouldn't be able to get those two this year, but try pitchers Bret Saberhagen and Bud Black and outfielder Gary Thurman. Then the Sox can turn around and trade pitchers Floyd Bannister and Bob James, no longer the stopper now that Bobby Thigpen has arrived, to San Francisco for Jeffrey Leonard, who's expendable but very valuable. In the meantime, the White Sox can send the disenchanted Carlton Fisk to Toronto for third baseman Kelly Gruber and outfielder Louis Thornton.

In retrospect, Ken Harrelson didn't do too badly. Although he traded away prospects like Edwin Correa, he had a knack for picking up useful rejects like Steve Carlton, Jose DeLeon, and Ivan Calderon. Anything can happen in the AL West, and maybe it'll happen to the White Sox.

## OPENING DAY LINEUP

| Williams | LF | Hulett | 2B |
| Boston | CF | Gruber | 3B |
| Leonard | RF | Karkovice | C |
| Walker | 1B | Guillen | SS |
| Calderon | DH | Saberhagen | P |

# Their Turn at Bat

## CLEVELAND INDIANS

It's no secret by now that the past six AL East titles have been won by six different teams. The Indians are the seventh, and this year they will have more going for them than the fact that it's their turn. Last season they put *the* best offensive lineup in baseball on the field, and it was a swampy field at that. Because Cleveland Stadium, hard by Lake Erie, harbors all sorts of vermin—Joe Charboneau, to name just one—it takes a special breed of player to play there, one who is not the least bit squeamish, one who is not particularly susceptible to athlete's foot, one whose bodily enzymes do not attract bird-sized mosquitoes, one who likes to play with spiders. That's probably why it has taken the Indian front office 33 years to bring the team back into contention. We're just as nostalgic as the next fantasy league, but they should have razed the place a long time ago.

Where were we? Oh, the Indians have a terrific offensive team, but a terrible pitching staff. How terrible? Well, they weren't as bad as the Twins or the Mariners, but what do you say about a staff whose Big Three are Tom Candiotti, Ken Schrom, and Phil Niekro, and whose stopper, Macho Camacho, should be renamed Mucho Camacho for the number of hits and walks he gives up per innings pitched? What do you say about such a staff? You say it sucks.

But the Indians can do something about that because they have a wonderful new ballplayer named Cory Snyder, who not only can brand the old cowhide but also can play four or five different positions. The Indians are already overloaded in the outfield, so Snyder's emergence enables them to trade either second baseman Tony Bernazard, shortstop Julio Franco, or third baseman Brook Jacoby.

Since Jacoby could probably fetch the most, Cleveland should shop him for pitching. The best place to look is San Diego, where Trader Jack McKeon presides. Here it is: Jacoby for pitchers Dave Dravecky and Lance McCullers. McCullers was to have been the future stopper in San Diego, but now that Rich Gossage is stuffing his face with Chicken McNuggets again, he would be little more than a glorified setup man for at least another year. Jacoby would give the Padre offense a big boost, and McCullers and Dravecky would give the Indians a much-needed stopper and an even more-needed left-hander.

The Indians should also begin parcelling off their other spare parts for pitching. Carmelo Castillo can hit left-handers, and since everybody has trouble against lefties, they could trade him for a useful fifth starter like Randy O'Neal of the Tigers. It's time Chris Bando got a change of scene, so off to Minnesota for Allen Anderson. Maybe some team could use Otis Nixon's speed and defense. In any case, here are ten little Indians for Opening Day:

| Butler | CF | Franco | SS |
| Bernazard | 2B | Hall | LF |
| Carter | RF | Tabler | 1B |
| Snyder | 3B | Allanson | C |
| Thornton | DH | Dravecky | P |

# Changing Stripes

## DETROIT TIGERS

No one has thrown around the word "dynasty" in the American League—and good thing, too—since the '84 Tigers limped home third in '85. They squeaked into the same spot last season. Why did anyone think this was a club capable of repeating its championship season? Probably because Sparky Anderson mesmerizes sportswriters the same way Sparky, President Jim Campbell, and GM Bill Lajoie are bewitched by Tiger Stadium's short fences, and so load their club with sluggers to the detriment of defense and relief pitching. Campbell and Lajoie set their jaws firmly like the Old School baseball men they are, while Sparky talks a blue streak and can't seem to do anything effective about the problems he so garrulously analyzes. There are only scandalous gaffes like ruining Chris Pittaro by exaggerating his abilities, changing his position, and placing too much burden on him to produce at once.

No, there aren't any geniuses at human relations in the Tigers' organization. Fortunately, there are a few humans with outstanding baseball ability on the field—or, more precisely, at the plate and on the mound. And the Tigers have got to let some of them loose to acquire the right-handed relief pitcher and the sure-handed third baseman they need, among others. Darnell Coles and his iron hands to the Padres for the Goose—how about the Goose in Tiger Stadium?—and a package of outfielders to the Expos, to replace the stars they're losing to free agency, in exchange for Tim Wallach. Mookie Wilson from the Mets, who take Chet Lemon for their bench. It's going to take more than Sparky's blather and the front office's stern values to turn this club into a contender.

| Trammell | SS | Wallach | 3B |
|----------|-----|---------|-----|
| Whitaker | 2B | Fields | LF |
| Gibson | RF | Grubb | DH |
| Parrish | C | Wilson | CF |
| Evans | 1B | Morris | P |

# Royal Pains

## KANSAS CITY ROYALS

Hal McRae finally got old, Bret Saberhagen decided he was Bo Belinsky, Steve Balboni suffered a career-threatening back injury, Jim Sundberg hit 52 points lower than the guy he replaced (and had 7 fewer RBI in 125 more at-bats), Dan Quisenberry was put on the shelf for no apparent reason, and George Brett had only 441 at-bats (the third time in the past four years that injuries have limited him to less than 465).

So what else could happen to the 1985 World Champions? How about this: Bo Jackson points to the fish-or-cut-bait clause in his contract and says, "Play me every day in the big show starting this summer, or watch me strut my stuff on Sunday afternoons starting next fall."

And we say, play him. The Royals are in deep trouble, and they have nothing to lose by letting Bo learn about curves and sliders and split-fingers and brushbacks and knucklers from the big boys. And he just might see enough fast balls and other mistakes to make the experiment an instant success.

Next, if Balboni doesn't come back, move Brett to first base and give third to Danny Tartabull, stolen from the Mariners. Move Bud Black back into the rotation and trade a starter for a cracker-jack outfielder, or even a DH, with some thump. Chili Davis and Tom Brunansky come to mind. Everybody wants Mark Gubicza, so he may have to be the one to go.

(If Bye-Bye isn't forced to say farewell, keep Brett at third, play Tartabull in the outfield and use Gubicza to get a catcher who can take over for Sundberg. The most obvious choice would be Tony Pena of the Pirates. In addition, sign Tony Armas to DH and hold Hal McRae Day.)

Round up some outfielders—Rudy Law, Dave Leeper, Gary Thurman—and trade for some pitching; have a heart-to-heart with Saberhagen about his attitude; plead with Willie Wilson to run more; thank your lucky stars for Frank White; and, for goodness sake, give Quisenberry the ball. Give it to him over and over again, when the game is there to be saved, and don't panic if he blows a few while he works out the early-season kinks. He's the Man. Or else he's the highest-paid mop-up guy and stand-up comic in the business. We think he's the former.

One more thing: After the season is over, and send Bo down to the Instructional League and teach him to play shortstop. If he's the all-fired great athlete he's cracked up to be, that should be a snap.

## OPENING DAY LINEUP

| | | | | |
|---|---|---|---|---|
| Wilson | CF | Davis | LF | |
| White | 2B | Bo Jackson | RF | |
| Brett | 1B | Pena | C | |
| Tartabull | 3B | Salazar | SS | |
| Armas | DH | Danny Jackson | P | |

# A Winner on Tap

### MILWAUKEE BREWERS

The Brewers are in much the same position they were in at the turn of the decade, when they were on the verge of taking over the division. Right now, they are one good reliever, one starter, and a fielding shortstop away from serious contention. And they can't have any more injuries: Somebody important always seems to be on the disabled list.

Two of their needs can be satisfied by trading Cecil Cooper, who can still swing a bat. The Dodgers seem to hunger after aging veterans—in the past few years, they have acquired Al Oliver, Enos Cabell, and Bill Madlock—and Cooper is right up their alley. They would probably part with Tom Neidenfuer, who is shell-shocked in L.A., and shortstop Dave Anderson for Cooper. Since the Brewers don't have much else to trade without mortgaging their future, they should probably dip into the free agent pool and pick up a starter like David Palmer or Doyle Alexander.

You have to hand it to GM Harry Dalton. Two years ago, this club was a mess. A few familiar names—Robin Yount, Jim Gantner, Paul Molitor—remain, but the farm system has produced a very nice crop, and Dalton literally stole Teddy Higuera (20 wins) and Rob Deer (33 homers). Now that kindly but basically inept George Bamberger is gone, Milwaukee has a damn good chance.

## OPENING DAY LINEUP

| | | | |
|---|---|---|---|
| Felder | LF | Braggs | RF |
| Yount | CF | Surhoff | C |
| Molitor | 3B | Gantner | 2B |
| Brock | 1B | Anderson | SS |
| Deer | DH | Higuera | P |

# Over the Humpdome

## MINNESOTA TWINS

What's wrong with this picture? You have a leadoff hitter who bats .328 with 31 homers and 96 RBIS, a third baseman who clubs 34 homers and knocks in 108 runs, a first baseman with 29 homers and 91 RBI, and two other guys with 20-plus homers. You also have four, maybe five perfectly good starting pitchers. Yet you spend most of your season last in the worst division in baseball. What's wrong with the Minnesota Twins?

The obvious answer is pitching, since they were last in the league in that. The Twins must have driven Ray Miller, a man brought in to manage on the strength of his pitching wizardry, crazy. Still, most teams wouldn't mind going to war with Bert Blyleven, Frank Viola, Mike Smithson, Neal Heaton, and latecomer Mark Portugal. The rest of the staff, though, is the worst possible dreck. George Frazier? Frank Pastore? Keith Atherton? Juan Disgusto?

The first thing the Twins should do is trade one of their starters for two less proven but potentially valuable pitchers. Smithson to Cincinnati for Ron Robinson and Ted Power would be a good beginning: Power was a legitimate stopper only two years ago and made a few nice starts last year after he lost his bullpen confidence, and Robinson is a very good setup man. Blyleven might fetch two decent starters himself—say, Storm Davis and Andy Hawkins from the Padres. If the Twins make those trades, then their staff of five automatically becomes a staff of seven. They also have a kid in their Farm System with the wonderfully apt name of Steve Gasser.

There is another, more subtle problem with the Twins. They lack a clubhouse leader of the Don Baylor variety, a player who can show them how to win. They could probably pry Gary Matthews loose from the Cubs for a prospect like Alex Marte, install Matthews as the DH, and let him take over the clubhouse. He'll also hit a lot of homers in the Dome.

The Twins might be thinking about trading Gary Gaetti, but the plain fact of the matter is that the teams that need a third baseman do not have the pitching to offer, and if Minnesota can't get pitching, it should keep Gaetti.

There is one more little thing the Twins can do. They have been searching for a catcher for so long, and Mark Salas is clearly not the one. So trade Salas and/or Tim Laudner along with Mickey Hatcher to Cleveland for Chris Bando, a switch-hitting catcher who can handle a pitching staff. Any team with Kirby Puckett, Kent Hrbek, Tom Brunansky, and Gaetti is not that far away. This lineup will give the fans in that oversized rec room called the Hubert H. Humphrey Metrodome something to cheer about:

## OPENING DAY LINEUP

| Puckett | CF | Matthews | DH |
| Beane | LF | Bando | C |
| Hrbek | 1B | Gagne | SS |
| Gaetti | 3B | Lombardozzi | 2B |
| Brunansky | RF | Viola | P |

# Who's the Boss?

## NEW YORK YANKEES

There are two main things wrong with the Yankees: Their pitching staff has only two legitimate 15-game winners outside of the guy they're using as their relief ace, and their management doesn't have a legitimate three-digit I.Q. anywhere in the organization.

Let's savage their management first.

It used to be said that rooting for the Bronx Bombers was like rooting for U.S. Steel. In the 1980s Steinbrenner era, rooting for the Yankees is a lot more comparable to rooting for the Ayatollah. Except the Iranis are probably a little bit more forthcoming about their injuries and have a better sense of humor.

Take a look at 1986 for a minute. What did the Yankees need

desperately? Pitching and catching. What did they have? Plenty of power. What did they trade away? Their second-best starting pitcher (shocking but true—check Cowley's stats for last season) and their only decent catcher. What did they get? One cripple, a journeyman shortstop, and . . . power. Not first- or even second-rate power. Ron Kittle is basically Dave Kingman with a decent personality.

Since the glory years of 1977 and '78, Steinbrenner and his crack "baseball people" have managed to overpay for mediocre players, degrade those players so thoroughly they can't/won't perform, then go out and tell the world how lousy the players are so they can't get any trade value for them. (Do the names Ed Whitson, Ken Griffey, Dave Collins, etc., etc., mean anything to you?)

Management also doesn't understand baseball fundamentals. In the middle of a pennant race—and, hard to believe, the Yanks easily could have beaten the Red Sox in '86; all they needed was a starting pitcher the caliber of, oh, say, Rick Aguilera—a good team doesn't switch catchers. Or shortstops. Or fire their pitching coach. Or . . . oh, what's the use?

The only good thing management has done recently is to rehire Lou Piniella, who did one helluva job. Considering the talent he had to work with and the pressure coming from the Fat Man, Piniella easily could have been Manager of the Year.

One of the problems with the Yankees is that you usually wind up talking about their management instead of their players; that's also one of the reasons they're so hard to root for. Who wants a George Steinbrenner baseball card? So let's do the worst thing we can do to George and ignore him for the rest of this discussion.

On to the pitching staff—which, with the exception of Dave Righetti, was possibly the worst staff in major league baseball. Getting Rick Roden was a big coup—the Yankees found a dumber front office in Pittsburgh. Dennis Rasmussen is no ace. He's a 15-game winner at best—but at least he's a winner. Who else do the Yanks have? You gotta love Ron Guidry, bless his Cajun heart, but he's a Number Four starter, maybe even Number Five for a good team (he'd pitch long relief for the Mets). Joe Niekro should retire. And everyone else on the staff sounds like they should have an 8–14 record pitching for the Minnesota Twins.

With any pitching at all, the Yanks could win in '87. Their offense is awesome. But they don't have anything to give, unlike their crosstown rivals, who can afford to give up two or three *starting players* to get the power-hitting outfielder or shortstop they need.

Quite simply, the Yanks need to rebuild around Henderson and Mattingly and Pags and Rags. But rebuilding is unheard of to George. It would certainly be the end of Sweet Lou's managerial run with the team. They should trade Winfield to the Twins for Tom Brunansky, Mark Portugal, Mickey Hatcher, Tim Laudner, and Chris Pittaro (then Winfield becomes 1987's "five-for-one"). They should trade Willie Randolph to any contending team who needs a solid second baseman (how about to the Angels for McCaskill?). They should then trade Joe Niekro to the Indians so he can pitch with Phil, and take anything they can get, even a decent minor league prospect. Then Steinbrenner should sell the team, preferably to the National Association of Rotisserie League Owners, go buy a football team, and hire George Allen and Richard Nixon to run it.

### OPENING DAY LINEUP

| | | | |
|---|---|---|---|
| Henderson | CF | Pasqua | LF |
| Tolleson | SS | Kittle | DH |
| Mattingly | 1B | Skinner | C |
| Brunansky | RF | Pittaro | 2B |
| Pagliarulo | 3B | Rhoden | P |

# There's No There There*

## OAKLAND A'S

Not so long ago the A's seemed to have the major league front office of the future. Computer programs to analyze player performance, innovative training techniques (an aerobics dance instructor at spring training, so help us John McGraw!), imaginative and witty marketing (Billy Ball, *et al.*), and a certified boy genius—V.P./ Baseball Operations Sandy Alderson—to call the shots, subject to the enlightened review of team President Roy Eisenhardt. Hell, Roger Angel even wrote about them in *The New Yorker*.

So what happened? They canned manager-*cum*-nice guy Steve Boros, who had the audacity to suggest that maybe Rickey Hen-

---

*That's what Gertrude Stein-Gertrude Stein-Gertrude Stein once said about Oakland, and if the A's don't get a break and make a buck this season or next, some of your better-educated sportswriters will be saying it again as the Oakland A's become the Tampa/Denver Athletics.

derson should concentrate less on stealing bases when they didn't matter and more on his home-run swing (Rickey's 52 dingers in the past two years as a Yankee suggest that Henderson may have been listening, despite his griping and whining at the time). They kept Dwayne Murphy around until his trade value fell through the floor. And they figured Dave Kingman's attitude was a fair price to pay for Dave Kingman's 35 home runs a year. As of this writing, they were thinking of signing one Reggie Jackson to be their new DH. If so, there will be a there there.

Okay, so they're human. But they got a bundle for Henderson, they got Alfredo Griffin for nothing, and they got Jose Canseco. They've built a good team over there on the other side of the Bay. So what do they have to do to win a pennant?

Nothing. Or practically nothing. Trade Mickey Tettleton for a little something (so long as they have some pop, catchers will always get you a decent middle-innings reliever, maybe a fourth outfielder). Break Mark McGwire in slowly. Hire a keeper for Joaquin Andujar. Sign Murphy again but don't be afraid to give Stan Javier a good shot. Sign up a faith-healer to help Moose Haas and Jay Howell heal. Figure out a way to give Rob Nelson enough playing time. Tip your hat to a pro like Carney Lansford. And watch Jose hit.

## OPENING DAY LINEUP

| | | | | |
|---|---|---|---|---|
| Phillips | 2B | McGwire | | 3B |
| Mike Davis | RF | Murphy | | CF |
| Lansford | 1B | Steinbach | | C |
| Canseco | LF | Griffin | | SS |
| Jackson | DH | Andujar | | P |

# My Kingdome for Some Horses

## SEATTLE MARINERS

If last year's late-season swap with the Red Sox—Dave Henderson and Spike Owen for Rey Quinones, Mike Brown, and Mike Trujillo—is indicative of what's to come, the Mariners may finally become the contenders they were supposed to be in 1984. Henderson's pop can be replaced, Quinones is miles better at short than Owen, and Brown and Trujillo could make Dick Williams smile once in a while (well, maybe that's going too far, but they do have live arms). George Argyros for Executive of the Year? Nah. He's too cheap.

There are other things left to do. Put Ken Phelps on first and trade Alvin Davis for pitching help. With 500 at-bats, Phelps will put 30 homers and 90 RBI in the bank. Sure, Davis is younger, but for that reason (along with his sweet swing, of course) he'll fetch a lot more. The Reds would give up Kal Daniels (Take him! Take him!) and a good starter (Ted Power?) or even two for the likes of Davis.

But the problem with dealing Davis is that it won't help a darned bit unless a few big "ifs" can go the Mariners' way:

- *If* Mickey Brantley is the real McCoy that Ivan Calderon wasn't (we're still scratching our heads over that one)
- *If* Ed Nuñez can deliver on the promise he showed as a closer two years ago
- *If* Harold Reynolds can figure out a way to steal first base
- *If* Mike Moore can figure out what went wrong—and fix it
- *If* no one notices that Seattle has been playing without a catcher for the entire history of the franchise

And, hey, the new insignia on the cap can't hurt.

## OPENING DAY LINEUP

| | | | |
|---|---|---|---|
| Brantley | CF | Kingery | LF |
| Bradley | RF | Coleridge | C |
| Daniels | DH | Quinones | SS |
| Phelps | 1B | Reynolds | 2B |
| Presley | 3B | Moore | P |

P.S.: Have you noticed that with the departure of Al Cowens and Gorman Thomas, not a single Mariner is even very old, much less Ancient?

# They Went Thataway

## TEXAS RANGERS

You have to admire Rangers' General Manager Tom Grieve and Manager Bobby Valentine. They took a terrible last-place team and said, What have we got to lose? We can't get any worse, let's play our rookies. They made a couple of smart trades—acquiring Ed Correa and Scott Fletcher in a single deal with the White Sox and snaring the rights to Pete Incaviglia from the Expos. They turned around the team's attitude and made themselves look like geniuses as the Rangers stayed in the AL West race nearly to the end and finished strong in second place.

The question they face is what to do to make the next move up. Is this a team that will mature naturally into champions, or are there further steps that have to be taken? Will Correa, Jose Guzman, and Bobby Witt (respectively, 20, 24, and 23 at the start of the 1987 season) become not just rookie survivors but also the kind of dominating, .500-plus pitchers a championship team needs? Can Charlie Hough, even with an ageless knuckle ball, continue to anchor the starting staff at 39 years old?

It says here that the Rangers just might make the leap with pretty much what they have now. The only significant problem area looks to be second base, where Toby Harrah has reached the end and Curtis Wilkerson isn't the answer. If Jeff Kunkel is ready to be a major league shortstop, there's enough versatility among the infielders for him, or Scott Fletcher, or even Steve Buechele to take over at second. Another option, and this one may make more sense, is to trade one aging DH who still has a lot of thunder in his stick—Larry Parrish, we mean—for the help needed up the middle.

This was an exciting team to watch in 1986; look for more in 1987.

### OPENING DAY LINEUP

| | | | |
|---|---|---|---|
| Fletcher | 2B | Sierra | RF |
| McDowell | CF | Slaught | C |
| O'Brien | 1B | Buechele | 3B |
| Incaviglia | LF | Kunkel | SS |
| Parrish | DH | Hough | P |

# Sitting in the Jaybird Seat

## TORONTO BLUE JAYS

If you watched the Blue Jays blow seven of their final eight games in '86 and drop from second to fourth place, you saw a team that didn't care about winning. And it was only a repeat of the '85 ALCS, when the Jays couldn't win any of the last big ones, even at home. There's something about this club that doesn't want to be a winner. Maybe management doesn't want to pay higher salaries in U.S. dollars to championship players. Maybe the players, both North Americans and Latin Americans, have imbibed the Canadian ethos that frowns on success as vulgar. Their fans love them better as losers than as winners.

This is an organization of faceless organization men. It badly needs shaking up. Pat Gillick, Executive Vice President–Baseball, had a great idea when he picked unprotected minor leaguers off other teams' rosters—he got George Bell, among others, that way—but turned it into a fetish, leaving his team without a solid bench, and exposing himself and his manager as rigid thinkers when Dick Howser shamelessly outmaneuvered Bobby Cox in the '85 ALCS. The guess here is that Cox resigned out of shame, in the Japanese manner, and the certainty is that Jimy Williams replaced him because he was cut from the organization mold. What this team needs foremost is to break the mold. Move Williams into front office Valhalla and hire an outsider as manager, not a good ol' boy but a tough man with championship smarts like Frank Robinson. Then bring in a veteran to be a leader—Reggie comes to mind if his ego wouldn't get in the way—and do what Cliff Johnson couldn't, show the team how to be fighters, instead of fighting with the team.

In personnel, the Jays don't need much to make a run for the flag (but that's been the case for two years). They do, however, need to make some moves. Get rid of the third-base platoon and let Kelly Gruber play himself out of the job (we don't think he will). Trade Damaso Garcia for bench power or a quality starter. Sit down Willie Upshaw for Rick Leach if Upshaw can't drive in runs anymore (neither is worth much in a trade). And cross your fingers on the return to form of Dave Stieb, who needs a tough manager more than anybody else on the club.

## OPENING DAY LINEUP

| | | | |
|---|---|---|---|
| Moseby | CF | Campusano | LF |
| Fernandez | SS | Whitt | C |
| Bell | DH | Gruber | 3B |
| Barfield | RF | Lee | 2B |
| Upshaw | 1B | Stieb | P |

## 15 DEALS THAT OUGHT
## TO BE MADE FOR OBVIOUS REASONS

1. Sax for Viola
2. Washington for Boston
3. Lynn for Shirley
4. Swift for Walker
5. Smiley for Witt
6. Moses for Mormon
7. Fields for Woods
8. Deer for Lyons
9. Nixon for Jefferson
10. Brown and Blue for White and Black
11. Quirk for Plunk
12. Gross for Grubb
13. Mookie for Pookie
14. Chili for Rice
15. Trout for Bass

# Bronx Cheer

## The Hard Life and Slow Times of a Rotisserie Wife, by Mrs. Fleder of the Fledermice

*There is another side to almost every story, even the Founding Fathers of Rotisserie League Baseball would agree, but we aren't necessarily the ones to tell it. After all, how does one talk about life outside or "beyond" the Rotisserie League? Sure, we maintain the fiction that we continue to be exemplary breadwinners, friends, lovers, spouses, fathers, in spite of—because of, even—the Greatest Game for Baseball Fans since Baseball. But even when that's true, it's also a fact that our lives have been profoundly, irrevocably altered. Most of us can't even remember what it was like back then, much less contemplate a Rotisseless future. How can we possibly be expected to assess the impact of our peculiar obsession on those nearest and dearest to us?*

*Enter Mrs. Fleder of the Fledermice. Yes, she has another name, but for some reason was reluctant to have it used here (she said something about "not having told my parents yet; I don't think they would understand.") But she did agree to seek out her Rotissesisters across the land, and chronicle their reactions to having their family room transformed into a front office. Here's her report.*

Women play a small role in the Rotisserie League, perhaps

smaller than necessary. We look up at our men to see them beating their hairy chests and calling themselves by grandiose titles: Commissioner, General Manager, Owner. Sometimes they let us have a title, too. My title in the Fledermice franchise is Vice-President in Charge of Owner Development. I have a friend whose Rotisserie identity is Water Girl. (After a successful season, she was promoted to Liquid Woman.) What does this mean? Do we attend the annual awards banquet in glitter, on the arms of our men? Do we behave like cheerleaders and wear his logo on our heart? Do we explain to all our puzzled friends just what a Rotisserie League is and why our particular husband is so significant in it? No, no. Our role is to be as invisible as possible. We watch. We wait. We toss out the empty beer cans of his life.

I try my best to explain what it is he is doing. Take my word for it, I always end up saying: It's an amazing phenomenon, and I'm on the fringe of it. A Rotissewife exists on the fringe of Rotisserie baseball, just as all of us who know about this sport exist on the fringe of society. But we wives are strictly fringe. We send our men into the middle of something we can barely describe, and then we stand on the fringe of our marriage.

*Where did he go? I don't know. He was drafted for something. He had a minute so he named the baby Thurman Goose Catfish. He could be a missing person, I don't rule that out. He has dark hair. I think. If you see him, say "Yo."*

Someday, we may be able to lie down on the psychiatrist's couch and talk about our hard lives and slow times, but not yet. We're still in the dark ages, floundering between ignorance and disbelief. Vot is dis Rotisserie ball? a shrink would say. Who is dis Pedro Guerrero your husband adores? Ah, he is pretending to own him. I see. You are making dis up with him, yes? It's all in your head, no?

No, it's all in *his* head, but we would truly go insane if we reminded ourselves too frequently that he's making it all up, and just pretending to own a team. The stakes are much higher than those of some friendly little poker game. This is the Dungeons and Dragons of the Dad set. This is the Swami Rotisserie League, knocking on your door and holding open his empty sack. Won't you please contribute to the cult of Rotisserie Baseball? Won't you give us your husband?

Spring, summer, and part of the fall, the owner of the Fledermice lives for the Swami. He walks around with a telephone cord around his neck. Baseball is his video wallpaper. He gazes at the flickering images of his big, happy family—a Cub here, an Astro there, a couple of Pirates—and pats his belly. What has he wrought!

I am his phone maiden. The other owners call all the time, to brag about their team and to insult the Mice. Insults are the small talk of the Rotisserie League. I feel it's my duty to insult them back. One brazen owner offered me a bribe once—he said I could sing backup on his garage band's single if only I would tell him who the Mice were going for in the draft. I always have to be on guard—it's Rotisserian eat Rotisserian out there. No wife has the luxury of being neutral. Even the children are trained like dogs. The five-year-old son of another owner came up to me once at a softball game and actually asked me, "Do you belong to the hated Mice?"

I do. At night I return to our nest and watch him compulsively flip channels, looking for baseball games, any baseball games, cruising for moments when a Mice runner steals a base or a Mice pitcher squeaks to victory. One night he flipped in vain past *Dallas* and *Miami Vice* and all the fun programs I used to watch. The only ball game was in the process of being rained out. "Honey," he said finally, "do you mind if we watch the rain delay?"

My life is slow. My life is hard.

I rarely get a chance to chat with the other wives at league social functions, perhaps because there aren't any league social functions. Oh, one year in the original Rotisserie League, the Eisenberg Furriers celebrated victory by throwing a party for the losers and their spousal units. The owner of the Furriers made his appearance in a tux and had a woman in a mink coat on either arm. I spent my party time getting to know one of the Furry women; it turned out she'd been rented for the occasion. I never saw her again.

I did, however, recently steal the league rosters for the two leagues in which the Mice compete—the original Rotisserie League in New York and the expansion Great Lakes Bush League in Chicago—and wrestled the phone away from the Mice long enough to call some of my counterparts. We have something powerful in common: Our husbands belong to the same Raccoon Lodge.

A few of the Rotissewives in these two leagues have husbands who are in other leagues as well—the obsession has a way of feeding itself—and so I learned of heroic Rotissewives from the Junior League and from a league in California that has neither a computerized stat service nor a name. I also learned of a woman who qualifies as the first saint of Rotissewives. Her name is Mrs. Capozzalo, she lives in New Jersey, and her husband not only fields teams in three separate leagues (Tiffany, Marshall, and Stardust) but also computes all the stats for all three leagues with an adding machine. Mrs. Capozzalo is full of wisdom. "Just ignore them," she says.

The first Rotissewife in history is Mrs. Okrent of the Okrent Fenokees in the original league. For six years she has been tilling the land of western Massachusetts and raising two children while Mr. Okrent attends to his team. What has she learned?

"I've learned it's the season of little pieces of paper all over the floor, that I don't know if I'm supposed to save or throw out. Numbers. Hieroglyphs. I've learned that we have to have three different newspapers in the morning. At least three different calls to New York every day. Two telephones. We now have a Porta-Phone, in case I should be in the blueberry bushes when the call comes in with the late box scores Dan has phoned in each day from the Coast. Do you know the other owners call me L.S.B., Long Suffering Becky?"

She has a revenge fantasy. "What if I was more obsessed than I am with gardening? What if I dragged Dan off to garden shows constantly, and every night, when I finally got into bed, I'd turn on the radio and then a voice like Julia Child's would discuss what's in bloom in this crackly little voice from a distant town—you know, that horrible reception on the radio from baseball games in Milwaukee or Pittsburgh? Will I ever have something that equals his obsession? No, nothing could equal it. Nothing.

"You've got to admire them," she says firmly. "But what can you do? I was duped. Grin and bear it. I have no advice."

## REACH OUT AND TOUCH SOMEONE

Definitely get another telephone. As a matter of fact, when the husband of a friend of mine joined a league, I said you must get another telephone, and I credit that with saving her marriage.

Mrs. Waggoner of the Goners
New York, New York

I know if Harry's making a call in the middle of the night, he's calling Sports Phone. He calls them constantly, sometimes every ten or fifteen minutes. If it's a crucial day and we're walking through the city, he'll stop and call from pay phones.

Mrs. Stein of the Stein Brenners
Hastings-on-Hudson, New York

It's impossible to control the telephone problem. There is one guy in the Great Lakes Bush League who calls constantly. He's impossible to discourage. He'll call once and you'll tell him Hank's not home, he'll be back in an hour. Forty-five minutes later, he'll call again. Also, he spreads vicious rumors about my husband in the league.

Mrs. Neuberger of the Peorians
Evanston, Illinois

Please quote me anonymously. I don't want him to come across as insane to his business colleagues. But he pretty much supports Sports Phone. All over the United States. There are pages, just pages of the very same phone calls. I mean it's the exact same number, except different area codes. He calls all night, *all night*. My daughter—it's just standard for her to see him get on the phone and not say a word.

Name withheld by request

During the period of time when they're trading, you have men calling you at all hours of the day. You have men calling you at the office. Don't get me wrong—nice men, nice men. But they want Ken to get off the phone with a client to trade with them. And they make long-distance calls to the stadiums! Sometimes I go off the deep end.

> Mrs. Thomas of the T-Birds
> Woodland Hills, California

Ah, we are lucky. We look at our phone bills and see each other's numbers, the same numbers every month. Look, at least you know who he's calling.

> Mrs. Capozzalo of many teams
> Jersey City, New Jersey

Ordinarily, the Rotissewife is confined to a zone between the television and the telephone. She hears about such rituals as the draft, but she rarely witnesses them. When she does, she is shocked.

"Well, I was very surprised because J. had talked about what a great night it was and what fun he had," reports one Rotissewife, who asked to remain anonymous. "This year I stopped by—I had to pick something up at the restaurant where they were holding their Draft—and it was quite serious. Based on J.'s information, I thought it would be one big party, but it was real serious business. I didn't dare interrupt it."

Mrs. Stein of the Steinbrenners, the only two-time winners in the original Rotisserie League's history, agrees: "It's become such a big thing for the kids, Draft Day. It's like seeing their Dad go off to war. I went to the Draft once. It was like a state of siege, like a bunch of generals sitting around. The bunker mentality."

"Before the Draft, they work like they're getting ready for their senior prom. There's a lot of tension. We're talking heavy-duty," Mrs. Mitchell of the Farley Grangers reflected in her Gig Harbor, Washington, home. "I've given up going to the party the Junior League throws at the end of the season. It's real silly stuff. Strictly boys' stuff. They pour a can of Yoo-Hoo over the winner, and then everybody rehashes every trade. The wives are all catatonic at that point. Even if our husband is the winner, there's no reflected glory. We're sort of nonpeople; they're not concerned with us at all. I feel like I know how a politician's wife must feel. At Junior League events, I feel like I'm wearing an imaginary pillbox hat."

The exclusivity of the Rotisserie League can be maddening, but experienced Rotissewives have learned to step over their husbands as New Yorkers step over bums on their streets. Mrs. Waggoner, a charter member of the women's auxiliary in the original Rotisserie League, has learned to sleep at the ball park; and next year, when her husband goes South to spring training, she'll go to Paris. Mrs. Thomas of the T-Birds in the unnamed California League takes advantage of her husband's inattention. "I read. I watch television. I go off with my girlfriends. I do what I want to do—and he can't complain." He makes it all up to her when he wins. "Last year he won and we went to Canada. We thought the World Series was going to be there, but that's okay. I still got to see Niagara Falls and Toronto on the money he won."

It is the fresh, new, young wives whose plunges into the world of Rotisseball that are the most traumatic. You run into them at the supermarket and they look stunned. "Officially, I have no comment," says the new Mrs. Eisenberg of the Furriers. Unofficially, her tone spoke volumes.

I talked to Mrs. Scott of the Doug-Outs, a first-year team in the Great Lakes Bush League, and she said she felt as if she had run a marathon. "It hasn't really been that bad, not as bad as I thought," she said. "But it does go on forever. It's the only thing that gets Doug up in the morning, the sports section, because normally he'd sleep in. But it just seems to drag on forever. When is it over?"

I wanted to put my arm around her and say, Mrs. Scott, it's *never* over. In the spring, they read their scouting reports and go on scouting missions and gather at the Draft. Then all through the summer, they trade and scrutinize box scores and argue and insult each other. September is a month of depression, heartache, tantrums. Then they pour Yoo-Hoo over somebody's head. Then they start building for next year. Mrs. Stein says her husband talks perfectly seriously about passing his team on to their two-year-old.

Some men can't take it, and they drop out, and perhaps you think their wives are the lucky ones. But Mrs. Telander, formerly of the Peorians in the Great Lakes Bush League, is an ex-Rotisserie ball wife who yearns for the good old days when her husband had a team. She fondly remembers reading the sports pages first thing in the morning and using yellow highlighter on the relevant lines of the box scores. She also turned her energy to drawing up charts on butcher paper that traced the stats of the Peorians every week; she decorated their living room with these charts. "I was the perfect Rotissewife," she says now. "Unfortunately, my husband wasn't the perfect owner."

When Mr. Telander gave up his team to return to life as an ordinary baseball fan, Mrs. Telander acknowledges there was a void in her life. There are women who are brave enough and thick-skinned enough to run their own franchises, but Mrs. Telander wasn't one. "I didn't want the responsibility, but I loved being involved." Fortunately, Mrs. Telander is a doctor of psychology and sees a future for herself in counseling troubled Rotissewives.

"I could call myself Dr. Judy," she says. "I could do group therapy—separate groups for those whose husbands have good teams, and those with bad teams. I could write an advice column. 'Dear Dr. Judy, My husband hasn't been to bed in three days. He's pacing around, mumbling something about a 'Draft.' And it's not even cold. Distressed.' 'Dear Distressed. Have you tried the black negligee? The one with the Cubs' insignia?' "

*Get involved* is her whole message. "Perhaps I was more involved than is healthy, but a little involvement gives you something to share with him. Ask your husband if he'll draft a player just for you—a cute hometown player, maybe, who you can root for on his team."

For the record, the *Fledermausmeister* was appalled by this suggestion. "No Rotisserian in his right mind would draft a player just because he was cute," says my husband.

Then Mrs. Okrent, the original Rotissewife, called with some advice she had thought up. "Don't join a support group," she said. "A bunch of guys in our town got obsessed about basketball, and their wives formed a support group to meet on the night the men played. Before you know it, they were all divorced."

The owner of the Mice was puzzled. Why would women who formed a support group for the men suddenly change their minds and get divorced, he wondered.

How sweet—he thought they got together to support the men.

## Rotisserie League—the Family Game

Are you a remarkable single person? Join a Rotisserie League and become a staid married one. . . . Wait, Take Two: Major league baseball has the effrontery to call itself The Family Game and play World Series games after midnight—maybe it's The Addams Family Game—while the fact is that Rotisserie League Baseball is the true Family Game. When the Original Rotisserie League was founded back in 1980, fully 60% of its members were lonely guys (and gals), looking perhaps to fill their empty hours with improving thoughts about the National Pastime. The training and discipline required to be a Rotisserie League owner/GM turned these wretches into full-scale, some would even say outsized, human beings. The inspiring story of Bob Sklar's romance with Adrienne Harris beginning at a Rotisserie League awards event has already been told in our first book, *Rotisserie League Baseball*. Since the Gazer chief took a bride, four more nuptials have followed: Glen Waggoner of the Goners married Sharon McIntosh, despite a 17-inning game at Shea that almost sidetracked their storybook courtship; Rob Fleder of the Mice took Marilyn Johnson's hand in marriage; Steve Wulf wooed and won Jane (Bambi) Bachman; and Lee Eisenberg of the Furriers invited Linda Reville to share his cold storage. What with several franchises changing hands since the early days, now fully nine of the Original ten are community property. Only Peter Gethers remains outside the marriage fold. Peter would probably tell you that marriage has an adverse effect on a team's Rotisserie League standings, but that can be explained . . . it's only during the honeymoon period.

# Scorecard

## How to Keep Score

In the RL's rookie season our Beloved Founder took on the task of compiling official standings. He also wrote the constitution, called meetings, prepared news releases, made up new rules, met with the press, established a League archive, and finished eighth. That last fact, as Former Commissioner-for-Life Okrent admits, had a direct impact on the first. In the early weeks of the season, when the Fenokees were still in the race, we got stat reports . . . well, if not regularly, at least often enough to know where we stood, what strengths we could trade from, what weaknesses needed shoring up. As his team sank into the swamp, Bogmaster Okrent lost interest in quantifying the decline. From early July until the end of the season the League had no official standings to guide us—only the "Okrent Unofficials" (perversely, the Beloved Founder continued to tabulate, as he still does, unofficial standings *each day* from newspaper box scores) to monitor our first pennant drive.

At the Rotisserie League's winter meetings, team owners voted unanimously to relieve the Beloved Founder of scorekeeping responsibilities the next season. Sharing the task was briefly considered, but passing the records around is cumbersome, and it still meant that someone would have to devote seven to ten hours per reporting period to get the stats out. So we took the smart way out: we hired someone reliable to do it for us.

Enter Sandra Krempasky, the unsung heroine of the Rotisserie League. A music producer in her other job, Sandra was named Director of Statistical Services of the Rotisserie League (and of the Junior League, whose appreciative owners named their championship trophy after her). Armed with only a calculator and a penchant for perfection, she provided the RL with accurate, neatly organized standings on a regular schedule for three seasons. She did such a terrific job, it's a criminal shame that we fired her. But that's a later story. Right now, here's what you need to know to keep score yourself.

# Rotisserie League Scoring—The Basics

**STEP 1:** Nail down your source for *USA Today*—by subscribing, by bribing a newstand dealer to save you a copy on Tuesday or Wednesday, or—if necessary—by hanging out at airports (you'll always find a copy of McNewspaper there).

**STEP 2:** Prepare work sheets for the players and pitchers on each team. Here's a model you can use:

WORK SHEET

TEAM: __Okrent Fenokees__          OWNER: __Dan Okrent__

PERIOD:_____ GAMES THROUGH:_____ USA Today DATED:_____

## PLAYERS

| Name | NL Team | AB | H | HR | RBI | SB | Trade/Reserve Status |
|------|---------|----|----|----|-----|----|----------------------|
|      |         |    |    |    |     |    |                      |
|      |         |    |    |    |     |    |                      |
|      |         |    |    |    |     |    |                      |
|      |         |    |    |    |     |    |                      |
|      |         |    |    |    |     |    |                      |
|      |         |    |    |    |     |    |                      |
|      |         |    |    |    |     |    |                      |
|      |         |    |    |    |     |    |                      |
|      |         |    |    |    |     |    |                      |
|      |         |    |    |    |     |    |                      |
|      |         |    |    |    |     |    |                      |
|      |         |    |    |    |     |    |                      |
|      |         |    |    |    |     |    |                      |
|      |         |    |    |    |     |    |                      |
|      |         |    |    |    |     |    |                      |
|      |         |    |    |    |     |    |                      |
|      |         |    |    |    |     |    |                      |
|      |         |    |    |    |     |    |                      |
|      |         |    |    |    |     |    |                      |
|      |         |    |    |    |     |    |                      |
| Totals |       |    |    |    |     |    | BA:                  |

TEAM: __Okrent Fenokees__          OWNER: __Dan Okrent__

PERIOD:_____   GAMES THROUGH:_____   USA Today DATED:_____

## PITCHERS

| Name | NL Team | IP | H | BB | ER | W | S | Trade/Reserve Status |
|------|---------|----|----|----|----|----|----|----------------------|
|      |         |    |   |    |    |   |   |                      |
|      |         |    |   |    |    |   |   |                      |
|      |         |    |   |    |    |   |   |                      |
|      |         |    |   |    |    |   |   |                      |
|      |         |    |   |    |    |   |   |                      |
|      |         |    |   |    |    |   |   |                      |
|      |         |    |   |    |    |   |   |                      |
|      |         |    |   |    |    |   |   |                      |
|      |         |    |   |    |    |   |   |                      |
|      |         |    |   |    |    |   |   |                      |
|      |         |    |   |    |    |   |   |                      |
|      |         |    |   |    |    |   |   |                      |
|      |         |    |   |    |    |   |   |                      |
|      |         |    |   |    |    |   |   |                      |
|      |         |    |   |    |    |   |   |                      |
|      |         |    |   |    |    |   |   |                      |
|      |         |    |   |    |    |   |   |                      |
|      |         |    |   |    |    |   |   |                      |
|      |         |    |   |    |    |   |   |                      |
|      |         |    |   |    |    |   |   |                      |
|      |         |    |   |    |    |   |   |                      |
|      |         |    |   |    |    |   |   |                      |
| Totals |       |    |   |    |    |   |   | RATIO:    ERA:       |

If you follow the revolving door policy of the Furriers and the Coronas, or if you have a lot of injuries and Reserve List activity, you'll need all this space—and maybe more.

**STEP 3:** It's early May, and *USA Today* has finally decided that the batters have enough at-bats and the pitchers enough innings pitched to give us their first round of cumulative stats. You take a deep breath, gird your loins, throw back a neat shot the way Randolph Scott always did before a gunfight—and discover that taking the numbers from the neat *USA Today* charts and entering them on the work sheets is a snap.

So, what's the big deal? A few hours of adding, multiplying, and dividing—where's the problem?

Easy does it, rookie. The first reporting period is a snap because there haven't been any player changes to give the scorekeeper grief yet. The players on a team's work sheet are the players a team started with on Draft Day. Any trades, call-ups, or other transactions made in the intervening weeks *do not take effect until the day after the first reporting period ends*. The first reporting period *is* easy by comparison to what follows.

**NOTE:** Careful readers will note that some of the players on the Fenokees have been out of baseball for a while. The same can be said for the team's front office, of course, but in fact the players listed in the next few pages are from the *1983* Fenokees, exactly as listed in our first book. Call us lazy, but Fenokee teams just don't change that much from year to year. The idea here is to show you how to keep score, not keep you up to date on the Fenokees' sad performances.

# WORK SHEET

TEAM: __Okrent Fenokees__          OWNER: __Dan Okrent__

PERIOD: __1__   GAMES THROUGH: _____   USA TODAY DATED: _____

## PLAYERS

| Name | NL Team | AB | H | HR | RBI | SB | Trade/Reserve Status |
|---|---|---|---|---|---|---|---|
| Foster | NY | 50 | 11 | 2 | 4 | 0 | |
| Monday | LA | 4 | 0 | 0 | 0 | 0 | |
| Horner | ATL | 61 | 14 | 5 | 10 | 0 | |
| Clark | SF | 63 | 12 | 0 | 4 | 1 | |
| Lacy | PITT | 64 | 20 | 1 | 3 | 12 | |
| Sax | LA | 69 | 19 | 1 | 7 | 9 | |
| Virgil | PHIL | 5 | 1 | 0 | 0 | 0 | |
| Scioscia | LA | 18 | 4 | 0 | 0 | 0 | |
| Bergman | SF | 14 | 2 | 0 | 0 | 0 | |
| O'Malley | SF | 44 | 12 | 0 | 4 | 0 | |
| O. Smith | ST L | 55 | 16 | 0 | 2 | 2 | |
| Bowa | CHI | 60 | 15 | 0 | 2 | 0 | |
| Cedeno | CIN | 53 | 19 | 1 | 10 | 2 | |
| Youngblood | SF | 24 | 5 | 0 | 2 | 0 | |
| | | | | | | | |
| | | | | | | | |
| | | | | | | | |
| | | | | | | | |
| | | | | | | | |
| | | | | | | | |
| Totals | | 584 | 150 | 10 | 48 | 26 | BA: .257 |

## WORK SHEET

TEAM: __Okrent Fenokees__     OWNER: __Dan Okrent__

PERIOD: __1__   GAMES THROUGH: _____   USA Today DATED: _____

## PITCHERS

| Name | NL Team | IP | H | BB | ER | W | S | Trade/Reserve Status |
|------|---------|-----|-----|-----|-----|-----|-----|----------------------|
| Minton | SF | 9 | 9 | 9 | 8 | 1 | 3 | |
| Show | SD | $29^1$ | 29 | 10 | 11 | 3 | 0 | |
| Swan | NY | $14^2$ | 17 | 13 | 11 | 1 | 0 | |
| Forsch | ST L | $28^2$ | 25 | 11 | 11 | 1 | 0 | |
| Monge | PHIL | $7^1$ | 13 | 4 | 3 | 2 | 0 | |
| Denny | PHIL | 31 | 27 | 6 | 10 | 2 | 0 | |
| Ruhle | HOUS | $18^1$ | 16 | 6 | 5 | 0 | 1 | |
| Ownbey | NY | $10^2$ | 7 | 10 | 6 | 0 | 0 | |
| McGraw | PHIL | 5 | 7 | 0 | 0 | 0 | 0 | |
| | | | | | | | | |
| | | | | | | | | |
| | | | | | | | | |
| | | | | | | | | |
| | | | | | | | | |
| | | | | | | | | |
| | | | | | | | | |
| | | | | | | | | |
| | | | | | | | | |
| | | | | | | | | |
| Totals | | 154 | 50 | 69 | 65 | 10 | 4 | RATIO: 1.422 ERA: 3.80 |

But halfway through the season, the picture has become a little more complicated.

**WORK SHEET**

TEAM: __Okrent Fenokees__    OWNER: __Dan Okrent__

PERIOD: __7__   GAMES THROUGH: _____    USA Today DATED: _____

## PLAYERS

| Name | NL Team | AB | H | HR | RBI | SB | Trade/Reserve Status |
|------|---------|----|----|----|-----|----|----------------------|
| Foster | NY | 305 | 76 | 15 | 45 | 0 | |
| Monday * | LA | 52 | 11 | 3 | 7 | 0 | Trade 6/17 |
| Horner | ATL | 271 | 82 | 15 | 51 | 4 | |
| Clark | SF | 311 | 77 | 14 | 45 | 2 | |
| Lacy | PITT | 192 | 58 | 4 | 11 | 20 | |
| Sax | LA | 313 | 87 | 4 | 22 | 31 | |
| Virgil | PHIL | 84 | 18 | 3 | 12 | 0 | |
| Scioscia * | LA | 35 | 11 | 1 | 7 | 0 | Reserve 5/20 |
| Bergman | SF | 57 | 10 | 1 | 5 | 0 | |
| O'Malley * | SF | 189 | 56 | 2 | 17 | 1 | Trade 6/17 |
| O. Smith | ST L | 292 | 63 | 0 | 24 | 16 | |
| Bowa | CHI | 295 | 76 | 2 | 28 | 2 | |
| Cedeno * | CIN | 134 | 32 | 4 | 17 | 5 | Trade 6/17 |
| Youngblood | SF | 157 | 43 | 8 | 20 | 5 | |
| Strawberry* | NY | 69 | 17 | 6 | 20 | 3 | Acquire 6/17 |
| Maldonado* | LA | 0 | 0 | 0 | 0 | 0 | Acquire 6/17 |
| Ashford * | NY | 0 | 0 | 0 | 0 | 0 | Acquire 6/17; Release 6/24 |
| Roenicke * | LA | 48 | 11 | 2 | 7 | 1 | Acquire 6/17 |
| Esasky * | CIN | 65 | 17 | 4 | 9 | 1 | Call up 6/24 |
| Bilardello * | CIN | 88 | 22 | 1 | 8 | 0 | Call up 5/20 |
| Totals | | 2957 | 767 | 89 | 355 | 91 | BA: .259 |

TEAM: __Okrent Fenokees__          OWNER: __Dan Okrent__

PERIOD: __7__   GAMES THROUGH: _____   USA Today DATED: _____

## PITCHERS

| Name | NL Team | IP | H | BB | ER | W | S | Trade/Reserve Status |
|------|---------|----|----|----|----|----|----|----------------------|
| Minton | SF | 53 | 59 | 30 | 25 | 2 | 8 | |
| Show * | SD | $86^2$ | 80 | 27 | 26 | 7 | 0 | Trade 6/17 |
| Swan | NY | $64^1$ | 72 | 28 | 36 | 1 | 1 | |
| Forsch * | ST L | 81 | 76 | 26 | 36 | 4 | 0 | Trade 6/17 |
| Monge | SD | $36^2$ | 42 | 11 | 13 | 3 | 4 | |
| Denny | PHIL | $124^2$ | 110 | 36 | 30 | 7 | 0 | |
| Ruhle | HOUS | 64 | 75 | 24 | 35 | 2 | 1 | |
| Ownbey * | NY | $29^2$ | 28 | 20 | 18 | 0 | 0 | Release 6/17 |
| McGraw * | PHIL | 6 | 7 | 0 | 0 | 0 | 0 | Trade 5/13 |
| Diaz * | NY | 26 | 19 | 15 | 7 | 1 | 0 | Acquire 5/13 |
| Welsh * | MONT | 14 | 14 | 8 | 8 | 0 | 0 | Acquire 6/17 |
| Reed * | PHIL | $16^1$ | 17 | 4 | 7 | 0 | 0 | Acquire 6/17 |
| Hernandez* | PHIL | 22 | 18 | 6 | 7 | 2 | 3 | Acquire 6/17 |
| | | | | | | | | |
| | | | | | | | | |
| | | | | | | | | |
| | | | | | | | | |
| | | | | | | | | |
| | | | | | | | | |
| | | | | | | | | |
| Totals | | $624^1$ | 617 | 235 | 248 | 29 | 17 | RATIO: 1.365 ERA: 3.58 |

**STEP 4:** Take a look at the difference between the Fenokees' work sheets for Period 1 and Period 7. What's happened is that the Swampmen, like any big league team, have had injuries, and call-ups from the Free Agent Pool to replace disabled players, and one activation from their Farm System. And, like any good GM who wants to improve his team's chances, Okrent has acquired some new players in trades. This means that he has *pieces* of certain players' years. And this means that whoever keeps score for the league has to keep tabs of those pieces and take them into account when compiling the standings. Attached to each work sheet, then, will be another tabulation sheet that contains the names of players and pitchers who have been with the Fenokees only part of the season, and the numbers for each of them that must be deducted from the cumulative stats carried each week in *USA Today*, or simply carried as part of the Fenokees' total statistics, as with Rick Monday, for example, who was traded away. Not as tricky as $e = mc^2$, but you will need someone who's careful with numbers—or our official Stats Service (see page 191).

**STEP 5:** If you allow trading, call-ups, waiver moves, and Farm System activity between reporting periods, and you should, it is imperative that scoring records be updated routinely. One reporting period might end July 14 and the next one August 4, but there could be transactions that are effective July 21 and July 28. Appropriate notations (along with numbers to be deducted at the next reporting period) must be made on the backup work sheet.

**STEP 6:** You've figured BA, HR, RBI, SB, ERA, Ratio, W, and S for every team, so now you rank them in each category from first to last, assign points accordingly (10 down to 1 for 10-team leagues, 12 down to 1 for those with 12 teams), add up the points each team accumulates in all the categories, and tote up the period's standings.

Then you double-check everything.

All that's left to do is type up the results, prepare a list of transactions since the last period so teams can keep tabs on each other's rosters, make copies of everything, and mail a set of standings and transactions to each owner.

TEAM: __Okrent Fenokees__          OWNER: __Dan Okrent__

## PLAYERS

| Trans-action date(s) | Name<br><br>CARRY or DEDUCT | NL Team | Stats apply from -- to |  |  |  |  |
|---|---|---|---|---|---|---|---|
| | | | AB | H | HR | RBI | SB |
| 5/20 | Scioscia | LA | Opening Day–5/19 | | | | |
| | CARRY | | 35 | 11 | 1 | 7 | 0 |
| 5/20 | Bilardello | Cin | 5/20–current | | | | |
| | DEDUCT | | −59 | −12 | −1 | −4 | −1 |
| 6/17 | Monday | LA | Opening Day–6/16 | | | | |
| | CARRY | | 52 | 11 | 3 | 7 | 0 |
| 6/17 | O'Malley | SF | Opening Day–6/16 | | | | |
| | CARRY | | 189 | 56 | 2 | 17 | 1 |
| 6/17 | Cedeno | Cin | Opening Day–6/16 | | | | |
| | CARRY | | 134 | 32 | 4 | 17 | 5 |
| 6/17 | Strawberry | NY | 6/17–current | | | | |
| | DEDUCT | | −118 | −22 | −3 | −12 | −6 |
| 6/17 | Maldonado | LA | 6/17–current | | | | |
| | DEDUCT | | −20 | −3 | −0 | −1 | −0 |
| 6/17 & 6/24 | Ashford | NY | 6/17–6/23 | | | | |
| | CARRY | | 0 | 0 | 0 | 0 | 0 |
| 6/17 | Roenicke | LA | 6/17–current | | | | |
| | DEDUCT | | −95 | −21 | −0 | −5 | −2 |
| 6/24 | Esasky | Cin | 6/24–current | | | | |
| | DEDUCT | | −19 | −7 | −0 | −1 | −1 |

## TABULATION SHEET
## FOR PARTIAL STATS

TEAM: __Okrent Fenokees__          OWNER: __Dan Okrent__

### PITCHERS

| Trans-action date(s) | Name / CARRY or DEDUCT | NL Team | Stats apply from – to | | | | | |
|---|---|---|---|---|---|---|---|---|
| | | | IP | H | BB | ER | W | S |
| 5/13 | McGraw | Phil | Opening Day–5/12 | | | | | |
| | CARRY | | 6 | 7 | 0 | 0 | 0 | 0 |
| 5/13 | Diaz | NY | 5/13–current | | | | | |
| | DEDUCT | | –16 | –19 | –5 | –6 | –1 | –0 |
| 6/17 | Show | SD | Opening Day–6/16 | | | | | |
| | CARRY | | $86^2$ | 80 | 27 | 26 | 7 | 0 |
| 6/17 | Forsch | St L | Opening Day–6/16 | | | | | |
| | CARRY | | 81 | 76 | 26 | 36 | 4 | 0 |
| 6/17 | Ownbey | NY | Opening Day–6/16 | | | | | |
| | CARRY | | $29^2$ | 28 | 20 | 18 | 0 | 0 |
| 6/17 | Welsh | Mont | 6/17–current | | | | | |
| | DEDUCT | | –14 | –14 | –8 | –8 | –0 | –0 |
| 6/17 | Reed | Phil | 6/17–current | | | | | |
| | DEDUCT | | $–16^1$ | –17 | –4 | –7 | –0 | –0 |
| 6/17 | Hernandez | Phil | 6/17–current | | | | | |
| | DEDUCT | | –22 | –18 | –6 | –7 | –2 | –3 |

We never said keeping score was complicated, just that it is a lot of work. By season's end, you're up to seven to ten hours per reporting period.

How many reporting periods? The more you play, the more you want. In our earlier days, the RL schedule was weekly from early May until the Trade Deadline, every three weeks through August, then weekly again in September when the pennant race heated up. But that wasn't enough. If we didn't have weekly stats from early May right on through to the end of the season, we'd probably have to resort to hang gliding for kicks.

# Rotisserie League Baseball Enters the Computer Age

What's really needed is weekly stats, and that's why the Rotisserie League replaced the estimable Sandra and her accurate but unavoidably slow way of keeping score with a computerized method. The basic elements of scoring outlined above remain unchanged; it's just that the computer cuts the task from seven to ten hours of computation to two to three hours of data entry. (And sentimentalists need not fret: Sandra Krempasky was recently voted into the Rotisserie League Hall of Fame, the very first year she was on the ballot.)

As you form your own league and address the issue of keeping score, you will have four options:

1. Do it yourself.
2. Hire someone to do it for you.
3. Develop your own computer program and put the family computer to a better use than prepping for the SATs or solving math problems.
4. Subscribe to the Rotisserie League Baseball Association Statistical Service. (YES, WE'LL DO IT FOR YOU—see page 191 for full details.)

# Give Me This Day My Daily Box Score

Some owners scan the box scores for a sense of how their players are doing, then wait for the weekly standings to find out for sure. If you think that's a sign of a shoddy front office, you can track your squad's performance on a daily basis. Here's how:

### THE 1983 GETHERSWAG GONERS BASEBALL CLUB
### DAILY PERFORMANCE CHART

Games of_____

| Players | | AB | H | HR | RBI | SB | Pitchers | | IP | H | BB | ER | W | S |
|---|---|---|---|---|---|---|---|---|---|---|---|---|---|---|
| Brown | lf | — | — | — | — | — | Welch | s | — | — | — | — | — | — |
| Van Slyke | 3b | — | — | — | — | — | McWilliams | s | — | — | — | — | — | — |
| Dawson | cf | — | — | — | — | — | Reuss | s | — | — | — | — | — | — |
| Kennedy | c | — | — | — | — | — | LaPoint | s | — | — | — | — | — | — |
| Knight | 1b | — | — | — | — | — | Scott | s | — | — | — | — | — | — |
| Hayes | rf | — | — | — | — | — | Price Res | s | — | — | — | — | — | — |
| Templeton | ss | — | — | — | — | — | Holland | r | — | — | — | — | — | — |
| Garner | 2b | — | — | — | — | — | Dawley | r | — | — | — | — | — | — |
| Pocoroba | c | — | — | — | — | — | Scherrer | r | — | — | — | — | — | — |
| Brooks | if | — | — | — | — | — | Scurry | r | — | — | — | — | — | — |
| Oberkfell | if | — | — | — | — | — | Hume Res | r | — | — | — | — | — | — |
| Morrison | if | — | — | — | — | — | | | | | | | | |
| Easler Res | of | — | — | — | — | — | | | | | | | | |
| Hall | of | — | — | — | — | — | Totals | | — | — | — | — | — | — |
| Maddox | of | — | — | — | — | — | | | | | | | | |
| _____ | | — | — | — | — | — | Notes:_____ | | | | | | | |
| Totals | | — | — | — | — | — | | | | | | | | |

### SEASON TO DATE

| | AB | H | HR | RBI | SB | | IP | H | BB | ER | W | S |
|---|---|---|---|---|---|---|---|---|---|---|---|---|
| Before Today | — | — | — | — | — | Before Today | — | — | — | — | — | — |
| Today | — | — | — | — | — | Today | — | — | — | — | — | — |
| TOTALS | — | — | — | — | — | TOTALS | — | — | — | — | — | — |

BA: __ HR: __ RBI: __ SB: __

ERA: __ RATIO: __ WINS: __ SAVES: __

A chart like this is fine for keeping track of your team, but you may need more as the trade deadline nears, or in the last stages of a pennant race when your nerves can't stand the suspense. Chances are you'll find yourself tracking key stats for a few other teams as well as your own. It means a bit more time with the box scores every day, but what else are your waking hours for?

# The Rotisserie League Baseball Association

You've collared nine other fanatics, memorized this book, subscribed to *Baseball America* and *The Sporting News,* bought every baseball mag on the racks, and appointed someone else to work on the logistics of your first Draft Day. What's next? Membership in the Rotisserie League Baseball Association seems sensible. Join now and beat the Christmas rush. Here's what your new league gets with RLBA membership:

1.  A complete, up-to-date, attractively presented Position Eligibility List (American or National League), sent to you by first-class mail (what else would you expect from the Rotisserie League?).

2.  Official Opening Day Rosters (American or National League), compiled by the RLBA's crack research department and mailed to you within 48 hours after Opening Day. Includes last-minute disabled list moves.

3.  Special announcements regarding a complete line of genuine, officially authorized Rotisserie League products (e.g. caps, patches, T-shirts, cars, vacation homes, etc.), all bearing the famous RL logo.

4.  Two annual updates, with information on rule changes, new wrinkles, variations on the game, news from other leagues, and other happenings around the RLBA world.

5.  A can of Yoo-Hoo mailed to you for your league's awards ceremony if you have the ill fortune to live outside the Yoo-Hoo Belt.

6.  A certificate signed by Beloved Founder and Former Commissioner-for-Life Okrent to be awarded to your league's pennant winner.

Here's how to join. Send the name and mailing address of your new league, along with $50 (check or money order only, please, no cash), to:

> The Rotisserie League Baseball Association
> 211 West 92nd Street, Box 9
> New York, NY 10025

# Official Rotisserie League Stats Service

The best way to be sure that you get accurate standings reports every week of the season is to subscribe to the official RLBA Stats Service. We compile stats, compute standings, and mail a report to your league the same day the numbers appear in *USA Today* (Tuesdays for American League teams, Wednesdays for National League). You report weekly Transactions on a form we provide; they take effect immediately.

For more information about the RLBA Stats Service, including current price, a sample standings report, and an application form, write: RBLA Stats, 211 West 92nd Street, Box 9, New York, NY 10025.

Owner: Lee Eisenberg

Owner: Rob Fleder

Owner: Peter Gethers

Owner: Daniel Okrent

Owner: Michael Pollet

Owner: Cary Schneider

Owner: Robert Sklar

Owner: Harry Stein

Owner: Glen Waggoner

Commissioner for Life: Cork Smith

Owner: Steve Wulf

# FINAL 1986 ROTISSERIE LEAGUE STANDINGS

| | | | | |
|---|---|---|---|---|
| 1. STEIN BRENNERS | 67.0 | 6. SKLAR GAZERS | 39.5 |
| 2. EISENBERG FURRIERS | 60.5 | 7. SMOKED FISH | 29.0 |
| 3. WULFGANG | 56.5 | 8 (TIE). FLEDERMICE | 28.0 |
| 4. OKRENT FENOKEES | 55.5 | 8 (TIE). GLENWAG GONERS | 28.0 |
| 5. POLLET BURROS | 50.0 | 10. CARY NATIONS | 26.0 |

## PITCHING RECORDS

| | WINS | | | SAVES | |
|---|---|---|---|---|---|
| STEIN BRENNERS | 106 | 10.0 | EISENBERG FURRIERS | 77 | 10.0 |
| WULFGANG | 96 | 9.0 | GLENWAG GONERS | 70 | 9.0 |
| POLLET BURROS | 90 | 8.0 | SKLAR GAZERS | 66 | 8.0 |
| SKLAR GAZERS | 88 | 7.0 | OKRENT FENOKEES | 47 | 7.0 |
| CARY NATIONS | 86 | 6.0 | WULFGANG | 42 | 6.0 |
| EISENBERG FURRIERS | 80 | 4.5 | SMOKED FISH | 33 | 5.0 |
| OKRENT FENOKEES | 80 | 4.5 | FLEDERMICE | 32 | 4.0 |
| FLEDERMICE | 66 | 3.0 | STEIN BRENNERS | 30 | 3.0 |
| SMOKED FISH | 62 | 2.0 | POLLET BURROS | 27 | 2.0 |
| GLENWAG GONERS | 55 | 1.0 | CARY NATIONS | 10 | 1.0 |

| | ERA | | | RATIO | |
|---|---|---|---|---|---|
| WULFGANG | 3.1165 | 10.0 | POLLET BURROS | 1.1952 | 10.0 |
| POLLET BURROS | 3.1675 | 9.0 | WULFGANG | 1.2120 | 9.0 |
| STEIN BRENNERS | 3.3808 | 8.0 | STEIN BRENNERS | 1.2187 | 8.0 |
| GLENWAG GONERS | 3.5544 | 7.0 | OKRENT FENOKEES | 1.3016 | 7.0 |
| OKRENT FENOKEES | 3.6824 | 6.0 | EISENBERG FURRIERS | 1.3073 | 6.0 |
| EISENBERG FURRIERS | 3.7204 | 5.0 | GLENWAG GONERS | 1.3222 | 5.0 |
| CARY NATIONS | 3.7788 | 4.0 | CARY NATIONS | 1.3351 | 4.0 |
| SKLAR GAZERS | 3.8190 | 3.0 | SKLAR GAZERS | 1.3641 | 3.0 |
| SMOKED FISH | 3.9746 | 2.0 | SMOKED FISH | 1.3914 | 2.0 |
| FLEDERMICE | 4.2540 | 1.0 | FLEDERMICE | 1.3950 | 1.0 |

## BATTING RECORDS

| | AVERAGE | | | HOME RUNS | |
|---|---|---|---|---|---|
| STEIN BRENNERS | .27414 | 10.0 | OKRENT FENOKEES | 177 | 10.0 |
| FLEDERMICE | .27405 | 9.0 | EISENBERG FURRIERS | 170 | 9.0 |
| EISENBERG FURRIERS | .27248 | 8.0 | STEIN BRENNERS | 164 | 8.0 |
| POLLET BURROS | .26887 | 7.0 | SKLAR GAZERS | 143 | 6.5 |
| SMOKED FISH | .26285 | 6.0 | WULFGANG | 143 | 6.5 |
| OKRENT FENOKEES | .25728 | 5.0 | SMOKED FISH | 142 | 5.0 |
| WULFGANG | .25642 | 4.0 | POLLET BURROS | 125 | 4.0 |
| SKLAR GAZERS | .25632 | 3.0 | FLEDERMICE | 114 | 3.0 |
| GLENWAG GONERS | .25415 | 2.0 | CARY NATIONS | 111 | 2.0 |
| CARY NATIONS | .24386 | 1.0 | GLENWAG GONERS | 83 | 1.0 |

| | RBI | | | STOLEN BASES | |
|---|---|---|---|---|---|
| STEIN BRENNERS | 805 | 10.0 | STEIN BRENNERS | 332 | 10.0 |
| EISENBERG FURRIERS | 780 | 9.0 | EISENBERG FURRIERS | 208 | 9.0 |
| OKRENT FENOKEES | 772 | 8.0 | OKRENT FENOKEES | 202 | 8.0 |
| WULFGANG | 702 | 7.0 | POLLET BURROS | 171 | 7.0 |
| SMOKED FISH | 667 | 6.0 | CARY NATIONS | 161 | 6.0 |
| SKLAR GAZERS | 666 | 5.0 | WULFGANG | 146 | 5.0 |
| FLEDERMICE | 619 | 4.0 | SKLAR GAZERS | 128 | 4.0 |
| POLLET BURROS | 616 | 3.0 | FLEDERMICE | 127 | 3.0 |
| CARY NATIONS | 476 | 2.0 | GLENWAG GONERS | 102 | 2.0 |
| GLENWAG GONERS | 423 | 1.0 | SMOKED FISH | 101 | 1.0 |

## FINAL 1985 ROTISSERIE LEAGUES STANDINGS

| | | | | | |
|---|---|---|---|---|---|
| 1. CARY NATIONS | 58.0 | | 6. STEIN BRENNERS | 43.5 |
| 2 (Tie). SMOKED FISH | 53.0 | | 7. FLEDERMICE | 42.0 |
| 2 (Tie). EISENBERG FURRIERS | 53.0 | | 8. SKLAR GAZERS | 39.5 |
| 4. GLENWAG GONERS | 49.0 | | 9. POLLET BURROS | 33.5 |
| 5. WULFGANG | 48.0 | | 10. OKRENT FENOKEES | 20.5 |

## PITCHING RECORDS

| WINS | | | SAVES | | |
|---|---|---|---|---|---|
| CARY NATIONS | 92 | 10.0 | WULFGANG | 77 | 10.0 |
| FLEDERMICE | 90 | 9.0 | SKLAR GAZERS | 62 | 9.0 |
| GLENWAG GONERS | 88 | 8.0 | CARY NATIONS | 52 | 8.0 |
| STEIN BRENNERS | 85 | 6.5 | SMOKED FISH | 47 | 7.0 |
| SKLAR GAZERS | 85 | 6.5 | STEIN BRENNERS | 39 | 6.0 |
| EISENBERG FURRIERS | 84 | 5.0 | GLENWAG GONERS | 38 | 5.0 |
| OKRENT FENOKEES | 78 | 4.0 | FLEDERMICE | 27 | 4.0 |
| SMOKED FISH | 74 | 3.0 | EISENBERG FURRIERS | 25 | 3.0 |
| WULFGANG | 73 | 2.0 | OKRENT FENOKEES | 21 | 2.0 |
| POLLET BURROS | 66 | 1.0 | POLLET BURROS | 15 | 1.0 |

| ERA | | | RATIO | | |
|---|---|---|---|---|---|
| STEIN BRENNERS | 3.0587 | 10.0 | CARY NATIONS | 1.2346 | 10.0 |
| CARY NATIONS | 3.1992 | 9.0 | POLLET BURROS | 1.2452 | 9.0 |
| SMOKED FISH | 3.3141 | 8.0 | STEIN BRENNERS | 1.2523 | 8.0 |
| POLLET BURROS | 3.4072 | 7.0 | SMOKED FISH | 1.2714 | 7.0 |
| EISENBERG FURRIERS | 3.4291 | 6.0 | SKLAR GAZERS | 1.2727 | 6.0 |
| SKLAR GAZERS | 3.4516 | 5.0 | GLENWAG GONERS | 1.2752 | 5.0 |
| WULFGANG | 3.5423 | 4.0 | EISENBERG FURRIERS | 1.2982 | 4.0 |
| GLENWAG GONERS | 3.5979 | 3.0 | WULFGANG | 1.3008 | 3.0 |
| FLEDERMICE | 3.6748 | 2.0 | OKRENT FENOKEES | 1.3216 | 2.0 |
| OKRENT FENOKEES | 3.7469 | 1.0 | FLEDERMICE | 1.3423 | 1.0 |

## BATTING RECORDS

| AVERAGE | | | HOME RUNS | | |
|---|---|---|---|---|---|
| WULFGANG | .27184 | 10.0 | SMOKED FISH | 182 | 10.0 |
| EISENBERG FURRIERS | .26751 | 9.0 | EISENBERG FURRIERS | 173 | 9.0 |
| GLENWAG GONERS | .26516 | 8.0 | WULFGANG | 170 | 8.0 |
| POLLET BURROS | .26454 | 7.0 | FLEDERMICE | 125 | 7.0 |
| SMOKED FISH | .26346 | 6.0 | GLENWAG GONERS | 124 | 6.0 |
| FLEDERMICE | .26295 | 5.0 | SKLAR GAZERS | 120 | 5.0 |
| CARY NATIONS | .25931 | 4.0 | CARY NATIONS | 118 | 4.0 |
| OKRENT FENOKEES | .25724 | 3.0 | OKRENT FENOKEES | 101 | 2.5 |
| SKLAR GAZERS | .25701 | 2.0 | POLLET BURROS | 101 | 2.5 |
| STEIN BRENNERS | .25489 | 1.0 | STEIN BRENNERS | 84 | 1.0 |

| RBI | | | STOLEN BASES | | |
|---|---|---|---|---|---|
| WULFGANG | 783 | 10.0 | STEIN BRENNERS | 222 | 10.0 |
| FLEDERMICE | 751 | 9.0 | EISENBERG FURRIERS | 218 | 9.0 |
| EISENBERG FURRIERS | 750 | 8.0 | CARY NATIONS | 176 | 8.0 |
| GLENWAG GONERS | 698 | 7.0 | GLENWAG GONERS | 173 | 7.0 |
| SMOKED FISH | 664 | 6.0 | SMOKED FISH | 163 | 6.0 |
| CARY NATIONS | 599 | 5.0 | FLEDERMICE | 133 | 5.0 |
| POLLET BURROS | 588 | 4.0 | OKRENT FENOKEES | 127 | 4.0 |
| SKLAR GAZERS | 570 | 3.0 | SKLAR GAZERS | 113 | 3.0 |
| OKRENT FENOKEES | 554 | 2.0 | POLLET BURROS | 103 | 2.0 |
| STEIN BRENNERS | 482 | 1.0 | WULFGANG | 68 | 1.0 |

# FINAL 1984 ROTISSERIE LEAGUE STANDINGS

| | | | | |
|---|---|---|---|---|
| 1. SKLAR GAZERS | 61.5 | 6. OKRENT FENOKEES | 40.0 |
| 2. GLENWAG GONERS | 57.5 | 7. WULFGANG | 35.0 |
| 3. STEIN BRENNERS | 56.0 | 8. EISENBERG FURRIERS | 32.0 |
| 4. POLLET BURROS | 51.0 | 9. SMOKED FISH | 30.5 |
| 5. FLEDERMICE | 46.5 | 10. SALEMBIER FLAMBÉS | 30.0 |

## PITCHING RECORDS

| WINS | | | SAVES | | |
|---|---|---|---|---|---|
| GLENWAG GONERS | 89 | 10.0 | STEIN BRENNERS | 79 | 10.0 |
| SKLAR GAZERS | 88 | 9.0 | EISENBERG FURRIERS | 61 | 9.0 |
| WULFGANG | 86 | 8.0 | WULFGANG | 56 | 8.0 |
| POLLET BURROS | 84 | 7.0 | POLLET BURROS | 52 | 7.0 |
| SMOKED FISH | 81 | 5.5 | SKLAR GAZERS | 46 | 6.0 |
| STEIN BRENNERS | 81 | 5.5 | SALEMBIER FLAMBÉS | 38 | 5.0 |
| FLEDERMICE | 79 | 4.0 | OKRENT FENOKEES | 30 | 4.0 |
| OKRENT FENOKEES | 71 | 3.0 | FLEDERMICE | 28 | 3.0 |
| SALEMBIER FLAMBÉS | 70 | 2.0 | GLENWAG GONERS | 16 | 2.0 |
| EISENBERG FURRIERS | 67 | 1.0 | SMOKED FISH | 15 | 1.0 |

| ERA | | | RATIO | | |
|---|---|---|---|---|---|
| STEIN BRENNERS | 3.2544 | 10.0 | SKLAR GAZERS | 1.2405 | 10.0 |
| SKLAR GAZERS | 3.3145 | 9.0 | GLENWAG GONERS | 1.2429 | 9.0 |
| WULFGANG | 3.3486 | 8.0 | STEIN BRENNERS | 1.2554 | 8.0 |
| FLEDERMICE | 3.3796 | 7.0 | OKRENT FENOKEES | 1.2841 | 7.0 |
| OKRENT FENOKEES | 3.4222 | 6.0 | SMOKED FISH | 1.3148 | 6.0 |
| GLENWAG GONERS | 3.4234 | 5.0 | FLEDERMICE | 1.3163 | 5.0 |
| SALEMBIER FLAMBÉS | 3.6644 | 4.0 | EISENBERG FURRIERS | 1.3367 | 4.0 |
| SMOKED FISH | 3.6947 | 3.0 | WULFGANG | 1.3454 | 3.0 |
| POLLET BURROS | 3.7374 | 2.0 | SALEMBIER FLAMBÉS | 1.3465 | 2.0 |
| EISENBERG FURRIERS | 3.8497 | 1.0 | POLLET BURROS | 1.3479 | 1.0 |

## BATTING RECORDS

| AVERAGE | | | HOME RUNS | | |
|---|---|---|---|---|---|
| FLEDERMICE | .27643 | 10.0 | GLENWAG GONERS | 152 | 10.0 |
| SKLAR GAZERS | .27221 | 9.0 | POLLET BURROS | 131 | 9.0 |
| POLLET BURROS | .27149 | 8.0 | FLEDERMICE | 130 | 7.5 |
| GLENWAG GONERS | .27088 | 7.0 | SKLAR GAZERS | 130 | 7.5 |
| STEIN BRENNERS | .27018 | 6.0 | SALEMBIER FLAMBÉS | 118 | 6.0 |
| EISENBERG FURRIERS | .26555 | 5.0 | OKRENT FENOKEES | 114 | 5.0 |
| SMOKED FISH | .26444 | 4.0 | SMOKED FISH | 109 | 3.5 |
| WULFGANG | .26352 | 3.0 | STEIN BRENNERS | 109 | 3.5 |
| OKRENT FENOKEES | .26012 | 2.0 | WULFGANG | 92 | 2.0 |
| SALEMBIER FLAMBÉS | .25557 | 1.0 | EISENBERG FURRIERS | 72 | 1.0 |

| RBIS | | | STOLEN BASES | | |
|---|---|---|---|---|---|
| GLENWAG GONERS | 763 | 10.0 | EISENBERG FURRIERS | 190 | 10.0 |
| POLLET BURROS | 740 | 9.0 | OKRENT FENOKEES | 186 | 9.0 |
| FLEDERMICE | 677 | 8.0 | POLLET BURROS | 174 | 8.0 |
| SLEMBIER FLAMBÉS | 668 | 7.0 | STEIN BRENNERS | 167 | 7.0 |
| STEIN BRENNERS | 654 | 6.0 | SKLAR GAZERS | 157 | 6.0 |
| SKLAR GAZERS | 642 | 5.0 | SMOKED FISH | 152 | 4.5 |
| OKRENT FENOKEES | 614 | 4.0 | GLENWAG GONERS | 152 | 4.5 |
| SMOKED FISH | 604 | 3.0 | SALEMBIER FLAMBÉS | 142 | 3.0 |
| WULFGANG | 544 | 2.0 | FLEDERMICE | 140 | 2.0 |
| EISENBERG FURRIERS | 460 | 1.0 | WULFGANG | 136 | 1.0 |

# FINAL 1986 JUNIOR LEAGUE STANDINGS

| | | | | |
|---|---|---|---|---|
| 1. WAGGONER WHEELS | 78.0 | 7. SHURE-BO CREATIONS | 57.0 |
| 2. STEVIE'S WUNDERS | 72.0 | 8. GETHERS YE ROSEBUDS | 45.5 |
| 3. CHARLIE ABEL BAKERS | 71.0 | 9. GARR FIELDERS | 42.5 |
| 4 (Tie). FARLEY GRANGERS | 60.5 | 10. HARRIS TWEEDS | 32.5 |
| 5 (Tie). FILIAL FOLLIES | 60.5 | 11. BRUCE LOUIS ALL-STARS | 24.5 |
| 6. FLINN STONES | 58.5 | 12. FALKLAND ISLANDERS | 21.5 |

## PITCHING RECORDS

| WINS | | | SAVES | | |
|---|---|---|---|---|---|
| WAGGONER WHEELS | 95 | 12.0 | FILIAL FOLLIES | 60 | 12.0 |
| CHARLIE ABEL BAKERS | 89 | 11.0 | CHARLIE ABEL BAKERS | 48 | 11.0 |
| FARLEY GRANGERS | 83 | 9.5 | HARRIS TWEEDS | 45 | 10.0 |
| GETHERS YE ROSEBUDS | 83 | 9.5 | FARLEY GRANGERS | 43 | 9.0 |
| SHURE-BO CREATIONS | 78 | 8.0 | WAGGONER WHEELS | 38 | 8.0 |
| FLINN STONES | 77 | 7.0 | GARR FIELDERS | 36 | 7.0 |
| STEVIE'S WUNDERS | 75 | 6.0 | BRUCE LOUIS ALL-STARS | 35 | 5.5 |
| FILIAL FOLLIES | 73 | 5.0 | FLINN STONES | 35 | 5.5 |
| BRUCE LOUIS ALL-STARS | 70 | 4.0 | STEVIE'S WUNDERS | 30 | 4.0 |
| FALKLAND ISLANDERS | 62 | 3.0 | SHURE-BO CREATIONS | 27 | 3.0 |
| HARRIS TWEEDS | 60 | 2.0 | FALKLAND ISLANDERS | 24 | 2.0 |
| GARR FIELDERS | 58 | 1.0 | GETHERS YE ROSEBUDS | 14 | 1.0 |

| ERA | | | RATIO | | |
|---|---|---|---|---|---|
| WAGGONER WHEELS | 3.2083 | 12.0 | WAGGONER WHEELS | 1.1538 | 12.0 |
| STEVIE'S WUNDERS | 3.5856 | 11.0 | CHARLIE ABEL BAKERS | 1.2799 | 11.0 |
| CHARLIE ABEL BAKERS | 3.8847 | 10.0 | STEVIE'S WUNDERS | 1.2954 | 10.0 |
| FILIAL FOLLIES | 3.8871 | 9.0 | FILIAL FOLLIES | 1.3139 | 9.0 |
| GARR FIELDERS | 4.1740 | 8.0 | GETHERS YE ROSEBUDS | 1.3599 | 8.0 |
| GETHERS YE ROSEBUDS | 4.1775 | 7.0 | SHURE-BO CREATIONS | 1.3704 | 7.0 |
| FARLEY GRANGERS | 4.1991 | 6.0 | FARLEY GRANGERS | 1.3740 | 6.0 |
| FLINN STONES | 4.2632 | 5.0 | FALKLAND ISLANDERS | 1.3754 | 5.0 |
| SHURE-BO CREATIONS | 4.3494 | 4.0 | GARR FIELDERS | 1.3882 | 4.0 |
| HARRIS TWEEDS | 4.3554 | 3.0 | FLINN STONES | 1.3900 | 3.0 |
| BRUCE LOUIS ALL-STARS | 4.5280 | 2.0 | BRUCE LOUIS ALL-STARS | 1.4499 | 2.0 |
| FALKLAND ISLANDERS | 4.6964 | 1.0 | HARRIS TWEEDS | 1.4827 | 1.0 |

## BATTING RECORDS

| AVERAGE | | | HOME RUNS | | |
|---|---|---|---|---|---|
| STEVIE'S WUNDERS | .28313 | 12.0 | FILIAL FOLLIES | 210 | 11.5 |
| WAGGONER WHEELS | .27552 | 11.0 | SHURE-BO CREATIONS | 210 | 11.5 |
| FLINN STONES | .27181 | 10.0 | FLINN STONES | 205 | 10.0 |
| GARR FIELDERS | .26539 | 9.0 | FARLEY GRANGERS | 199 | 9.0 |
| HARRIS TWEEDS | .26427 | 8.0 | CHARLIE ABEL BAKERS | 191 | 8.0 |
| SHURE-BO CREATIONS | .26180 | 7.0 | WAGGONER WHEELS | 189 | 7.0 |
| BRUCE LOUIS ALL-STARS | .25939 | 6.0 | STEVIE'S WUNDERS | 187 | 6.0 |
| FARLEY GRANGERS | .25656 | 5.0 | GETHERS YE ROSEBUDS | 186 | 5.0 |
| CHARLIE ABEL BAKERS | .25509 | 4.0 | HARRIS TWEEDS | 145 | 3.5 |
| FILIAL FOLLIES | .25505 | 3.0 | GARR FIELDERS | 145 | 3.5 |
| FALKLAND ISLANDERS | .25479 | 2.0 | FALKLAND ISLANDERS | 130 | 2.0 |
| GETHERS YE ROSEBUDS | .25467 | 1.0 | BRUCE LOUIS ALL-STARS | 121 | 1.0 |

|  | RBI |  |  | STOLEN BASES |  |
|---|---|---|---|---|---|
| SHURE-BO CREATIONS | 907 | 12.0 | STEVIE'S WUNDERS | 193 | 12.0 |
| STEVIE'S WUNDERS | 860 | 11.0 | CHARLIE ABEL BAKERS | 149 | 11.0 |
| FILIAL FOLLIES | 848 | 10.0 | FLINN STONES | 132 | 10.0 |
| FARLEY GRANGERS | 795 | 9.0 | WAGGONER WHEELS | 131 | 9.0 |
| FLINN STONES | 782 | 8.0 | GETHERS YE ROSEBUDS | 123 | 8.0 |
| WAGGONER WHEELS | 774 | 7.0 | FARLEY GRANGERS | 120 | 7.0 |
| GETHERS YE ROSEBUDS | 759 | 6.0 | GARR FIELDERS | 118 | 6.0 |
| CHARLIE ABEL BAKERS | 754 | 5.0 | FALKLAND ISLANDERS | 104 | 4.5 |
| GARR FIELDERS | 705 | 4.0 | SHURE-BO CREATIONS | 104 | 4.5 |
| HARRIS TWEEDS | 649 | 3.0 | BRUCE LOUIS ALL-STARS | 96 | 3.0 |
| FALKLAND ISLANDERS | 611 | 2.0 | HARRIS TWEEDS | 65 | 2.0 |
| BRUCE LOUIS ALL-STARS | 528 | 1.0 | FILIAL FOLLIES | 57 | 1.0 |

# THE ULTIMATE ROTISSESTAT

You've heard, no doubt, of particle physicists who are spending their professional lives and no small amount of federal research grant money trying to discover the smallest, simplest form of matter. In so doing, they figure, they will unlock the ultimate secret of the universe, win several Nobel prizes, and be invited to appear on the Carson show.

Enter Walt Allan, owner of the Blue Danube Walts in the DECENT League up there in Maine. (DECENT stands for "Down East Cheap and Economical National League," which gives you some idea of how clever those lobster wrestlers are with words.) Walt—or Dr. Allan, as he's know to close friends and family— "practices" medicine in Falmouth, Maine (sure, and Bill Buckner practices taking ground balls at first before big games). But he dabbles on the side in a number of areas, including First Principles and Scenic Overviews, and while on a recent dabble claims to have stumbled on something of such magnitude as to make what the physicists are doing look like remedial arithmetic.

Walt Allan, the Sir Isaac Newton of Rotisserie League Baseball, claims to have discovered—and will explain here, in his own words—no less than "The Ultimate Rotissestat." Dr. Allan, proceed:

Yeahup [Editor's note: Even—or especially—Maine residents who were born somewhere else say things like "Yeahup" a lot. Ignore it.], we humbly refer to it as the ULTIMATE ROTISSESTAT, which we always say in all caps.

This single numerical gem lets you know how your team would stack up in a "real" game. (Satchel Paige once asked, "What is 'real'? 'Cause them big leagues ain't." I don't know for sure what he meant, but I think he was anticipating Rotisserie League Baseball.) Just because the Founding Fathers wanted to have eight categories doesn't mean we have to believe that they tell us more than who is going to get the Moxie poured down her blouse (bring some old clothes, Kathy).

[Editor's note: Here Dr. Allan seems to be referring to

a bizarre sexual rite involving a foul-tasting Maine soft drink called "Moxie," which is sometimes used to remove seagull excrement from dockside restaurant tables.]

Games are won by scoring more runs than you give up, right? Right! The closest you can come in Rotisseball to runs scored per game is what we modestly call your Runs-Batted-In Average, or RBIA. Multiply your total RBI by 27 (that's the minimum at-bats in game, deahh). [Editor's note: "dear."] Then divide by your total number of at-bats. It's like the ERA. See the symmetry of it? Beautiful!

[Editor's note: Dr. Allan raves on in this vein for five pages, which have been omitted for fear you would stop reading and go buy Peter Golenbock's book.]

But, brilliant as the RBIA is, I wasn't satisfied. There had to be more. I had to push the envelope, dare to go where men had never gone before, give 110%, but stay within myself. And the result was simplicity itself. All you do is divide your RBIA by your ERA, *et voilà* [Editor's note: Maine is near Montreal.] . . . THE ULTIMATE ROTISSESTAT!

For those of you who passed high school algebra, here's the formula:

$$\frac{RBI \times 27}{Total\ AB} = RBIA \qquad \frac{ER \times 9}{Total\ IP} = ERA$$

$$\frac{RBIA}{ERA} = ULTIMATE\ ROTISSESTAT$$

Now, tell me. Do you think I should donate my brain to the Smithsonian? Later, of course, that is.

Hey, Doc, we don't know, but it sure would look good in the Rotisserie League Hall of Fame. Maybe display it next to Harry Stein's lucky sweater.

# The Year of Living Stupidly:

## Confessions of a Rebuilding Team

Dallas Green figured he knew all there was to know about rebuilding. First he gets Ryne Sandberg and Bob Dernier from the Phillies for a couple of old jock straps. Hey, sign up free agent Scott Sanderson. Then it's Billy Bucks to the Red Sox for Dennis Eckersley. Good-bye, Joe Carter and Mel Hall (yeah, *that* Joe Carter); hello, Cy Young Sutcliffe. Presto chango. Nothing to it. A division championship and near-pennant in 1984, and then . . . and then. . . .

The moral? Not even Rome was built in a day, much less the Chicago Cubs—although both franchises have been at it about the same number of years. Hail, Nero Green!

Hear this, Rotisserie League owners who take a look at their rosters in the off-season, scream in horror, and contemplate rebuilding: It isn't easy, it takes a lot of psychic energy, it's costly (somehow, if you think you have a chance at a first-division finish, those outlays for player call-ups don't seem real; if you know you're out of it, you feel every penny). But most important, there's no—read our lips—NO sure formula for success.

Ask the President and General Manager of the once-mighty Glenwag Goners, the most successful franchise in Rotissehistory with six—count 'em—*six* straight first-division finishes. Winners of the first-ever Rotisserie League pennant, the Goners rattled off four successive second-place finishes before finally falling to fourth in 1985. It was after that season, which saw the Goners edge the Wulfgang for the last money position amid charges of stats manipulation and shady dealings, that Boss Goner Glen "Iron Horse" Waggoner took a deep breath, looked deep into his own soul, and decided to rebuild. It was that or throw up.

Now, for the first time ever in print (except for the transcript of a seminar published in *Daedelus*), and as a direct consequence of the Rotisserie League's official news policy ("Open Covenants, Openly Arrived At, Except for the Furriers"), we offer a direct, firsthand explanation of the famous GORP—Goners Overnight Rebuilding Program. Here it is, straight from the Iron Horse's mouth.

# "It Was Sudden Pete's Fault"

Looking back—and yes, damnit, I recollect what Satchel Paige said about that—that thing would never have happened if that Mr. Uppity Snot-Nose Movie-TV Screenwriting Big Shot Peter "Sudden Pete" Gethers hadn't gotten too big for his britches. Wasn't satisfied being cofounder and visiting team batboy for the best doggone ball club in the Free World, oh, no. Had to be Top Gun, *Número Uno*, the Kingfish. Had to have his own team, is what it is.

It all started when Cork Smith, bless his heart, decided to give up the Smith-Coronas to become Commissioner for Life (the former Commissioner for Life, our Beloved Founder Dan Okrent, became Former Commissioner for Life while retaining his title as Beloved Founder). Next thing you know, Sudden Pete has taken over and renamed the ball club after the St. Petersburg Beach restaurant where we were having a postgame repast, a roadside joint named Peter's Famous Smoked Fish.

"Holy mackerel!" (I remember him shouting.) "I'll take over the Coronas! They'll be my team! Mine! No more kowtowing to the Iron Horse! No more kissing his catcher's mitt! I'll get rich! I'll be famous! I'll get the best seat in the ball park!"

Stark, raving mad he was, but it came to pass. Sudden Pete

quit the Goners to become Sturgeon General of the Smoked Fish.

Well, good riddance, I figured at the time. More for me when it came time to cash another one of them second-place-finish checks. Who knows, I reckoned, maybe there'd be another flag flying over Goner Field pretty soon. Sudden Pete knows about as much about baseball as a hog does about tap dancing, and I figured he'd be bottom feeding so regular he might as well change his team name to Carp. The only thing to keep him from coming in last was the Cary Nations, which is what Cary Schneider decided to call the Salembier Flambes when Val the Gal left the league to powder her nose.

My biggest worries would continue to be the Okrent Fenokees (the Beloved Founder would someday learn how to play the game he invented, wouldn't he? Wouldn't he?), the Sklar Gazers (they won in 1984, the year after the Stein Brenner sweep), and the ever-dangerous Eisenberg Furriers. The owners of the Wulfgang and the Fleder Mice were getting married, and that would take them out of the action. The Pollet Burros were too busy chasing torts to read the box scores. And the Stein Brenners win only in years that the Rotisserie League decides to write a book.

Well, I figured wrong. The Cary Nations, who had come in dead last in 1984, when they were the Flambés, finished first in 1985; the Smoked Fish finished in a tie for second; and the Goners just barely sneaked into fourth. It was along about then that I came to two conclusions: I decided I missed old Sudden in the front office, even if he was a swine; and I was going to rebuild in 1986.

To say that you're going to tear your team apart and start from scratch sounds brave, particularly since it means for sure that you're going to be out of contention for at least a year. Well, I got to admit that my decision was based on the fear that I had only two options: try my damndest to be good and end up being mediocre; or be terrible and say I planned it that way. What would you have done in my shoes?

Change 'em, that's what, and so I did.

# The Goners' Overnight Rebuilding Program

You can't tell the players without a scorecard, and you can't rebuild without a plan. Mine evolved over the winter of 1985–86. "Evolved," in this context, means a lot of fits and starts, backfires, and zigzagging, with all sorts of misgivings, second-guessing, and dead ends. I blame my baseball people.

The first order of business, of course, was to trade off anything of short-term value for future considerations. I had the Goose at a good price—$33—but I figured his arm would be gone by 1987, so I shopped him all winter. Funny, but most everybody figured he was cooked already, until I finally swallowed my pride and rang up the Smoked Fish. It was time to cut bait.

My former partner had Darryl Strawberry at $25, Mike Marshall at $20, and a lot of garbage. I traded him the Goose for the garbage. That's right, his entire team, plus his Farm System, plus a First-Round Farm System draft choice, for the Goose. In terms of bodies, it was the biggest trade in Rotissehistory, though it will probably get an asterisk in the record books because not all the bodies were alive.

The idea was to package small groups of ex-Fish and trade them quick for draft choices, Farm System players, and other marginalia before the smell got too strong. For details on how that came out, see Transactions 5–6 below.

Next I had to work out a Draft strategy. In past seasons, the Goner front office just sat down at the table, bought players at the right prices, and figured on trading later to balance things out. Simple. Rebuilding called for something different.

After many hours of heavy thinking and primal therapy, I came up with the key: Corner the market on stoppers. Everybody needs a bullpen ace, almost all of the National League's best were available in the Draft, and it seemed to make good sense to buy a couple of the big guns and trade them later for cheap talent who would blossom in 1987. Welcome, Jeff Reardon and Bruce Sutter, to the Goner clubhouse—but keep your bags packed.

Next I wanted to be sure to get Pedro Guerrero. He didn't figure to play until late summer, if then, and there was a chance that he might never be his old before-injury self. But he was sure to go for way less than the $40 he usually fetches, and risk-reward ratio was good (the Goner clubhouse attendant has a Harvard M.B.A.—it's the Goner Way). *Bienvenida,* Pedro—the whirlpool's over there.

Once the Valenzuelas and Goodens have fallen, starting pitchers usually go cheap, particularly late in the Draft, so I planned to hang back and pick up some young ones at good prices. You need to put on a few pounds, Bob Kipper. Sure beats being a Yankee, right, Jim Deshaies? This the year you break through, Jay Tibbs?

With my primary goal of cornering the market on relief at whatever price, I knew I wouldn't be able to buy much of an offense, and I was sure right. Flannery, Templeton, Trevino, and Foley might make a fine law firm, but Murderers' Row they ain't. John Kruk at $5 was nice, and Terry Puhl at $2 looked like a steal. But it was pretty obvious I wasn't going to win any home-run titles.

A firm believer in a strong Farm System, I traded *four* draft choices to the Fenokees to get the Number One pick in the 1986 draft. Shawn Abner or Bobby Bonds? Both were can't-miss blue chippers, but so was Clint Hartung once upon a time. My baseball people said, "Bonds, he has the speed." On Draft Day I said, "Abner." The way Shawn hit last season at Jackson, I'd have been better off with L'il.

# Goner Draft Day Roster, 1986

| PITCHERS | BATTERS |
|---|---|
| Jeff Reardon 39 | Alex Trevino 1 |
| Bruce Sutter 43 | Dave Van Gorder 1 |
| Jim Deshaies 12 | Will Clark 30 |
| Pat Perry 7 | Tim Flannery 1 |
| Paul Aasenmacher 9 | Garry Templeton 8* |
| Jay Tibbs 8 | Pedro Guerrero 22 |
| Scott Sanderson 3 | Tom Foley 1 |
| Bob Kipper 3 | Andres Galarraga 20 |
| Duane Ward 1 | Von Hayes 32 |
|  | R. J. Reynolds 10* |
|  | John Kruk 5 |
|  | Terry Puhl 2 |
|  | Tony Walker 1 |
|  | Brian Dayett 2 |

*Player owned prior to Draft.

Sounds neat, huh? Well thought out? Just according to GORP? Well, take a closer look.

Who drafted Will Clark at $30 and Andres Galarraga at $20? Those guys may be worth that someday, but no owner in his right mind would keep them at those prices in 1987 unless they had superstar years. (P.S.: They didn't.) Tony Walker, even at $1, figures to be overpriced unless the Rotisserie League adds a new category for Late-Inning Defensive Replacement. And who in the hell bought Von Hayes at $32? I must have been out of the room—or out of my mind. Rebuilding? No, *reliving*. The team that bought old Five-for-one for $37 the year he came over to the Phillies from Cleveland did it again. Aaah, shoot, look at the bright side: At least I saved me $5 this time.

# The Hard Part

The day after the draft was over, it began to sink in that summer was going to be winter. With a team like the 1986 Goners, there seems little point to reading the box scores in the morning, which means there's no point in getting out of bed. But therein is a classic trap. Ennui, malaise, and lassitude all have their place, but not in the front office of a rebuilding team. For GORP to have a chance of success, I had to force myself to pay attention, to spend precious dollars to fill open positions with the best available players, to cut unbalanced deals that would (won't they?) pay future dividends at the price of present performance, to follow the waiver wire the way *Gesundheit* follows a sneeze—in other words, to stay in the game despite having a team that would end up dead last in four categories. A little slice of baseball heaven, it wasn't.

So there you have it. Frankly, I'm tired of talking to the media about GORP. They distort everything a person says, no doubt because they are a bunch of lowlifes and sniveling pointyheads who've never held a bat or a gun in their hands. Sometimes I wonder why I bother holding daily press conferences.

## PRESEASON TRADES

1. TRADE Steve Sax and Tim Burke to FURRIERS for Howard Johnson, Bruce Sutter, and Garry Templeton.

Sax is overpriced at $16, and Burke faded at the end of 1985. HoJo's sure to hit 20–25, Tempy's a keeper at 8, Sutter will go back in the Draft if I can't palm him off on some sucker. Now what is the Burros' new telephone number . . . ?

2. TRADE Johnny Ray, Bob Brenly, and Second-Round Farm System draft pick to FURRIERS for Rick Schu and Steve Sax.

Schu's sure to start at third for the Phillies, and maybe Sax is a keeper after all. Hate to lose Ray, but Brenly's pricey at $19.

3. TRADE Jim Morrison to FURRIERS for Scott Sanderson.

Morrison's only $2, but he's probably not worth that, and Sanderson is a quality pitcher who'll give good ratio no matter what. [Postseason note: I was half right: Sanderson's ratio was 1.191. Who figured Morrison for 23 dingers?]

4. TRADE Goose Gossage for a whole school of SMOKED FISH —the entire team, including the FISH Farm System and First-Round Farm System draft choice, *except* for Mike Marshall and Darryl Strawberry.

A lot of chaff, very little wheat—but maybe enough to package in for other deals.

5. TRADE Steve Sax and three former FISH—Vance Law, Eric Show, and Rick Reuschel—to FURRIERS for R. J. Reynolds and Lance McCullers.

On second thought (third? fourth?), Sax is a bum. Law is a marginal player, Show is too expensive, and Reuschel has no chance of repeating his 1985 second half. McCullers, at $20, will have to go back into the Draft, but R.J., at $10, is a budding superstar.

6. TRADE four dead FISH—sub-.235 Glenn Hubbard, wild Jim Gott, too-old Davey Lopes, and pricey Nolan Ryan—to WULFGANG for Terry Pendleton, Mike Brown, and a First-Round Farm System draft pick.

Take this to the bank: Pendleton will hit .290 and steal 40 bases, Brown will drive in 95 runs—and what's all this talk around the front office about rebuilding? The future is now!

7. TRADE HoJo to FURRIERS for Jay Tibbs.

Tibbs is a lock to win 15 games.

8. TRADE Scott Sanderson to NATIONS for Jerry Reuss.

A steal! The Dodgers will win the West, and Reuss is good for 15, maybe more. Plus Sanderson's too fragile.

9. TRADE Mike Scott to BURROS for *two* First-Round Farm System draft choices 1986 and 1987.

No way Scott's going to win 18 again. He had one fluke year. I'm better off with unknowns.

**10–15.** TRADE frenzy in last hours before pre-Draft Roster Freeze. Bill Hatcher comes and goes; Rick Honeycutt goes; four Farm System draft choices to FURRIERS for Number One pick in 1986.

Rotissefever—I caught it!

## POSTDRAFT DEALS

**16.** RESERVE Brian Dayett, CALL UP Danny Heep.

Dayett was supposed to be a $2 steal; how can he hit 18 Wrigley Field homers from Iowa?

**17.** RELEASE Dave Von Gorder, CALL UP Mike Fitzgerald.

Maybe Fitzgerald will be worth something as part of a package in a trade.

**18.** WAIVE Tom Foley, ACTIVATE Terry Puhl.

Puhl is going to have a big year.

**19.** TRADE Jeff Reardon, Bill Sample, Mike Fitzgerald, and a 1987 First-Round Farm System draft chioce to FURRIERS for Mark Davis, Shawon Dunston, Bob Melvin, and Drew Denson (Farm System).

If Denson is half as good as the Furriers' and Braves' front office say he is, the Goners' dynasty is reborn. [Note: He's not; it isn't.]

**20.** TRADE Bruce Sutter to FENOKEES for Carlos Diaz, a 1987 First-Round Farm System draft choice, and José Gonzalez (Farm System).

If Gonzalez is half as good as the Fenokees' and Dodgers' front offices say he is, the Goners' dynasty is reborn again. [Note: The jury's still out, but Willie Mays he ain't.]

**21.** RELEASE Carlos Diaz, CALL UP José DeLeon.

A cinch to be the Pirates' bullpen stopper.

**22.** TRADE Von Hayes and José DeLeon to GAZERS for Reggie Williams and Todd Worrell.

Hayes is fading, DeLeon will stink so long as he's with the Pirates, Reggie Williams is another José Gonzalez, and Todd Worrell is a young Goose.

**23.** RESERVE Jim Deshaies, CALL UP Mike Bielecki.

Deshaies is good, but Bielecki was on the cover of *Baseball America* a year ago.

**24.** WAIVE Mike Bielecki, ACTIVATE Jim Deshaies.

And Mark Grant was on *Baseball America*'s cover a year before that.

**25.** TRADE Terry Puhl, Jay Tibbs, and Gary Templeton to FURRIERS for Cesar Cedeno, Ed Vande Berg, and Andres Thomas.

Tim McCarver says, "Most rookies you see come up are Parkay; Andres Thomas is butter."

**26.** WAIVE Ed Vande Berg, CLAIM José DeLeon on waivers.

Give the kid another chance.

**27.** WAIVE José DeLeon, CALL UP Don Robinson.

So how was I supposed to know the Pirates were going to give DeLeon another chance—with the White Sox?

**28.** WAIVE Cesar Cedeno, CALL UP Ron Roenicke.

Had a hot first week; he'll fetch something in trade.

**29.** RESERVE Duane Ward, CALL UP Andy McGaffigan.

Rebuilding is expensive.

**30.** RESERVE Will Clark, CALL UP Randy Kutcher.

Had a hot first week; he'll fetch something in trade.

**31.** TRADE Ron Roenicke to FE-NOKEES for Tito Landrum and 1987 Second-Round Farm System draft choice.

See Transaction 28.

**32.** WAIVE Tito Landrum, ACTIVATE Dave Martinez from Farm System.

The Farm System begins to pay off sooner than expected!

**33.** RESERVE Bob Kipper, CALL UP Frank Williams.

Williams has the stuff to be the Giants' closer, so long as all opposing hitters bat right-handed.

**34.** WAIVE Pat Perry, ACTIVATE Barry Jones from Farm System.

Hate to give up on Perry, but Jones is Pirates' stopper of the future, and I have to activate him or lose him.

**35.** WAIVE Mark Davis, CLAIM Rick Sutcliffe on waivers.

Dreaming of 1984.

**36.** WAIVE Danny Heep, CLAIM Dan Gladden on waivers.

Gladden was on the last year of his contract with the Mice, who had to choose between him and Jeff Stone. They keep Stone; the Goners print 1987 World Series tickets.

**37.** TRADE Jim Deshaies and Will Clark to FURRIERS for Charles Kerfeld and Terry Puhl.

Clark at $30 is not a keeper, and Kerfeld as a reliever at $10 will be more valuable in 1987 than Deshaies as a starter at $12. And who knows—Terry Puhl might *still* have a big year!

# Was It Worth It?

The Year of Living Stupidly was the most miserable season in Goner history. The team's owner-GM was so distraught at being out of the race for the first time ever, and had so much free time on his hands, that he actually took up golf—and heaped new insult to the ego onto the injury of finishing out of the money. As the Goner point total fell, his golf score soared, and he was even heard mumbling that perhaps he would give up both and start following the USFL more closely.

But there is no gain without sacrifice, no real learning without hard knocks, no pleasure without pain, no north without south. What, objectively, did the Goners' Rebuilding Program accomplish? What lessons of Rotisselife are to be learned from this grand, audacious experiment? Is there tit for tat in the great scheme of things? What hath the Iron Horse wrought?

Take a look at the Goners *après le déluge* and judge for yourself:

| PITCHERS | BATTERS |
|---|---|
| Paul Aasenmacher 9D | Bruce Benedict 1D |
| Barry Jones 10D | (RL) Brian Dayett 2D |
| Charlie Kerfeld 10D | Shawon Dunston 10C |
| Bob Kipper 2D | Tim Flannery 1D |
| Don Robinson 10D | Andres Galarraga 20D |
| Scott Sanderson 3D | Dan Gladden 10B |
| Rick Sutcliffe 10B | Jose Gonzalez 10D |
| Frank Williams 10D | (RL) Pedro Guerrero 22D |
| Todd Worrell 20D | John Kruk 5D |
| | Dave Martinez 10D |
| | Bob Melvin 1D |
| | Terry Puhl 2D |
| | R. J. Reynolds 10C |
| | Andres Thomas 2D |
| | Tony Walker 1D |
| | Reggie Williams 10D |

Contract status code: B = expires 10/87; C = renewable 4/87; D = renewable 4/88; (Note: Contracts that are *not* renewed expire in October.) RL = reserve list

No wonder the Goners finished tied for eighth. But what about 1987? Here's a preliminary scouting report.

**BULLPEN.** In Worrell, Robinson, Kerfeld, and Aasenmacher, the Goners have a first-rate relief corps. Enough strength here to trade Kerfeld or Aasenmacher. Jones might be packaged in a deal if the Goners can convince somebody that the setup job on the Pirates is worth $10.

**STARTING ROTATION.** Could be okay, could be awful. Kipper is a keeper, and Sanderson at $3 *still* gives good ratio. But what do you do with Sutcliffe? He'll pitch a lot, and in Wrigley, and his numbers might be horrendous again. But he could also find whatever he lost after 1984 and be a $10 Cy Young and MVG (Most Valuable Goner). Tough call.

**SPEED.** After Gladden, no one can be counted on for 20. Martinez? Gonzalez? You can't steal first, not even in Rotisseball. But if they hit. . . .

**POWER.** Guerrero, Galarraga, and Dunston should be good for 70 homers, but that's it. The Goners will have to draft power.

**TRADE BAIT.** Kerfeld or Aasenmacher and Jones for a starter or speed. Gonzalez, Martinez, Reynolds, and Williams might attract a rebuilding team. Not a whole lot to deal.

**FARM SYSTEM.** Shawn Abner, Chris James, and Drew Denson aren't shabby, but only James has much chance of helping in 1987.

**DRAFT CHOICES.** Goners have *four* First-Round Farm System draft choices in 1987. Look for all of them to be traded by Draft Day.

**CERTAIN KEEPERS.** Worrell, Robinson, Kerfeld, Aasenmacher, Kipper, Sanderson, Guerrero, Galarraga, Gladden, Dunston, Kruk, Thomas. Benedict, Dayett, Walker, and Frank Williams go back into the Free Agent Pool. The rest are "Maybes."

"You don't ever want to go through what I went through this season," admitted the haggard owner-GM of the Glenwag Goners in a leisurely 19th-hole interview after a postseason round of lights-out golf. "It even got to where I was reading the front page of the newspaper before turning to the box scores in the morning. My wife wanted to call the doctor; I wanted it to be next year."

Was it worth it? Will the Goners be in the race in 1987?

"I wish I knew," said the Iron Horse as he fired a stream of tobacco juice in the general direction of the broken 3-wood lying next to a bent putter, the only clubs left after another day's outstanding round. "I guess it all boils down to whether Terry Puhl has a great year."

"But I will say this," he added, "and you can quote me:

REBUILDING INHALES BACKWARD!"

# Postgame Show

## A Yoo-Hoo to Arms

*This is the way we ended our first book. This is the way we are ending this book. And this is the way we'll end our next book(s).*

Unseen hands hold you, force your head down and pour water, dairy whey, corn sweetener, non-fat milk, sugar, coconut oil, cocoa, sodium caseinate, salt, sodium bicarbonate, dipotassium phosphates, calcium phosphates, guar gum, natural flavors, xantham gum, vanillin (an artificial flavor), sodium ascorbate, ferric ortho-phosphate, palmitate, niacinamide, vitamin D, and, yes, *riboflavin* all over your hair. The bizarre ritual is a Yoo-Hoo shampoo, and it is what you get for winning the Rotisserie League pennant.

The chocolate-flavored rinse will not leave your locks radiant and soft to the touch, and squirrels will probably follow you around for a day or two. All and all, the ritual is pretty distasteful. But there's not a member of the Rotisserie League who wouldn't gladly suffer the rite so long as it came at the end of a championship season.

Since we traditionally end each Rotisseseason with an out-pouring of the chocolate drink of our youths, we figured we may as well end the book the same way. Besides, as the beverage company's former executive vice-president for promotions, Lawrence Peter Berra, once noted, or at least we think he noted, "Yoo-Hoo tastes good. And it's good for you, too."

Yoo-Hoo does taste good if your taste buds also happen to be impressed with the nose on strawberry Fizzies. To sophisticated palates, Yoo-Hoo tastes a little like the runoff into the gutter outside of a Carvel store.

As for Yoo-Hoo being good for you, well, Yogi says he let his kids drink it, and one of them grew up to be the .255-hitting shortstop for the Pittsburgh Pirates. But then maybe if Dale *hadn't* touched the stuff, he might actually be worth more than the $7 the Fledermice paid for him in 1983.

Yoo-Hoo is not unlike the Rotisserie League. Both of them taste good, and both of them are good for you. Just don't tell anybody that. Whenever one of us tries to explain just what the Rotisserie League is, we all get the same kind of look. It's the look one might get from a bartender if one ordered, say, a Kahlua and Yoo-Hoo. The look says, "Aren't you a little too old to be partaking of that stuff?" Our look invariably replies, "But it tastes good, and it's good for you."

Yoo-Hoo's current slogan is, "Yoo-Hoo's Got Life." Catchy, isn't it? But then, Yogi Berra used to be a catchy. The Rotisserie League's got life, too. It enlivens not only box scores, but Kiner's Korner, as well. Why, the game adds color to every fiber of your being, it gives you a sense of purpose in this crazy, cock-eyed world, it puts a spring in your step and a song in your heart, and it makes you care, deeply care, for your fellow man, especially if your fellow man's name is Biff Pocoroba. So the Rotisserie League is childish, is it? Yoo-Hoo and a bottle of rum, barkeep.

In case you're wondering where Yoo-Hoo comes from, we thought we'd tell you. It comes from Carlstadt, N.J. Yoo-Hoo also goes back to the days of Ruth and Gehrig. It first arrived on the American scene as a fruit drink named after a popular greeting of that day. Founder Natale Olivieri was obsessed with making a stable chocolate drink, and after years of experimentation, he hit upon the idea of heating the chocolate. The rest is soft-drink history.

In the fifties, Yoo-Hoo's Golden Age, the product came to be associated with Yogi. A billboard of Yogi and a bottle of Yoo-Hoo greeted fans in Yankee Stadium. And Yogi wasn't the only Yankee who endorsed Yoo-Hoo—Whitey, Mickey and the Moose could all be seen on the insides of Yoo-Hoo bottle caps. Nowadays, nobody inhabits the inside of the bottle cap. However, if you turn the cap upside down, it reads, 'ooh-ooy,' which is Yiddish for Rod Scurry's ERA.

Yoo-Hoo is also like baseball: you don't want to know too much about it. In the interests of this chapter, we sent an envoy out to Yankee Stadium to talk to Yogi. Yes, you've read all those funny Berra quotes over the years, about how it's not over until it's over and about how nobody goes to that restaurant any more because it's too crowded. To tell you the truth, Yogi is not the man that people suppose him to be. He is actually two different people, depending on his mood. When he is on guard, he is full of monosyllables, and when he is relaxed, he can be genuinely engaging. But the star of "The Hathaways," he is not.

We—actually, it was only one of us, who shall remain nameless, and if *The New Yorker* can do it, why can't we— asked Yogi if he would mind talking about Yoo-Hoo. He said, "Sorry, I can't." This caught us by surprise, but being quick on our tongue, we said, "You can't?" Yogi said, "Nope. Ask Cerone."

At which point, we approached Rick Cerone, the catcher who took Yogi's place as executive vice-president for promotions. For all their sterling qualities, Berra and Cerone do not strike us as being pillars of the corporate structure, but Yoo-Hoo obviously saw through to their executive talents. We asked Cerone if he would mind talking about Yoo-Hoo. He said, "I can't." This time, we said, "Why?" and Cerone said, "Because I'm suing them, that's why."

As it turns out, the company has changed hands, and Cerone claims that Yoo-Hoo never paid him for certain appearances. Yogi ran into similar problems, but he settled out of court. So that's why Yoo-Hoo is just like baseball: if you look too closely, it can get ugly on you.

We went back to Yogi and pleaded with him. All we cared about, we said, were the old days of Yoo-Hoo. He warmed to the subject in much the same way Natale Olivieri warmed Yoo-Hoo— slowly. In a series of grunts and moans, we determined that Yogi thought Yoo-Hoo tasted good, that his kids drank it, that he wishes he had some money invested in it, and that people still link him with Yoo-Hoo and vice-versa. Then he said, "What's this for, anyway?"

We explained to him about the Rotisserie League and the

book. When we said, "Then, at the end of the year, we pour Yoo-Hoo over the head of the winner," Yogi—dripping tobacco juice out of the left side of his mouth—gave us a look of partial disgust and said something like "ooh-ooy."

So, if you decide to take up baseball as played by the Rotisserie League, be warned. People will look at you funny. Pay them no mind. Just pay the treasurer.

We hate long good-byes. When we meet again, perhaps at a theater near you showing "The Rotisserie League Goes to Japan," let's just say, "Yoo-Hoo."